D1132817

A Guide to Elder Planning

_ST SLOPE COMMUNITY LIBRARY
(503)292-6416
MEMBER OF
WASHINGTON COUNTY COOPERATIVE
LIBRARY SERVICES

A Guide to Elder Planning:

Everything You Need to Know to Protect
Your Loved Ones and Yourself

Updated and Revised Edition

Steve Weisman

FT Press

Vice President, Publisher: Tim Moore
Associate Publisher and Director of Marketing: Amy Neidlinger
Executive Editor: Jim Boyd
Editorial Assistant: Pamela Boland
Development Editor: Russ Hall
Operations Specialist: Jodi Kemper
Marketing Manager: Megan Graue
Cover Designer: Alan Clements
Managing Editor: Kristy Hart
Project Editor: Elaine Wiley
Copy Editor: Sheri Cain
Proofreader: Sarah Kearns
Senior Indexer: Cheryl Lenser
Senior Compositor: Gloria Schurick
Manufacturing Buyer: Dan Uhrig

© 2013 by Pearson Education, Inc.
Publishing as FT Press
Upper Saddle River, New Jersey 07458

This book is sold with the understanding that neither the author nor the publisher is
engaged in rendering legal, accounting, or other professional services or advice by
publishing this book. Each individual situation is unique. Thus, if legal or financial advice
or other expert assistance is required in a specific situation, the services of a competent
professional should be sought to ensure that the situation has been evaluated carefully
and appropriately. The author and the publisher disclaim any liability, loss, or risk resulting directly or indirectly, from the use or application of any of the contents of this book.

FT Press offers excellent discounts on this book when ordered in quantity for bulk
purchases or special sales. For more information, please contact U.S. Corporate and
Government Sales, 1-800-382-3419, corpsales@pearsontechgroup.com. For sales outside
the U.S., please contact International Sales at international@pearsoned.com.

Company and product names mentioned herein are the trademarks or registered
trademarks of their respective owners.

All rights reserved. No part of this book may be reproduced, in any form or by any
means, without permission in writing from the publisher.

Printed in the United States of America
First Printing January 2013

ISBN-10: 0-13-309192-9
ISBN-13: 978-0-13-309192-2

Pearson Education LTD.
Pearson Education Australia PTY, Limited.
Pearson Education Singapore, Pte. Ltd.
Pearson Education Asia, Ltd.
Pearson Education Canada, Ltd.
Pearson Educación de Mexico, S.A. de C.V.
Pearson Education—Japan
Pearson Education Malaysia, Pte. Ltd.

Library of Congress Cataloging-in-Publication Data

Weisman, Steve.

  A guide to elder planning : everything you need to know to protect your loved ones and
yourself / Steve Weisman.—2e.

    pages cm

  ISBN 978-0-13-309192-2 (pbk. : alk. paper)

  1. Older people—Legal status, laws, etc.—United States—Popular works. I. Title.

  KF390.A4W45 2013

  646.7'9—dc23

                                    2012043869

"Grow old with me, the best is yet to be."
—Robert Browning

This book is dedicated, as is everything I do, to my dear wife, Carole.

Contents

About the Author

Steve Weisman is a lawyer who hosts the radio show "A Touch of Grey," syndicated to more than 50 stations nationwide, including AM 970 (NYC) and KRLA (LA). A senior lecturer at Bentley University where he teaches Elder Planning, he is a member of the National Academy of Elder Law Attorneys and is admitted to practice before the U.S. Supreme Court.

The legal editor for *Talkers* magazine and RadioInfo.com, he writes for publications ranging from *The Boston Globe* to *Playboy* and earned an ABA Certificate of Merit for excellence in legal journalism. His books include *Boomer or Bust*, *The Truth About Buying Annuities*, *The Truth About Protecting Your IRAs and 401(k)s*, and *The Truth About Avoiding Scams*, which was featured on *Dr. Phil* and CNN. Weisman received a J.D. degree from Boston College Law School. He also operates the website www.scamicide.com, which provides the latest information on scams and identity theft.

1

Asset Protection

"'Would you tell me, please,

which way I ought to go from here?'

'That depends a good deal on where you want to get to,'

said the Cat.

'I don't much care where,' said Alice.

'Then it doesn't matter which way you go,' said the Cat.

'So long as I get somewhere,' Alice added as an explanation.

'Oh, you're sure to do that,' said the Cat,

'if you only walk long enough.'"
—Lewis Carroll
  Alice's Adventures in Wonderland

It is not what you make that counts, it is how much you keep. Protecting your assets from the slings and arrows of outrageous lawsuits or divorces is a concern you share with many people. A single automobile accident or an injury to someone at your home could result in a financially devastating claim against you.

Insurance

At the cornerstone of any personal asset protection plan is insurance. You may be cynical about insurance and find yourself in agreement with Al Bundy of the old sitcom *Married with Children*, who said, "Insurance is like marriage. You pay and pay but you never get anything back."

However, the purpose of liability insurance is not to get anything back, but to protect your other assets if you find yourself in legal jeopardy. In addition, when it comes to your homeowner's insurance or your automobile insurance, you are not only protecting yourself if a claim is made against you; you are also insuring that if harm comes to you or your property, money is available to remedy the situation. This is money that you would prefer not getting, because it means that you have suffered a loss. Proper insurance coverage helps you sleep at night. It is a product that, if success is measured by money, you only win when you suffer a loss.

Homeowner's Insurance

Homeowner's insurance can protect you from losses due to fire, smoke, water, wind, hail, rain, theft, vandalism, or even pestilence. Well, maybe not pestilence, but it does cover a great many things beyond mere physical damage to your home; it may, for example, provide insurance coverage if the mailman slips and falls at your door.

The extent to which a homeowner's insurance policy may be stretched was illustrated by a decision of the Federal Eighth Circuit Court of Appeals (State Farm Insurance v. Burton J. Ewing), in which it interpreted Minnesota law to provide for insurance coverage under a homeowner's insurance policy when the homeowner's mentally ill son killed the homeowner's daughter. The man, who suffered from bipolar and schizoaffective disorders, lived in a cabin that his mother owned. The sister lived with her mother. During a psychotic episode, the man went to his mother's house and killed his sister.

At his murder trial, the man was found not guilty by reason of insanity. Although he was not held criminally responsible, the dead woman's executor sued the man for wrongful death and looked to the mother's homeowner's insurance policy for coverage. The insurance company, not surprisingly, tried to deny coverage, saying that the murder did not constitute a covered occurrence under the mother's homeowner's policy because it was not an accident.

The court, however, disagreed, saying that because the man was pronounced to be mentally ill, he could not possess the ability to control his conduct regardless of any understanding of the nature of the act or its wrongfulness. The court went on to say that because he lacked the ability to control his conduct, the bludgeoning to death of his sister was both unexpected and unintended and therefore qualified as an accidental occurrence, which would be covered under the mother's homeowner's insurance policy.

Life used to be so simple. Homeowner's insurance was a "no brainer." When you bought your home, the bank from which you obtained your mortgage loan required homeowner's insurance, so after a short conversation with an insurance agent, you were all set. But no more. Some insurance companies have actually stopped selling insurance in some parts of the country, particularly where they have experienced significant mold-related claims. Those companies still selling insurance often raise their premiums.

Credit Reports

One disturbing trend involves insurance companies setting premiums or even rejecting applications entirely on the basis of an applicant's credit report. The insurance companies argue that people with bad credit statistically file more claims. Critics of this method of setting rates and denying policy applications have numerous concerns, including a charge that this procedure is a thinly disguised statistical justification for racial bias. Moreover, the formula used by the companies to come up with the insurance credit score is a secret not even provided to the state insurance commissioners for evaluation as to its legitimacy.

It is also important to note that credit scores, as derived from credit reports of the three major credit-reporting agencies, are often inaccurate, which lead to people to be either denied insurance or forced to pay larger premiums through no fault of their own. Hawaii and Maryland ban the use of insurance credit scores for all underwriting purposes; California bans the use of such scores in regard to automobile insurance, while permitting them to be used in regard to homeowner's insurance policies. Many other states are investigating this practice. Although statistics do not lie, they may fib a bit. An Australian study indicates that Geminis had the worst driving records of any astrological sign, whereas Capricorns were the best drivers.[1]

Dog Ownership

According to an old saying, barking dogs don't bite. Unfortunately, the old saying gives no guidance as to a particular barking dog's propensities once it has stopped barking, at which point, the dog just might find it necessary to nibble on someone's leg. According to the Insurance Information Institute, the cost of home-insurance claims for dog bites is more than $300 million annually.[2] Some insurers refuse to insure certain breeds; the usual suspects are Pit Bulls, Rottweilers, Wolf Hybrids, Huskies, Dalmatians, and Great Danes. Other companies do not specifically discriminate by breed.

Generally, policyholders are required to answer questions about their pets on the insurance application. Be honest and forthright in responding to these questions, because an insurance company could deny you coverage in the event of a dog bite if the application contained erroneous information. Most often, the insurance company asks whether a dog is vicious, whether it has ever bitten anyone, or whether it has been trained specifically for attack. Merely because your dog has bitten someone in the past, you will not automatically be disqualified from receiving coverage if you take precautions to prevent a recurrence. The insurance company also looks at the seriousness of a previous attack and whether the attack was provoked or unprovoked.

If you have a dog, consult your insurance agent about the company's rules regarding dogs, and be ready to shop around for a policy with which both you and man's best friend will be comfortable.

Valuable Personal Property

If you have jewelry, antiques, or any other valuable personal property in your home, it is important to get a rider to your policy that will specifically cover those items. Without that rider, most homeowner's insurance policies will limit your coverage to around $1,000 for these items. Even then, there is usually a deductible amount before you receive anything.

Make a written inventory of your personal possessions and videotape them in the home. In addition, keep the receipts for any expensive items, because in the event of a theft or damage, you need to prove the value of your property. You may also want to consider getting an appraisal for very expensive items, such as jewelry or antiques that may be worth more than you originally paid for them (this includes collections that typically appreciate in value, such as stamps, books, or even Hummel figurines). The appraisal helps you in the event of a claim.

As always, the devil is in the details, lurking in the fine print of your policy. Some homeowner's insurance policies do not cover a "mysterious disappearance," which sounds somewhat eerie, but actually means that if your diamond ring fell into the toilet, you could be down the drain. Make sure that your coverage is not a mystery to you.

Liability Insurance

Most homeowner's insurance policies provide liability protection of around $500,000 in the event someone is hurt on your property. However, for a small additional fee of about $200 a year, you can get an extra million dollars of protection through the purchase of umbrella insurance, the ultimate protection in the event of a really rainy day.

Umbrella insurance supplements your homeowner's and automobile insurance coverage and kicks in after the full amounts of those insurance policies have been utilized. Umbrella insurance covers you for claims that relate to your personal and business activities. Generally, the insurance company with which you have your automobile insurance or your homeowner's policy will provide you with umbrella coverage after you acquire the maximum in coverage on your regular homeowner's insurance and automobile insurance. Umbrella insurance is perhaps the ultimate protection from lawsuits at a reasonable price.

When you apply for homeowner's insurance, the company looks at the claims history of the home you are buying. A large number of claims in recent years could result in the application being turned down or your premiums being raised. Insurance companies look for patterns suggesting the possibility of future claims. It is prudent to get a copy of the Comprehensive Loss Underwriting Exchange (CLUE—pretty clever, eh?) report of the property before you apply for insurance. A CLUE property report covers the history of the last seven years of claims regarding the home.

Loophole

Only the homeowner and the insurance companies can get this report, so have the seller provide this to you. It can be ordered online at www.personalreports.lexisnexis.com.

Homeowner's Insurance Tips

1. As Smokey Robinson suggested, shop around. Rates vary significantly.

2. Consider increasing the amount of your deductible to lower the amount of your premium.

3. Consider buying both your home insurance and your automobile insurance from the same insurance company, because some companies offer you a lower premium if you purchase both your insurance policies from the same company.

4. Consider installing a home security system, which will not only provide you with a greater home-security protection, but may result in the company lowering your premium.

5. Loyalty is a good thing. Many companies may drop your rates if you have been with them for a long time.

6. Ask your insurer if they give a discount for retirees. Many do.

Prenuptial Agreements

Prenuptial (or premarital) agreements can be of great assistance in protecting assets in the event of a divorce or when a person marries and wants to protect assets for the children of a previous marriage.

History

For many years, husbands and wives were legally prohibited from making any contracts between themselves. Then, in the 1800s, the laws gradually changed to permit husbands and wives to make contracts with each other by which they could agree about what assets would be held separately by either of them during the marriage. Other than that, prenuptial agreements, particularly to provide for property rights following a divorce, were prohibited. The thinking was that premarital agreements were against "public policy" because, it was argued, they encouraged divorce.

It is not a coincidence that, in 1970, Florida, which has a significant population of senior citizens, became the first state to allow spouses to make premarital agreements that would take effect upon a divorce or death. Florida then and now has a large number of senior citizens who marry after having had previous families. These remarrying senior citizens often make prenuptial agreements to preserve assets for children of an earlier marriage should the parent later divorce or die.

Think about it. Marriage is a contract between two people that can end in one of only two ways—either by death or divorce—neither of which sounds particularly attractive. Yet, we still marry. I guess love really does conquer all.

Enforcement

Generally, for a prenuptial agreement to be enforceable, there must be full and fair disclosure of all the assets of both people. An agreement will not be recognized if it was based on fraud, misrepresentation, duress, or compulsion. At the time of the signing of the agreement, the agreement should be fair and reasonable. Most states follow the standard that, for the agreement to be enforceable upon death or divorce, the agreement must not be unconscionable. This term has been defined as occurring when "the inequality is so strong, gross, and manifest that it must be impossible to state it to one with common senses without producing an exclamation at the inequality of it" (Kathleen Short v. Howard N. Short [Missouri Court of Appeals— Eastern District No. ED95663]). For a visual aid in interpreting the standard, I refer people to the scene in the movie *Home Alone* where Kevin slaps shave lotion on his face while staring in the mirror and contorts his face in pain. If the agreement would solicit that effect, it is unconscionable. It is also certainly advisable, although not strictly required, that each person be represented by his or her own lawyer.

Allowable Provisions

About half of the states follow the Uniform Prenuptial Agreement Act, which provides for a number of matters that may properly be the subject of a prenuptial agreement. These include

1. The right to make a contract in regard to property.

2. Disposition of property upon separation, a breakup of the marriage, death, or the occurrence or nonoccurrence of any other event.

3. Modification or elimination of spousal support.

4. Ownership rights and disposition of death benefits from a life insurance policy.

5. The making of a will, trust, or other arrangement.

Provisions for the making of a will are particularly important, because without appropriate provisions in a prenuptial agreement, your surviving spouse is permitted by law to claim a statutory share of your probate estate, usually one-third, if the survivor receives nothing in the will or is dissatisfied with the inheritance.

Loophole

You may want to leave your ERISA pension benefits (employer-sponsored profit-sharing or pension plans) to your children from a previous marriage rather than to your spouse. The law provides that ERISA pension benefits are payable to the surviving spouse of the pension holder unless the surviving spouse has given up the right to receive the pension. You would think that all you would have to do is to have your spouse waive rights to the pension in the prenuptial agreement. But, you would be wrong. Talk about technicalities! A spouse is allowed by law to waive those rights, but the about-to-be-married person is obviously not yet the spouse of the pension holder. The law says that if the prospective spouse signs the waiver before the official marriage ceremony, the waiver is ineffective. So, what do you do? In that situation, it is important to ensure that the appropriate waivers are signed after the marriage has occurred, to supplement the prenuptial agreement.

Medicaid Implications

Senior citizens may want a prenuptial agreement to protect assets for themselves and their children from previous marriages in the event that a spouse goes into a nursing home and Medicaid coverage is sought. Unfortunately, in this instance, the state goes by its version of the Golden Rule, namely, "The state has the gold, so the state makes the rules," and the rule here is that the states are not bound by the provisions of a prenuptial agreement and may consider the assets of both spouses if one requires long-term care through Medicaid.

Living Together Agreements

More older Americans are choosing to live together without getting married. According to Bowling Green State University demographer Susan Brown, in 2006, 1.8 million Americans above the age of 50 lived together as couples without being married, which is an increase of 50 percent from just six years earlier. These numbers may even be higher today. There are many reasons why seniors may choose to live together rather than get married, including, quite significantly, the possible loss of pension benefits from a previous spouse. Some people refrain from remarriage under the false belief that if they remarry, they would lose Social Security survivor benefits derived from the earnings of their deceased previous spouse, but this rule only applies if you remarry prior to the age of 60 (or 50 if you are disabled).

Perhaps the primary reason that many seniors live together rather than remarry is so that, in the event that one has to go into a nursing home, his assets will not be considered in determining eligibility for Medicaid coverage. If they are living together, the partner's assets would not be considered in determining Medicaid eligibility for the spouse entering a nursing home and applying for Medicaid benefits, while if they were married, the income and assets of both spouses are considered in determining the eligibility for either or both of them should either or both require long-term care to be paid for by Medicaid.

It is important for older couples living together without being married to have a cohabitation agreement that clearly provides what their respective responsibilities are in the event of death or separation. They should also be wary of combining assets in joint accounts, such as joint bank accounts, because in so doing, each opens himself or herself up to the debts and liabilities of the other.

Bank Accounts

The old cliché used to be "Safe as money in the bank," but with an increase in recent years of the number of banks failing, people are starting to ponder just what their FDIC insurance protection covers if their bank goes under. According to FDIC, prior to 2011, almost one-third of all bank deposits were not covered by FDIC insurance, thereby putting many people in serious jeopardy should their bank fail.

The Federal Deposit Insurance Corporation (FDIC) believed that three classes of people were uncovered by insurance. The first class was made up of those people who were aware that their funds exceeded the federal insurance protection levels, but had faith in their own particular bank. The second class was made up of those people who, frankly, were given the wrong information by their bank as to their coverage. The third class was made up of those people who just did not understand the FDIC rules.

In response to fears brought about by the recession, the FDIC made a temporary change in the amount of FDIC insurance coverage for bank accounts that would last for the years 2011 and 2012. Under this temporary change, all funds deposited in non-interest bearing accounts would be unlimited. Essentially, this unlimited coverage was limited to traditional non-interest earning checking accounts or demand deposit accounts upon which the bank paid no interest.

For interest-bearing accounts, such as interest-bearing checking accounts, savings accounts CDs, and money-market accounts, each depositor is covered by FDIC interest of up to $250,000 for the combined deposits in each individual bank, he or she may have such accounts.

However, additional FDIC coverage is also available for different types of accounts. For example, in addition to the $250,000 coverage you have for income-earning accounts held in your name individually, you also will be able to qualify for an additional $250,000 FDIC insurance coverage for amounts you have in your share of a joint bank account as well as an additional $250,000 FDIC insurance for your share as a beneficiary of a revocable trust you create.

Finally, you also receive FDIC insurance coverage of up to $250,000 for amounts you hold in retirement accounts, such as IRAs or Keogh plans at the bank.

Trusts

When it comes to asset protection, the motto of many people might be "In trusts we trust." A trust is an entity you can create that can hold title to (a fancy way of saying "own") assets for the benefit of yourself or anyone else you choose. There are many reasons for having trusts, from being able to have your assets managed for you, to avoiding estate taxes, to protecting your assets from the claims of creditors or people who may sue you. There are many different kinds of trusts and the terms and requirements of these many different kinds of trusts vary considerably.

Safeguards for Trusts

An important thing to remember is, as a general rule, if you can get at the assets in your trust, so can your creditors. So, if you have a living revocable trust from which you can get money whenever you wish and the terms of which you can change whenever you wish, the assets that you have in the trust are not protected from creditors. However, you can set up a trust with truly independent trustees who have sole discretion as to the right to assets in the trust and any income earned by those assets. With such a trust, you can protect those assets from the claims of creditors or people who might sue you.

A few states, led by Alaska in 1997, have enacted laws by which you can set up special trusts that can protect your assets from the claims of creditors for multiple generations. You do not have to be an Alaskan resident to establish such a trust, although you must meet specific requirements, including a provision in the law that requires anyone setting up an Alaskan Trust to have at least some money held in an Alaskan bank or other financial institution.

Qualified Terminable Interest Trust

As part of an estate plan, you can set up a special form of trust, called a Qualified Terminable Interest Trust (QTIP), that both saves on estate taxes and provides income for your surviving spouse while ensuring that the assets in the trust will pass to your children following the death of the surviving spouse. A QTIP is a good choice when you want to provide for your spouse after your death, but you have some concerns. For example, you fear that your spouse would not manage money well if left the assets directly. Or you may want to make sure that should your spouse remarry, children from an earlier marriage will be guaranteed to receive your assets after the surviving spouse has died.

Offshore Trusts

For people seeking the ultimate in asset protection, offshore trusts are increasingly popular because of the combination of financial privacy laws and asset protection laws in these foreign countries. Many of these offshore trust havens are located in beautiful Caribbean islands, such as the Cayman Islands or Nevis, where it can be most enjoyable to take a trip to visit your money. The Cook Islands provide the strongest laws for protecting assets from the claims of creditors. The Cook Islands are located in the Pacific Ocean, east of Australia and south of Hawaii. My theory is that if you cannot find a place on the globe, you should not have a trust there.

Establishing an offshore trust is unnecessary for all but the wealthiest of people. In addition, although utilizing such trusts is perfectly legal, a significant number of people abuse these trusts to avoid income taxes, thereby raising the ire and the interest of the IRS. You may remember from when you prepared your income tax return the specific section where you must state whether you have an offshore trust. Even if you are operating your trust entirely properly, you may be inviting greater scrutiny of your income tax return by indicating that you have an offshore trust. And if you indicate that you do not have an offshore trust although you really do, you have committed perjury, which is a serious crime.

Homestead Protection

When many people think of the word "homestead," they may think of where Roy Rogers and Dale Evans might have lived, but in fact, a homestead is a legal concept by which your home or a significant amount of the equity in it is protected from the claims of most creditors. Florida and Texas are two states that protect the entire value of the home from the claims of creditors. In addition, most states will allow you, subject to certain time limitations, to sell your home and take the proceeds from that sale to purchase another home, which in turn will be protected from your creditors through homestead protection.

Because the states, when they passed homestead laws, continued to adhere to their version of the Golden Rule (if you have the gold, you make the rules), the homestead protection laws do not protect your home from debts owed to any form of government for things such as real estate taxes or income taxes. Homestead protection and the procedures for establishing it vary from state to state.

In addition, and most important, many people mistakenly think that a homestead declaration protects their home from Medicaid. It will not.

Fraudulent Conveyances

In an effort to protect their assets from the claims of creditors and lawsuits, many people give those assets away, usually to other family members or friends. It is not against the law to do this to protect yourself from people who may have a claim against you in the future, but it is illegal to do so to shelter your assets from present and past creditors or other people who may already have a claim against you (for example, someone with whom you have had an automobile accident). Such a gift is called a *fraudulent transfer*.

In a famous divorce case, Yacobian v. Yacobian, a woman accused her husband of fraudulently giving away substantial amounts of his assets to his children from a prior marriage eight years before their separation to prevent her from having those assets considered for division in their divorce. The court denied her claim, saying that because the gift was made so long before their divorce, it constituted appropriate gift giving. However, the court did say that if gifts had been made at a time when a divorce was imminent, such gifts might qualify as fraudulent transfers.

The laws against fraudulent transfers go back to the Statute of Elizabeth, an English law passed in 1571. According to that law,

"...feofments, gift, grants that have been and are devised and contrived of malice, fraud, covin, collusion or guile to the end purpose and intent to delay, hinder or defraud creditors and others of their just and lawful actions, suits, debts, accounts, damages, penalties will result in forfeiture of the personal property transferred."

To ensure that I was not violating any old English laws (you just can't be too careful), I looked up the word "covin" in the dictionary. It means a treacherous conspiracy of two or more people to defraud someone. I just thought you should know. In an early version of the governmental Golden Rule, under the Statute of Elizabeth, the Queen got half of whatever was recovered through the use of that law.

Assets Protected by Law

With some variations and exceptions, all the states have laws that protect life insurance policies and annuities from the claims of creditors. As usual, the IRS has its own loophole that allows it to get at the cash value of a delinquent taxpayer's life insurance policy.

Another good way to protect life insurance from the claims of creditors is through an Irrevocable Life Insurance Trust (ILIT). This is a great estate and financial planning tool and is described in detail in Chapter 4, "Estate Planning." In addition, Employee Retirement Income Security Act (ERISA) pensions, which are employer-sponsored pension and profit-sharing plans, are protected by law from the claims of creditors, even in a bankruptcy. However, an important exception to this pension protection law is that the IRS is allowed to take pension assets for unpaid taxes. Protection of non-ERISA plans, such as IRAs and Keoghs, vary significantly from state to state.

Joint Ownership

Joint ownership means multiple people own the same property (which can be real estate, bank accounts, stocks, or whatever) in such a way that if one of the owners were to die, the others would automatically inherit the deceased co-owner's share without having to probate that person's co-ownership interest. Designation of joint ownership may be made by the words "joint owners," "joint tenants with right of survivorship" or "JTWROS."

Although many people choose joint ownership as a simple way of avoiding probate, there are considerable risks involved with this form of owning property. First, it drastically limits your ability to do estate tax planning with the property. Second, and perhaps more important, putting someone's name on your account may make your account subject to claims of that person's creditors (including, of course, the IRS, who, not surprisingly, have extraordinary powers to deal with assets held jointly by someone from whom they are trying to collect payments). For these reasons, one of my professors at Boston College Law School always advised, "Stay out of expensive joints." I think he also may have wanted us to be frugal, but that's another story.

Tenancy by the Entirety

Under old English law, a man and a woman became one person when they married. What a romantic concept. That one person, however, was essentially the man. Married women did not have the right to own property. Under this old law, known as tenancy by the entirety, the husband had a superior right of possession in the marital home. If he wanted to kick the wife out of the home, he could do so. In addition, any income earned from the marital home through rents or otherwise belonged to the husband. About the only right the wife had was the right to inherit the home should she outlive her husband. But, there was a significant advantage to the tenancy by the entirety, namely, the marital home was protected from the claims of the wife's or husband's creditors.

Note that a tenancy by the entirety will not protect the home from the claims of joint creditors of the husband and wife. So, if the husband owed a credit-card debt or was sued successfully, for example, as a result of an automobile accident, the house could not be reached by his creditors if title to the home were held through a tenancy by the entirety. However, if the husband and wife jointly owed a credit-card debt or both were held responsible for an automobile accident, the house could be reached by their creditors even if it were owned as a tenancy by the entirety.

In many states, this anachronistic law was abolished, although 25 states still allow it to be chosen as a way for a husband and wife to hold title to their home. In some states, such as Massachusetts, the sexist aspects of the law have been abolished so that husbands and wives have equal rights in the home during their lifetimes, but the survivorship and creditor protection provisions of the law have been maintained.

Family Limited Partnerships

A Family Limited Partnership is a valuable estate and financial planning vehicle, which also has significant asset protection capabilities. A Family Limited Partnership is an arrangement that permits the division of the partnership's interest between those partners designated as limited partners and those partners designated as general partners. General partners are those partners or entities, such as trusts, that manage and control the partnership's assets and actions. Limited partners have no say in the ordinary operations of the partnership and have no personal liability beyond their interest in the partnership for any of its debts. Portfolio management of investments may be the business of the partnership.

Establishment of the Partnership

A Family Limited Partnership is established by a general partner or partners having a general partnership interest in a small amount, usually between 2–5 percent of the value of the partnership. A trust may be the general partner so that you can avoid probate and reduce estate taxes on the general partner's interest. The remaining interest in the partnership is held by the limited partners. The general partner may also be a limited partner. In a family setting, the parents often will be the general partners and give limited partnership interests to their children.

Protection of the Partnership's Assets

Family Limited Partnerships afford great protection of assets from creditors. A creditor of a partner is not entitled to any of the assets that are in the name of the partnership, because the personal debt that a partner has is not a debt of the partnership. A creditor is generally only entitled to what is known as a *charging order* against the partnership interest of the indebted partner, meaning that the creditor can only receive the distributions from the partnership that the indebted partner would receive. In circumstances in which there are claims against a partner, it is common for the general partner to stop making distributions in an effort to thwart the collection efforts of the creditor. Often, this leads to a significant compromise of any claim against the indebted partner.

Endnotes

1. http://sitesninemsn.com.au/minisite/testaustralia/drivingknow.asp, quoting a Suncorp Metway 2002 study.

2. www.iii.org.

2

Senior Citizens and Credit

Senior citizens deserve a lot of credit. Although a creditor may not generally consider your age when determining whether to grant a loan or credit, a creditor may consider whether you are close to retirement and whether you will soon be receiving less income. However, a bank is also required by law to consider any pension income, retirement account income, or Social Security benefits you may be receiving as income in determining your ability to repay a loan.

A bank or mortgage company may also consider age as it directly relates to certain elements of creditworthiness. So, for example, a bank or mortgage company may consider the likelihood that an 80-year-old person may not live to pay back the 30-year mortgage for which he's applying.

Equal Credit Opportunity Act

Under the federal Equal Credit Opportunity Act, a bank or any other institution granting credit or a loan may not deny credit or terminate existing accounts due to age. If you are over 62 years old, you may not be denied credit because credit-related insurance is not available owing to your age. (Credit insurance pays off the creditor if you die or become disabled.) Lenders or credit-card issuers often offer this insurance to you when you take out a loan or a credit card; however, it generally is not a particularly good buy. You can usually do better on your own.

The Equal Credit Opportunity Act also provides some measure of protection for people who retire, reach the age of 62, or have a joint account with a spouse who predeceases them. In these instances, the law does not permit the creditor to automatically close or change the terms of the account. However, the creditor is allowed to ask you to update your information or to reapply if the creditor reasonably believes that your income will no longer be sufficient to support the particular line of credit. After you submit the new information or reapply, the creditor must give you an answer within 30 days. During this time, you may continue to use your account without any additional restrictions.

If your new application is rejected, you must be given the specific reason for the rejection. The Equal Credit Opportunity Act does not guarantee you credit, but it does offer some measure of protection.

Tip

If all of your accounts are held jointly with your spouse and you are concerned that, if your spouse dies, you may have difficulty getting credit, you should open some individual accounts while your spouse is still alive. When you apply for a credit card in your own name, request that the credit-card issuer consider your spouse's credit report as well as your own in determining your creditworthiness. This is relevant information if it shows your ability to handle credit; for example, if you have ever made out the check for payments to an account in your spouse's name, that demonstrates your creditworthiness.

Credit Reports

Some older people first applying for credit may find themselves in a Catch-22. They want to establish credit, but may be denied credit because they do not have a credit history. In the past, they may have pretty much paid for things without borrowing money or establishing credit, but now, they want to borrow money or get a credit card. However, if this problem is yours, it should not be insurmountable. Even if you never had a mortgage, you have most likely paid electric bills, telephone bills, and other regular bills over your lifetime and will have a credit report, which is the primary source of information used to determine whether you will be granted credit or not.

A substantial amount of otherwise confidential information is found in a credit report. The report includes personal information such as name, age, social security number, home and business address, employment, previous addresses, marital status, spouse's name, and number of children. It also contains financial information, such as estimated income, value of car and home, bank accounts, credit accounts, payment history, credit limits, and mortgages. Public information, such as tax liens, bankruptcies, or court judgments, is also included in this report. The material contained in your credit report is regularly updated.

Credit Bureaus and Your FICO Score

Credit bureaus, sometimes called credit-reporting agencies, gather and sell information as credit reports about individual consumers. Credit reporting agencies do not actually grant credit, but rather merely collect large amounts of information that they sell to third parties such as banks or stores, who, using their own criteria, determine whether the consumer will be granted credit or not.

Most credit-reporting agencies use a scoring system called FICO (Fair Isaac Company), which is a company that provides a creditworthiness scoring system used by the major credit reporting agencies, to measure your creditworthiness. Your FICO score is used by banks and other institutions that provide credit. It is also used by many insurance companies to set the premiums for your insurance or to determine whether they will even sell you insurance coverage, such as automobile insurance. Your FICO score can also affect the interest rate that will be available to you on a loan.

Knowing your FICO score and what affects it is important. FICO scores range from 300 to 900. The largest component of the FICO score is your credit history. Being timely with your bill payments is important. However, although late or missed payments will hurt your score, older missed payments do not count as much as recently missed payments. Bad credit information that is more than 7 years old will not appear on your credit report and will not affect your FICO score, but a bankruptcy can stay on your credit report for 10 years and can significantly affect your score.

The second most important factor is how much you owe now as well as how much you could owe. Having many credit cards with large credit lines that you could access at any time could come back to haunt you when you're looking for a loan. Lenders worry about your potential to run up your debt merely by using your existing credit-card credit lines.

The length of your credit history is the next important factor and one that obviously works in favor of many senior citizens. The next consideration is whether you are taking on new credit. Opening a large number of new credit cards or accounts can drop your score. Last and least important, the types of credit you have will have an effect on your score.

Tip

When settling with a creditor on an overdue bill, make sure that, as a part of any settlement you may make, your creditor agrees to report it to the credit reporting bureaus as "paid in full" rather than charged off or settled. It can help your score.

Presently, three major national credit reporting agencies—Equifax, Trans Union, and Experian—maintain records throughout the country. Each agency keeps files on an estimated 200 million Americans.

Credit Report Error Correction

One of the immutable laws of the universe is Murphy's Law, "What can go wrong, will go wrong." And, as would be expected with the accumulation of such huge amounts of information, mistakes happen. It has been estimated that about half of all credit reports have errors in them. Unfortunately, errors on your credit report can have potentially disastrous results.

The first step in finding out if there is a mistake in your credit report is to obtain a copy of it. The cost for such a report is small.

Federal law requires each of the three major credit reporting agencies to provide you with a free copy of your credit report annually. You can obtain your free credit report by going to www.annual creditreport.com. Make sure that you use this particular website to order your free credit reports, because there are many websites with similar names that seem to offer free credit reports, but in actuality, will enroll you in costly programs that you may not need if you order your "free" credit report through them. You can also order your free credit reports by calling 877-322-8228.

Because you are entitled to a free credit report from each of the three credit-reporting agencies annually, it is a good idea to order one free credit report from one of the credit-reporting agencies and then order another free credit report from one of the other two remaining agencies four months later and then finally order your free credit report from the last of the credit reporting agencies four months after that. This way, you can review your credit reports for free every four months and thereby keep a closer eye on your credit reports. Once you examine your credit report, you will see if it contains any errors.

If you find a mistake in your credit report (and there is a good chance that you will), bring it to the attention of the credit-reporting agency or agencies in writing. Remember, each credit reporting agency acts independently, so it is prudent to check each agency's report for mistakes. After you notify the credit-reporting agency of any inaccurate or incomplete information that you may have found in your credit report, the credit reporting agency is required by law to investigate your complaint at no cost to you. In accordance with federal law, this investigation must be completed within 30 days, although it may be extended an additional 15 days if, during the 30-day period, you provide additional relevant information for them to consider.

Once the credit-reporting agency's investigation is complete, it must notify you within five business days of the result of the investigation. At that time, the agency must also give you a revised credit report and notify you that, upon your request, it will provide you with a description of the credit-reporting agency's method used to investigate and determine the correctness and completeness of the information in the credit report.

At the same time, the credit-reporting agency must also notify you of your right to have included in your credit report your own explanation, of no more than 100 words, of any item contained in your credit report that you dispute, but that after investigation, the credit reporting agency refused to delete. If, following your complaint, the credit-reporting agency either agrees with you that the disputed information is incorrect or the credit-reporting agency is unable to confirm its accuracy, the disputed information must be removed from your credit report. Not only that, you must be informed of your right to require that the credit-reporting agency contact anyone who previously had received a copy of the credit report that contained the disputed information.

Judy Thomas was awarded more than $5 million by a Federal Court jury in Portland, Oregon, in a lawsuit she brought against Trans Union, one of the three major national credit reporting agencies (Judy Thomas v. Trans Union LLC). In 1996, Ms. Thomas first found listings of bad debts mistakenly included on her credit report. The debts were, in fact, those of a woman named Judith Upton. Similar first names, the same birth year and social security numbers that differed by only a single digit probably contributed to the mistaken inclusion of these debts on Ms. Thomas' credit report. After being informed of the mistakes by Ms. Thomas, Trans Union, the jury determined, failed to properly investigate and correct the matter, causing a three-month delay in the processing of a mortgage application of Ms. Thomas. Taking things into her own hands, Judy Thomas directly contacted the creditors listed by mistake in her credit report and, through them, fixed the credit report. A sympathetic jury awarded Judy Thomas $300,000 in compensatory damages and then added $5 million in punitive damages to make their point. A less sympathetic appeals court later reduced the amount of the punitive damage award to a still significant $1 million.

Credit Cards

Although the Federal Reserve Board reduced interest rates many times in recent years, many credit-card holders are surprised to find that the interest rate on their credit cards has not gone down correspondingly. In mid 2012, the average interest rate on credit cards was a still high 16.89 percent. The reason for this is simple. Although credit cards have variable rates that you would think would rise or fall with other interest rates, the truth is that, in the fine print of your credit card agreement, is a floor below which the interest rate will not fall and, not surprisingly, this floor rate is quite high, as reflected by the average interest rate of 16.89 percent in 2012 when this book was written.

Those of us with fixed-rate cards should not feel particularly smug, though, because the fine print is not our friend either. You would think that if you had a credit card with a fixed rate, the interest rate on the credit card would remain stable. But, that is not true. In fact, if your credit card carries a fixed rate, all that means is that the rate will not automatically rise or fall as other rates go up or down. The credit-card issuer has the power to raise rates whenever it wishes. It just does not happen automatically. The credit-card issuer also has the power to lower the rate as it chooses, but I would not suggest holding your breath waiting for that to happen. So, what about those offers we all receive in the mail to transfer our balances to a new card at a new lower rate? Again, the devil is in the details. Those new low rates are often only what are called teaser rates that are effective only for a few months after which the rate shoots up to a much higher rate. In addition, some credit card issuers charge a balance transfer fee of between 2–5 percent.

Did you know that the credit-card issuers also have written in their contracts that they have the right to change your interest rate, not only if you are late in your payments to them, but if you are late to any of your creditors? This is called a *universal default* provision. So, if you have another credit card or a car loan and you are late with a payment, the issuer of the credit card with which you are completely up to date in your payments can and often will raise your interest rate. The Credit Card Act of 2009 now limits the ability of the credit-card companies to utilize the universal default provision until you have been given at least 45 days notice of your interest rate change, but this is of little solace. This is not to say that you should not shop for the right credit card. Some are significantly better than others. As always, however, it makes sense to read the fine print when you are giving yourself a little credit. A good place to go to compare credit cards is www.creditcards.com.

3

Substitute Decision Making

In so many areas of financial and personal legal planning, if you fail to plan, the law, by default, will impose a plan on you. Often, that imposed plan is not only more costly than if you had done personal planning, but may not even approximate what you would have chosen had you done proper planning. In the area of wills, for example, if you neglect to have a will drawn, the law determines who gets your assets.

Nowhere is this failure to plan more important than in the area of planning for incapacity. If you do not have a *Durable Power of Attorney*, that is, a document by which you appoint the person you wish to make financial decisions for you and the conditions for exercising those decisions, the law requires that a guardian or conservator be appointed on your behalf. This person may or may not be the person whom you would have chosen to help manage your financial affairs. In addition, the process of a guardianship or a conservatorship is much more time consuming and costly than merely having a Durable Power of Attorney drafted for you.

Power of Attorney

For some people, a Power of Attorney conjures up images of being able to leap tall subpoenas in a single bound. In reality, a Power of Attorney is a written document that enables a person known as the principal to designate another person or persons as his attorney-in-fact, which means that this person can act on the principal's behalf. Although this person is called an attorney, in this context, the word *attorney* merely means agent. He or she does not have to be a lawyer. The scope of the Power of Attorney can be as broad or as limited as desired.

For many years, Powers of Attorney allowed you as principal to appoint someone to manage your financial affairs unless you were incapacitated. In other words, you could appoint someone to act on your behalf unless you actually needed someone to do so, at which time the Power of Attorney was automatically deemed void and invalid. It only took our legislators around 200 years to realize that when someone is incapacitated, that is precisely when they need someone to act on their behalf and when they want it to be the person of their choosing. The reasoning behind the older Power of Attorney laws was that because potentially people were giving someone else so much power over their finances, the law wanted this power to be always revocable and, it was thought, someone who was incapacitated would not be able to revoke the Power of Attorney. Finally, however, the legislatures around the country recognized that people wanted Powers of Attorney to be effective at just those times, so the Durable Power of Attorney was born.

Durable Power of Attorney

In 1954, Virginia became the first jurisdiction to enact a Durable Power of Attorney law; in 1987, the District of Columbia was the last. Most states passed Durable Powers of Attorney laws in the 1970s and 1980s patterned after the Uniform Durable Power of Attorney Act, which has been adopted in 48 states.

A Durable Power of Attorney might possibly be the most important legal document that you ever execute because, unlike a will, which takes effect only at death, a Durable Power of Attorney is a document that can turn over the control of your entire financial dealings to another person while you, the principal of the Durable Power of Attorney, are still alive. It is not unusual for a Durable Power of Attorney to provide for important Medicaid eligibility planning powers, the power to make gifts on your behalf and the power to make trusts, as well as to change beneficiary designations on life insurance, annuities, or retirement accounts. Although it is perhaps the most important document you may ever make, it also carries the most potential for abuse and is one that you should carefully consider before doing.

Terminology

Generally, the magic words that must appear in a Power of Attorney to make it a Durable Power of Attorney are words to the effect of "This Power of Attorney shall not terminate upon the disability or incapacity of the principal." Although other words and phrases are allowed to be used, lawyers as a group prefer to copy language that they are confident has the approval of the law, so it is most likely that your Durable Power of Attorney will have these exact words. Most states also permit another kind of Durable Power of Attorney that only becomes effective upon the incapacity or disability of the principal, in which case the words "This Power of Attorney shall become effective upon the disability or incapacity of the principal" will appear. Once again, although other words may be used to accomplish the same purpose, uncreative and risk-averse lawyers will most often use that exact language.

Unlike the immediate Durable Power of Attorney, which takes effect at its signing, the springing Durable Power of Attorney is like an insurance policy. It takes effect only upon the happening of a specified event, such as a physical or mental incapacity. Often, the determination of a physical or mental incapacity is left to the principal's primary care physician (PCP).

Provisions

A Durable Power of Attorney can be as broad or as narrow as you wish. It can (and should) be tailored to your own specific needs and should not be done with a cookie-cutter, one-form-fits-all. It is effective until either you revoke it or until it terminates by its own terms (such as when it is done for a specific purpose, such as signing papers for the sale of a house) or upon your death.

There are four items that must be in a Durable Power of Attorney. First, it must, of course, name the principal whose Durable Power of Attorney it is. Second, it must name the attorney-in-fact. It is also advisable to name a backup or successor attorney, although that is not required by law. Third, it must state the powers specifically being granted. Many General Durable Powers of Attorney are too sparse in this regard, and that can be a real problem, particularly in the area of effectiveness when dealing with the IRS on taxes, making gifts if not specifically authorized to do so, and dealing with retirement accounts. Fourth, and obviously of great importance, are the magic words to either indicate that the Power of Attorney is an immediately effective Durable Power of Attorney or a springing Durable Power of Attorney.

Some people want to place limitations on the types of investments that may be made on their behalf by their attorney-in-fact.

It is also common for a Durable Power of Attorney to provide for the naming of a guardian or a conservator if one is needed despite the existence of the Durable Power of Attorney and, generally, you will name the same person as your guardian or conservator (a guardian is a court-appointed person who makes personal and medical decisions on your behalf, while a conservator is a person who makes financial decisions on your behalf).

An important and often overlooked provision in many Durable Powers of Attorneys is a provision giving the attorney-in-fact authority under the Health Insurance Portability and Accountability Act (HIPAA), which provides for privacy in your healthcare records, and even though your attorney-in-fact may not be making decisions regarding your medical treatment, he or she may act on your behalf with medical insurance companies. Without such HIPAA authorization contained in your Durable Power of Attorney, your attorney-in-fact would not be able to have access to important health insurance records necessary to protect your interests.

It is easy to obtain a form for a Durable Power of Attorney online, but it is not a good idea because there may be provisions that do not comply with your particular state's laws as well as provisions that you do not wish, need, or understand. In fact, even some attorneys fail to adapt their standard forms for a Durable Power of Attorney to the needs and desires of their clients. There is not a one-size-fits-all Durable Power of Attorney. Your Durable Power of Attorney should be adapted to fit your own specific needs and wishes.

Attorney-in-Fact

More than one person can be named as the attorney-in-fact; however, if you do have more than one named attorney-in-fact, it is important to state in the document whether both attorneys must act together in agreement or if either is independently authorized to act on behalf of the principal. Either of these alternatives has obvious drawbacks. Getting both to agree to act in a timely fashion can present problems, as can allowing two or more people with different strategies to operate independently. My preference (in case you asked) is to have only one person at a time named as the attorney-in-fact, with a backup named if the original attorney-in-fact is unable to act.

It is common for married people to name each other as their attorneys-in-fact under their respective Durable Powers of Attorney; however, only a minority of states automatically remove that spouse as the attorney-in-fact in the event of a divorce, so it is important to remember to change your appointment of an attorney-in-fact in the event of a filing for divorce.

You and Will Robinson

In the late 1960s, a popular television series was *Lost in Space*, a science-fiction version of Swiss Family Robinson in which the Robinsons' space ship wandered the galaxy after blasting off from Earth in the far-off year of 1997. Among the cast was Guy Williams (Zorro without the mask) as Dr. John Robinson, June Lockhart (Lassie's Mom) as his wife, Billy Mumy as their young son Will Robinson, and Bob May as the Robot. Throughout the series' run, Will Robinson seemed to be constantly in danger. Fortunately, the robot was always there to warn him of imminent peril. Unfortunately, the robot knows nothing about Durable Powers of Attorney and legal planning, so I take over and warn you when danger lurks in your legal affairs.

Danger, Will Robinson!

Some people think that a way to avoid having to do any planning, including executing a Durable Power of Attorney, is to have all assets jointly owned with a spouse or other person. This is a dangerous and inadequate course of action. Again, as indicated in Chapter 1, "Asset Protection," it is important to heed the words a Boston College Law School professor used to say, "Stay out of expensive joints."

This statement has many levels of meaning. On one level, this professor recognized that having all assets jointly held could result in higher estate taxes. It could also jeopardize those assets because the creditors of the joint owner of a bank account, for example, can reach the entire bank account—even if the joint owner whose name was added to the account never put any money into the bank account. In addition, with some jointly owned assets, the joint owner would not be able to deal with the assets in the event of an incapacity of the other joint owner. So, for example, if one joint owner of real estate becomes incapacitated, you—the other joint owner—would not be able to sell that property on your own.

Danger, Will Robinson! Danger!

I am sometimes asked if people can just go to a legal stationary store or go to the Internet and obtain a "standard" Durable Power of Attorney that they can do for themselves. My answer is a qualified yes in the sense that I also believe that you can take out your own appendix with a penknife if you so choose, but I would not recommend either course of action. In fact, you might do yourself more harm doing your own Durable Power of Attorney than you would doing your own surgery, although again, I want to firmly go on record as saying that I do not think you should do either (no lawsuits for me). Although I am not qualified to speak on the surgery, I can to tell you why you should not do your own Durable Power of Attorney.

First, the laws that govern Durable Powers of Attorney vary from state to state, and you cannot be sure that the one you are using meets all of your state's requirements. Second, I have seen many Durable Powers of Attorney that are just plain defective when it comes to issues such as dealing with the IRS or making gifts, which are two important parts of a Durable Power of Attorney. Finally, a Durable Power of Attorney should be drafted to meet your own particular needs and desires when it comes to important matters, such as gift giving, to whom and with what limitations.

Oh, Will Robinson! Even More Danger!

Although many people have interpreted a broadly worded General Durable Power of Attorney to include the power to make gifts on behalf of the principal, many people would be wrong. In fact, the courts have uniformly rejected simple, broadly worded Durable Powers of Attorney that contained words to the effect that the agent was authorized to do "all that the principal might do" (a common catch-all phrase found in the boilerplate language of many Durable Powers of Attorney), such as authorizing the attorney-in-fact to make gifts on behalf of the principal. Courts that have dealt with this issue have generally required gift-giving powers to be specifically set out within the Durable Power of Attorney, which is a good thing because there are many ramifications to the ability to make gifts on behalf of someone else.

Income tax, estate tax, and gift tax considerations should be a part of any Durable Power of Attorney decisions. Again, what you do not know can sometimes hurt you or come back to bite you in the wallet. For example, if the person acting as the attorney-in-fact has an unlimited power to make gifts in any amounts to anyone at any time, the attorney-in-fact runs the risk of having his or her gifting powers be considered a "general power of appointment." This could have serious tax consequences for the estate of an attorney-in-fact who predeceases the principal.

Gift-giving through a Durable Power of Attorney can be a most effective tool for Medicaid planning on behalf of a person who has accumulated assets over a lifetime but is in a position where all of those assets are in jeopardy (I'll take potential financial ruin for $500, Alex) if the person is in need of expensive nursing home care. A carefully worked-out gift-giving program can preserve family assets while at the same time hastening eligibility of the principal for nursing home benefits through Medicaid. Again, the wording of the gift-giving power to enable the agent to do this kind of planning should be carefully enumerated within the Durable Power of Attorney.

IRS Dangers

You might think that if a provision in your Durable Power of Attorney authorized your attorney-in-fact to deal with the IRS on tax matters on your behalf, such provision would be clear enough for even those linguistically challenged people at the IRS. Unfortunately, the IRS often operate under its version of the Golden Rule, which is, "We have the gold, so we make the rules." The rule it has made applicable in this situation is that you must either use their own Power of Attorney Form or you must list in your Durable Power of Attorney the specific tax years for which you authorize the attorney-in-fact to act on your behalf. Although you can designate any specific years or periods of time that have already passed, the Power of Attorney is only good for three years into the future, thus making it necessary to update your Durable Power of Attorney every three years.

One problem that continues to arise is that of particular banks, brokerage houses, or other financial institutions making their own rules (the revised Golden Rule again) as to whether they will honor a Durable Power of Attorney. Like the IRS, they prefer that their own forms be used or alternatively, that your Durable Power of Attorney has been executed within a specific period of time, ranging from 60 days to 3 years of the time the Durable Power of Attorney is presented to the bank or other institution. These requirements exceed those imposed by the law in determining a valid Durable Power of Attorney; in many instances, attorneys, including me, have found themselves going to court to obtain an order requiring the particular institution, in my client's case, a bank, to honor the Durable Power of Attorney.

The problem to a great extent has been reduced in recent years by including provisions in the Durable Power of Attorney that provide both an incentive for these institutions to accept the Durable Power of Attorney and a disincentive to deny it. One new provision excuses the bank or other institution that accepts the Durable Power of Attorney from any liability for relying on the document in good faith. On the other side of the coin, another recent provision holds the bank or other institution legally and financially responsible for its failure to honor a Durable Power of Attorney that complies with state law. There is also a movement around the country to amend the

Durable Power of Attorney laws to reduce this problem with states, such as Massachusetts specifically amending their laws to provide that a Durable Power of Attorney does not become "stale" or invalid after any particular period of time.

Banks or other institutions to which a Durable Power of Attorney is presented also commonly require the attorney-in-fact to sign an affidavit that says that the Durable Power of Attorney is still in effect and valid. In fact, the law in about half the states specifically provides for an affidavit signed by the attorney-in-fact stipulating that the principal is still living and that the Durable Power of Attorney has not been revoked, these statements being sufficient to prove the effectiveness and validity of the Durable Power of Attorney.

All in all, a Durable Power of Attorney is an important document that should be a part of everyone's estate and financial planning. Just like the advertisement for American Express says, "Don't leave home without it."

Health Care Proxy

A few years ago, I gave a speech to a group of people in the middle of February in Boston about estate and financial planning in which I discussed Health Care Proxies. Health Care Proxies are called by different names from state to state. Some of the other names are Power of Attorney for Health Care and Advance HealthCare Directive. The fact that I gave the speech in February is a significant detail. My parents, who have lived in the Boston area all of their lives, are senior citizens (not to be confused with sophomore citizens or junior citizens). One of the little-known laws in the Northeast is that when people reach a certain age, they are required to retire to Florida. It's the law. All right, maybe it's not the law, but it certainly seems that way. In any event, my parents go to Florida for the winter and return to Massachusetts for the spring, summer, and fall. So, because my parents were in Florida, I thought I was safe making a little joke at their expense when I told the audience at my February speech that I was designated as the Health Care Proxy agent for my parents and that if my father so much as coughed, I would, as I delicately put it, pull the plug on him. The audience laughed, and I went on to complete my speech. Less than six hours later, I received a telephone call from Florida. My Dad wanted to know if I had said that, if he coughed, I would pull the plug on him. Being the good lawyer, I looked for a way out by inquiring who had told him that. His curt response was, "That is none of your business. Did you say that?" Softening my tone, I said, "Dad, you know me better than that." And then after a pause, "Of course, I said that. Was there any question?" "No, not really," he said, "It didn't even bother me. I just wanted you to know that you still can't do anything without me finding out about it." This was a recurring theme from my youth. It took me six months to learn that someone in the audience who knew my father's next-door neighbor in Florida called the neighbor, who then trotted over to tell my father what his son was saying about him in Massachusetts.

The Law

Many people remember the 1990 United States Supreme Court decision commonly known as the Cruzan decision [Cruzan v. Director, Missouri Department of Health 497 U.S. 261 (1990)], which did much to bring to the public attention the need for Health Care Proxies. The case involved the serious healthcare decisions faced by the family of Nancy Cruzan, who at the age of 25 was rendered comatose following a horrible automobile accident in 1983. Until her death in 1990, Nancy Cruzan's existence was maintained by a feeding tube that provided artificial nutrition and hydration without which she would have died. Year after agonizing year, her parents were dragged through the courts as they tried to have the feeding tube removed. It took a decision of the Supreme Court to finally allow the removal of the tube, whereupon Nancy quietly died the next day. The grave marker of Nancy Cruzan reads, "Born July 20, 1957; Departed January 11, 1983 and At Peace December 26, 1990." If Nancy Cruzan had a Health Care Proxy, this heart-wrenching scenario could have been avoided. Her case did much to both clarify the laws that existed at that time regarding Health Care Proxies and to encourage more states to pass such laws.

Following the Cruzan case, Congress passed the Patient Self-Determination Act, which, since 1991, has required that anyone admitted to a hospital or other healthcare facility receive at admission, written information regarding the advance care directive laws of that particular state. In addition, each state now has laws that authorize some form of advance care directive, although some states limit the application of such advance care directives to terminal illness care.

The Trusted Ones

In the area of healthcare, the right to make decisions pertaining to your own treatment is an important right. Each of us has the right to choose or refuse specific treatments and medicines. We do not lose that right if we become incapacitated. We only lose the ability to communicate what are or were our wishes. It is for that reason that a Health Care Proxy, sometimes called an advance directive for healthcare, is important. Like a stock proxy by which you appoint someone to vote on your behalf at a stockholders' meeting, a Health Care Proxy is your appointment of someone to make healthcare decisions on your behalf if you are unable to do so personally.

Without a Health Care Proxy, if you are unable to make your own healthcare decision, once again, as when there is no Durable Power of Attorney, a guardian will be appointed by the court to determine your medical care. Also, as when there is no Durable Power of Attorney, this process can not only be time consuming, privacy invading, and expensive, but once again, the person who is appointed may not be the person you would have wanted making these decisions for you.

Your Health Care Proxy can be written broadly or specifically; the decision is yours. A Health Care Proxy is a way for you to direct the person you appoint as your healthcare agent to make those decisions on your behalf when you are unable to do so. I believe that it is better to state your general principles in your Health Care Proxy rather than try to be too specific. Too much specificity as to the care you want to receive or not receive in a specific situation may create problems, because the directions contained in your Health Care Proxy may not precisely apply to your situation as it actually occurs. Your well-intended directive might serve to confuse the issue and involve the courts to determine exactly what your wishes would be in the real-life situation.

Moreover, being too specific is particularly risky because medical science is constantly advancing. The specifics you deal with in your Health Care Proxy today may not even be relevant tomorrow. Some of the standard Health Care Proxy forms used today have a confusing chart that is supposed to describe all possible situations and the kind of care you authorize or prohibit under those circumstances. Even if you understand all the information in that form (I sure didn't), the form was outdated the moment it was first printed because of continuing new developments in medical science. Once again, these kinds of forms can result in your healthcare agent having to go to court for instructions as to how to interpret the Health Care Proxy in the situation in which you are found.

As with your Durable Power of Attorney, an important provision that should appear in everyone's Health Care Proxy is provision giving your healthcare agent authority to view your medical records pursuant to the Health Insurance Portability Accountability Act (HIPAA). Otherwise, you could be left in the ridiculous position where your healthcare agent could be authorized to make healthcare decisions on your behalf, but not be authorized to have access to your medical records or speak with your physicians about your condition.

You may want to discuss your care with your primary care physician (PCP) while you are still healthy. Inquire as to what kinds of treatments are available under particular circumstances and what effects those treatments have. You can put whatever limitation you want on your healthcare agent's power. After all, it's your life. Some people do not want a feeding tube for nutrition or hydration, for example, under any circumstances. Others, with whom I concur, would let the healthcare agent decide so he or she can be flexible and adapt to any particular circumstances that occur. I believe it is best to state your general principles, such as not wanting to be maintained by extraordinary means when there is no hope of a meaningful recovery. That may seem like a vague standard and, with good reason, it is. However, the vagueness of this standard provides your healthcare agent with the flexibility to deal with individual circumstances that may occur consistent with your stated wishes and desires.

Early in his career, Johnny Carson had a quiz show titled *Who Do You Trust?* I know you English teachers out there are already thinking that it should be, "Whom do you trust?," but in any event, picking the person to make healthcare decisions on your behalf if you are incapacitated is an exceedingly important decision. For spouses, it is often an easy decision, with each naming the other, but whom (just in case Mrs. Gonson, my high-school English teacher is reading this book) you choose as a backup agent to a spouse can present more difficulty. If you have more than one child, can you name all of your children to act jointly? Would you want to do this? Some states specifically prohibit multiple healthcare agents, but it is wise not to do so even in the states that allow more than one person to serve as healthcare agents at the same time. A better option for many people is to name one child as the healthcare agent with a provision in the document requesting that child to consult with siblings whenever reasonably possible, but not binding him or her to such a consultation.

Free Advice (And Worth Every Penny)

It is not enough to make a Health Care Proxy. It is also important for it to be known that you have one. I advise that duplicate original versions of the Health Care Proxy be executed, with one duplicate original given to your PCP. It is also important to discuss your wishes regarding all areas of your healthcare and treatment with your healthcare agent. Also, the U.S. Living Will Registry operates a nationwide program for the storage of Health Care Proxies at no charge to the public. Once filed with them, your Health Care Proxy is available to hospitals and other healthcare providers at any time. More information about them can be found online at www.uslivingwillregistry.com.

Religious considerations are often important to people when they make a Health Care Proxy. Various religious organizations provide sample Health Care Proxies consistent with their faith. You can use these as written or, if you wish to vary them somewhat, you can incorporate some of their provisions into nonsectarian Health Care Proxy forms.

According to an old joke, an elderly man was talking with his friends about his plans to marry a much younger woman. Out of concern, one of his friends asked him, "Don't you know that could be fatal?" The elderly man quickly responded by saying, "If she dies, she dies." That joke came to mind when I read about a case in which an elderly man who married a much younger woman went into an irreversible coma not long after their wedding. There was no Health Care Proxy, and a prolonged court battle ensued between the young wife and an adult child from a previous marriage of the comatose man. The wife argued to the judge that her husband would want to be kept alive by all means necessary, while the son argued that his father would not want this kind of an existence prolonged. Unfortunately, there was no Health Care Proxy to provide guidance. You might question the wife's intentions, though, because of a prenuptial agreement that provided her with significantly more money if the marriage were to last longer. In any event, the judge never did make a decision because right before he was going to do so, the elderly man passed away. However, this story clearly indicates the importance of having a Health Care Proxy.

4

Estate Planning

According to the old adage (as if there are any new adages), your life can't go according to plan if you have no plan. Without an estate plan, state law determines who receives your property and who is in charge of settling your affairs. In addition, the administration of your estate can be needlessly complicated without a proper estate plan. With that complication comes increased costs. Proper estate planning, however, can give you control over your affairs while you are living as well as after your death.

Wills

Estate planning is a primary concern for many older Americans. At the cornerstone of any estate plan is a will. Everyone should have a will. Without a will, you let the laws of your state determine who gets your property, which might possibly be relatives whom you have never even met. Without a will, the determination of who will manage your estate is also left to the state. We all know we should have a will, but only a third of Americans actually have one.

Choosing an Executor

One of the key decisions in making a will is the choice of whom to name as the executor, who is the person you name and then the court appoints to oversee the probate process and the settlement of the estate. In some states, the executor is referred to as the *personal representative*. At its simplest, the job entails gathering the assets of the estate, paying the debts of the estate including any taxes that may be due, including income taxes and estate taxes, if applicable, and then distributing the estate's assets in accordance with the directions contained in the will. It would seem that specialized knowledge might be helpful, such as in accounting, investments, or the law. My opinion is that a knowledge of the family involved is even more important. And if the executor has that most uncommon of traits, namely, common sense, you may have yourself a proper executor.

A person does not need to be familiar with the tax laws, probate laws, or investment issues to be a good executor. When he needs help with those matters, he can hire a lawyer, an accountant, a financial planner, or a broker. What is important is that you have confidence in the person you name and that you trust the person to carry out your wishes.

Husbands and wives often name each other as executors. Sometimes, people name more than one person to act as co-executors. This can present difficulties, particularly if there exist the possibilities of disputes among those people you would name as co-executors.

So, who is the proper person to name as your executor? Should it be a bank trust department, a professional fiduciary, or a close relative or spouse? They all have their advantages and disadvantages, and what is right for the next person may not be right for you. The most important thing is to make that decision and have a will drawn. Otherwise, that decision is left up to the Probate Court.

Erasing Battle Lines

The old saying is, "Where there's a will, there's a way." However, probate lawyers have their own variation on that old saying, namely, "Where there's a will, there are relatives."

Money all too often brings out the worst in people, and it is not at all uncommon for relatives to have substantial disputes over who gets what when it comes to an estate. Obviously, this is something that no one wants, so the question is, "What can I do to prevent or at least lessen the chances of family battles over my estate?"

Above all else, your will should be as specific as possible. Take extreme care in naming your executor, and make the list of powers given to your executor in your will as detailed and extensive as possible.

An important clause, which you can put into your will in some states, is one referred to by the Latin name of "in terrorem." By making this clause a part of your will, you specify that if someone attempts to contest your will or any provision of it, any bequest to that person is revoked. This clause provides good insurance against a will challenge.

Famous Wills

Karl Tausch, a German businessman, left the shortest will. It read, "All to wife."

P.T. Barnum was estranged from his daughter Helen at the time he made his will and revoked a generous bequest contained in his previous will and instead substituted a provision, leaving her a worthless piece of real estate in Colorado. However, the worthless piece of real estate ended up having tremendously valuable mineral deposits, making it more valuable than all of the rest of his assets combined.

William Shakespeare made no mention of his literary works in his will, but did leave to his wife his "second best bed."

But the prize, if there were one, for the most unusual will would go to Canadian lawyer, Charles Millar, who died in 1927 and who wrote in his will, "This Will is necessarily uncommon and capricious because I have no dependents or near relations and no duty rests upon me to leave any property at my death and what I do leave is proof of my folly in gathering and retaining more than I required in my lifetime."

His will was filled with humorous bequests. He gave a vacation home he owned in Jamaica jointly to three men who despised each other. He left $700,000 worth of corporate stock in O'Keefe Brewery to seven prominent Protestant ministers and temperance advocates on the condition that they participate in its management and draw on the stock's dividends. But, his final bequest was the most unusual. It provided for a gift of the substantial remainder of his estate to the woman who gave birth to the most children in the ten years immediately following his death. The newspapers coined this bequest the Great Stork Derby. Attempts were made to invalidate this provision of his will as being against public policy, but the Supreme Court of Canada upheld the provision. Ultimately, $750,000 was divided among four Toronto women who each had nine children.

Letting the State Decide

What happens if you die without a will? In that circumstance, your state's laws of intestacy control the distribution of your estate. These laws differ greatly from state to state, but these laws could well pass your property to relatives whom you would not wish to inherit your assets. In New York, for example, if a married person with children dies without a will, his or her spouse receives the first $50,000 and half of the rest of the estate while the child or children equally divide the remainder of the estate.

Doing It Yourself

Can you write your own will? Take what anyone says with a grain of salt and take what I say, as a lawyer who prepares wills for a living, with a pound of salt, but that said, yes, you can write your own will. You also can take out your own appendix with a penknife, but I would not suggest that you try either. Wills are technical documents with precise rules as to their execution. It is easy for the layman to make a mistake that might have disastrous consequences.

A good example of the problems that can arise when someone fails to have a proper will is found in the estate of famed *On the Road* television correspondent, Charles Kuralt. Charles Kuralt, who apparently spent a great deal of time on the road, owned 90 acres of land in Montana, where the married Kuralt spent much time with his mistress of 29 years, Patricia Shannon. Following Kuralt's death, Ms. Shannon claimed that, in a letter to her from Kuralt written a mere two weeks before his death, he promised to change his will to give his Montana land to her at his death. Montana law provides for self-written informal wills. Ms. Shannon argued that his letter, particularly by the underlining by Kuralt of the word "inherit" in and of itself constituted a valid, informal will indicating Kuralt's intention to give her the property at his death. Not surprisingly, his wife as well as his children from a previous marriage disagreed, arguing instead that Kuralt was well aware of how to have a formal will prepared and that his intention was not to make an informal Montana will. The case went all the way to the Montana Supreme Court, which ruled in favor of Ms. Shannon, awarding her the 90 acres of land.

Living Trusts

When it comes to estate planning, one size definitely does not fit all. Although it is true that everyone should have a will, Health Care Proxy, and a Durable Power of Attorney, once you get beyond these documents, what you should have as a part of your own personal planning depends on your own particular situation, desires, and goals. There are many vastly different kinds of trusts that can serve many valuable purposes, including legitimate income tax avoidance, reducing estate taxes, probate avoidance, and liability protection.

In 2002, Congress held hearings on Living Trusts to determine whether federal regulation was needed for this particular estate-planning tool that has too often been oversold to the public, particularly to senior citizens. However, presently, there are no federal regulations governing the use of Living Trusts.

There are many variations of a Living Trust; in fact, the term itself merely means any trust that is created during your lifetime as opposed to being created through your will after your death.

Deciding on a Living Revocable Trust

The most basic form of a Living Trust, one that is most often pitched to senior citizens by aggressive salespeople, who often are not even lawyers, is a Living Revocable Trust, in which you can act as your own trustee during your lifetime and can revoke or amend it any time you wish. At your death, the assets contained in the trust are distributed to the beneficiaries whom you designate in the trust outside of probate. But, probate in many states, particularly for smaller estates, is not as expensive or time consuming as people often assume. Almost all the states have simplified procedures for the settlement of smaller estates, which range from as little as $3,000 estates in Alabama to as much as $100,000 estates in Ohio. That said, Living Revocable Trusts are appropriate for many people.

If your assets are more than what would allow you to be eligible for your state's small estate settlement procedure, or if you wish the privacy that a trust will provide as to your assets, a Living Revocable Trust may be for you. If you set up a trust and put assets into the trust during your lifetime, all the assets contained within the trust will pass to the people you name as beneficiaries of the trust at your death, without the delays or costs involved in the probating of an estate. In addition, a trust is totally private, unlike probate records, which are available to anyone who inquires.

If you have young or even not-so-young children, or grandchildren, you may wish to have a trust that can manage and distribute your assets over a timetable you determine. If you do not have a trust, assets that are left to children or grandchildren, for example, must be given to them when they reach the age of majority, generally 18 years old.

A trust can also allow you to name the person whom you would want to manage the assets in the trust on your behalf if you were to become incapacitated. This can be done without the involvement of the courts, avoiding additional costs and maintaining privacy as to your affairs.

The most basic form of a Living Revocable Trust allows you to be your own trustee and the beneficiary during your lifetime. Therefore, you can manage the trust assets for your own benefit during your lifetime without anyone's interference. With this type of trust, you do not even need to get a tax identification number for the trust or file income tax returns for the trust during your lifetime. You can use your own Social Security number as an identifying number for the trust, and you report the income from the trust on your own Form 1040 income tax return.

Important Reminder

One of the most common mistakes made by people who have trusts created mainly to avoid probate is that they neglect to put their assets into the name of the trust. For real estate, you need to have a deed drafted, transferring title to the property into the trust. However, for just about everything else, all you need do is send to the bank, brokerage house, or wherever your assets are being held a letter requesting that the title to your property be put into the name of the trust. If you fail to do this, you will have an empty trust that will be of little use for avoiding probate.

Important Reminder Number Two

If you use a Living Revocable Trust to avoid probate, it is important to remember to have your will be a *pourover* will, which will take whatever assets are not in your trust at the time of your death and pour them over into the trust so that the trust will have all of your property, including anything you might have omitted putting into the trust before your death or assets which came to your estate following your death.

Important Reminder Number Three (In Case You Are Keeping Count)

A Living Revocable Trust is not a substitute for a will, but rather supplements and works with your will. A will is necessary not just to deal with property that may not have been contained in your trust at the time of your death, but also to serve as a document by which someone of your choice is appointed by the Probate Court to represent your estate in matters relating to income taxes and estate taxes as well as to deal with any other claims or matters with which your estate may be involved.

Choosing a Trustee

One of the most important decisions in creating a trust is the choice of a trustee. The *trustee* is the person who manages your trust. Although with the most basic Living Revocable Trust, you may choose to be the trustee for yourself during your lifetime, you should name a successor trustee to act for you later if you are unable to act as trustee or to manage the trust upon your death.

Sometimes, people choose a bank trust department as trustee; other times, they may choose a relative or friend in whom they have great faith. Each choice has advantages and disadvantages. A bank trust department or other corporate fiduciary is, most likely, not personally familiar with your family's interpersonal dynamics and relationships. Cost is also a factor in picking a corporate trustee. The fees charged by corporate fiduciaries are often high. In their favor is the fact that they are pretty sure to be around when you need them. Family members or friends may be more familiar with your family but may be susceptible to influences within the family, which you may not wish. They also are mortal, unlike banks, which have no heart. (Oops, my personal bias is showing.) Your human friends or relatives, unfortunately, could themselves die before your trust is fully administered; you take this risk when you name a friend or relative as trustee. As to investment and money management acumen, bank trust departments and corporate fiduciaries certainly have that expertise, although if your friend or relative serving as a trustee has "common sense" (which I must admit is sometimes not that common), he or she can retain independent lawyers, accountants, or investment brokers with whom to consult. Sometimes, a compromise solution is to name a personal friend or relative as a co-trustee with a bank trust department.

Choosing a Trust Protector

Although the use of what is now called Trust Protectors has been with us for a while, only recently has it become popular. A Trust Protector is someone other than the primary trustee, who is named in the trust and given special powers, such as the authority to remove a trustee or amend the trust in response to changing laws or other changed circumstance.

Most often, a person creating a trust will name a friend, relative, accountant or lawyer as a Trust Protector. This person, although now often referred to as a Trust Protector, is actually just another trustee with specific, limited powers. "Trust Protector" sounds so much better, though, than "Just Another Trustee with Specific, Limited Powers." The Trust Protector may be a person whom you might not consider qualified to manage the trust on a regular basis, but in whom you have extreme faith to oversee the trust's operation to make sure that it is managed in a way that is most consistent with your goals in establishing the trust.

Some examples of special powers given to Trust Protectors are the power to change distributions to beneficiaries when individual circumstances warrant such a change; the power to remove the primary trustee when that person or institution, such as a bank trust department, is not acting in a manner that you, as the creator of the trust, would have wished; and the power to amend the trust to ensure that it complies with laws that may change from time to time. This last is particularly important in the area of trusts used for long-term care planning and to preserve Medicaid eligibility, for which the laws have changed often in recent years, leaving people who previously created irrevocable trusts in the lurch when new laws were applied to older trusts. Trust Protectors may provide greater flexibility and protection of your trust and are worth considering.

Incentive Trusts

It certainly is true that you can't take it with you. But, with an Incentive Trust, you can have a continuing influence on the people to whom you leave your assets even after you are gone. A recent trend in estate planning involves the use of an Incentive Trust, which is a type of trust that distributes your assets after your death upon the fulfillment of conditions that you establish with the trust. In this way, the trust can be used to either reward and encourage actions or to discourage other actions. For example, you may wish to leave money to a beneficiary on the condition that he or she completes some particular level of education. Or you may wish to condition the payment of money from the trust on the successful completion of a drug or alcohol treatment program. The range of behavior or achievements that you can encourage or discourage by use of an Incentive Trust is practically limitless and, of course, can be tailored to your own particular family situation. The only limitation is the vague legal standard that the condition not violate "public policy."

The choice of trustee for an Incentive Trust is particularly important, because you want someone who is both familiar with the trust creator's intentions and the people involved, yet independent enough of the beneficiaries so as not to be unduly subject to their influence.

The trust's language must also be carefully crafted to be clear. Most problems with Incentive Trusts come when the terms and conditions of the trust are not sufficiently clear.

But, with these issues being understood, if you feel the need to have a continuing influence in certain people's lives after your death, an Incentive Trust might be the way to go.

Estate Taxes

"Over and over again courts have said that there is nothing sinister in so arranging one's affairs as to keep taxes as low as possible. Everybody does so, rich or poor; and all do right for nobody owes any public duty to pay more than the law demands; taxes are enforced exactions, not voluntary contributions. To demand more in the name of morals is mere cant."

—Judge Learned Hand

By the way, for those unfamiliar with the word "cant" as used by Judge Hand, a federal judge from the early 1900s, it means hypocritical and sanctimonious speech.

Estate taxes are still a concern of many senior citizens. Congress' attempt at estate tax reform has done little to clarify the situation.

Benjamin Franklin said that the only things that were certain were death and taxes, which would seem to indicate that death taxes would be about the most certain thing of all, but Benjamin Franklin never met our present United States Senators and Congressmen.

In 2001, the federal estate tax exemption stood at $675,000 when the law was changed by the Economic Growth and Tax Relief and Reconciliation Act of 2001 (EGTRA) to increase the exemption amount to a million dollars in 2002 and 2003; 1.5 million dollars in

2004 and 2005; 2 million dollars in 2006–2008; and 3.5 million dollars in 2009. Then, the fun began. According to the provisions of EDTRA, starting on January 1, 2010, the estate tax was repealed (sort of). I say "sort of" because EGTRA also provided for the estate tax to magically reappear on January 1, 2011 at the reduced level of a one million dollar exemption and a maximum tax rate of 55 percent as compared to the 3.5 million dollar exemption level and maximum exemption level and maximum tax rate of 45 percent in effect in 2009. So in reality, EGTRA only provided for a 365-day repeal of the estate tax whereupon it would return in 2011 with a vengeance.

So, why would anyone do this?

The reason behind this apparently illogical behavior by our lawmakers is what is called "sunsetting." A sunset law occurs when Congress passes a particular law that will only be in effect for a specific period of time. It is not uncommon for tax laws to sunset. It is also not uncommon for there to be such an uproar when a particular law providing benefits to the electorate is about to go away that Congress makes the particular law permanent. The tortured reasoning behind a sunset law is that the government needs to project sufficient revenue to operate so when it computed that lost revenue that would occur as a result of the reducing of the estate tax, it also took into account that it would get the money back later when these tax benefits were taken back. The reality of the situation is that no one, not even members of Congress, ever thought it would come to that. It was widely assumed that Congress would take the ten years of EGTRA to thoughtfully debate and craft a more permanent resolution of the estate tax, which generally was thought to be a continuation of the 3.5 million dollar exemption, perhaps indexed to inflation.

But, although the House of Representatives managed to pass an extension of the 2009 rules for estate taxes that would have given Congress time to put together a more comprehensive resolution to the estate tax in 2010, partisan differences in the Senate prevented any legislation from being passed.

So, for the year of 2010, we had no federal estate taxes, although state estate taxes still applied during that time.

With the deadline of January 1, 2011, and a return of the estate tax with only a one million dollar exemption looming, Congress passed the Tax Relief, Unemployment Insurance Authorization and Job Creation Act of 2010 on December 17, 2010. This law provided an estate tax exemption of five million dollars and a lifetime gift tax exemption of five million dollars. Lost in the euphoria of this solution to the estate tax quandary was the fact that this law, too, was set to sunset on January 1, 2013, with a return of the one-million-dollar exemption again if Congress once again fails to act before that date.

Dealing with the uncertainties of estate taxes is important.

The Credit Shelter Trust

Maybe The Rolling Stones had it right when the band said, "Gimme Shelter." A credit shelter trust, sometimes called a bypass trust and other times an AB trust, is a trust that allows married couples to leverage their estate tax credit or exemption so that they double the protection of their assets from federal estate taxes.

Applying an Example

Principle: When a married person dies, leaving all assets to a spouse, there is no immediate federal estate tax on anything that passes to that surviving spouse regardless of the amount.

Example: Suppose Adam has an estate of $10 million. He could leave that entire amount to Eve, his spouse, without any kind of trust and not incur any federal estate tax liability. However, if Eve later dies with an estate of $10 million, her estate has an exemption from federal estate taxes of $5 million (in 2012), leaving $5 million of Eve's estate subject to federal estate taxes.

Principle: With a credit shelter trust, when the first spouse dies, the exemption of $5 million (in 2012) is placed into the credit shelter trust for the benefit of the surviving spouse and whomever else the deceased spouse named in the credit shelter trust.

Example: If Adam had a credit shelter trust, there would be no federal estate tax whatsoever either at his death or the later death of Eve. Here's how.

Principle: The assets in this trust can be used for the benefit of the spouse or other beneficiaries of the trust, but the assets can also be allowed to grow free from all federal estate taxes. When the surviving spouse later dies, whatever is then contained in the credit shelter trust, which may have substantially increased in value, will pass to the ultimate beneficiaries such as children designated in the credit shelter trust, free of all income taxes and estate taxes.

Example: Adam dies first and leaves an estate of $10 million. Half of the $10 million would go either directly or through a marital deduction trust (a trust to manage assets exclusively for a surviving spouse) to Eve and would avoid federal estate taxes. When Eve later dies, only the $5 million in her own name (or in the marital deduction trust) would be in her federal taxable estate. Since $5 million is by law (in 2012) exempt from federal estate taxes, Cain and Able, Eve's designated beneficiaries, would pay no federal estate taxes whatsoever.

Using a Disclaimer

A disclaimer is a provision of law that permits someone who would inherit either as a beneficiary of a retirement account, a beneficiary of a life-insurance policy, a surviving joint owner, a beneficiary of an estate or a beneficiary of a trust to disclaim or refuse to accept all or a part of his or her inheritance. Disclaimers help provide greater flexibility to be able to effectively deal with changing state and federal estate tax laws. For example, you can designate your spouse as the primary beneficiary of your IRA, your children as the secondary beneficiaries, and your grandchildren as the tertiary beneficiaries. After your death, it is then up to your surviving spouse to determine whether to take all or a portion of the inherited IRA or disclaim all or a portion of the IRA. Any amount disclaimed passes to the children, who, in turn, may choose to disclaim the money to the grandchildren without any gift tax. Thus, the benefits of tax avoidance could be stretched over the lifetimes of your descendants. For example, a ten-year old grandchild who inherited a Roth IRA from a grandparent would have 72.8 years to withdraw the money in the inherited Roth IRA income tax-free. The money remaining in the Roth IRA would continue to compound income tax-free during that time.

State Estate Taxes

As the federal estate tax laws gradually increased the amount of the exemption, the states, which generally took as their share of the estate tax a portion of the federal estate tax, found that their estate tax revenues were going down at a time when their need for revenue was increasing. In response to this situation, many states changed their estate taxes to tax estates with less money than would result in a federal estate tax. Massachusetts, for example, was faced with the unpopular position of either raising its estate tax or losing revenue if it kept its estate tax tied to a portion of the federal estate tax. With some creative thinking, what they came up with was a new law that allowed them to say that they were not raising taxes, but continuing to tie their estate taxes to the federal exemption amount; however, the federal exemption amount that they were tying itself to was not the present federal exemption amount, but rather the one-million dollar exemption of 2002. Many people are finding that their estates are subject to state estate taxes even if they do not require the payment of a federal estate tax. If you think you might be subject to a state estate tax, revisit your estate planning to make the necessary fine-tuning to provide for these changes in the state estate tax laws. Or you might want to consider moving. Alabama, Florida, and Nevada have specific provisions in their state constitutions that prevent the states from making separate estate tax laws.

Irrevocable Life Insurance Trusts

Many people are under the false impression that life insurance proceeds are not subject to estate taxes. Many people are under the false impression that a Boston Cream Pie (the official state dessert of Massachusetts) is a pie. It is not—it is a cake, but that is another subject. Some people even buy life insurance to have it available to pay for possible estate taxes when, if not done properly, all they succeed in doing is just increasing the amount of their taxable estate.

Life insurance is subject to estate taxes according to what the IRS refers to as "incidents of ownership." This means that it is irrelevant, for estate tax purposes, who you name as your beneficiary if you own the policy and pay the premiums. If you own the policy, regardless of whom you name as beneficiary, the entire amount of the life-insurance policy is included in your taxable estate for purposes of determining estate taxes.

Fortunately, there is a relatively simple solution to this problem. A specially constructed Irrevocable Life Insurance Trust allows you to shelter your life insurance proceeds from estate taxes for multiple generations and still permit you to pay the premiums if you so desire. At one time, the IRS took the position that a gift tax would have to be paid by the person setting up a life insurance trust whenever he or she paid the premiums, arguing that it was not an exempt gift, subject to the $10,000 per year gift tax exclusion. (In 2012, the exclusion amount is $13,000.) The reasoning of the IRS was that, because a person who benefited from a life insurance trust did not receive anything until after the person creating the trust had died, the annual payments of life-insurance premiums should be taxable gifts because the annual exemption for gift taxes only applies to gifts of present interests, not future interests.

A clever estate planner, however, came up with a loophole that would have pleased W.C. Fields. He argued that if the beneficiaries of the trust have the right to receive the money used to pay for the life-insurance premiums and if they do not take the money (and they never do), it still is a present interest because they could have asked for the money used to pay for the premiums and, therefore, the premium payments should be exempt from gift tax. When the IRS remained unconvinced by this argument, the trust creator appealed to the Federal Courts, which decided the case of Crummey v. Commissioner in 1968 in favor of the trust creator. The loophole has become forever identified with the name of the man whose trust was at the center of this controversy: Crummey. Some looked at this as somewhat unfortunate, because who would want something commonly known as a "Crummey Trust." I, however, prefer to look at the glass as half full and am grateful that the trust's creator was not named "Crappy."

When it came time to write my own trust, my life-insurance agent, Ron Nathan, had to convince the life-insurance company with which I have a policy that the name of the trust on the life-insurance application form was a legitimate trust and not a joke. Apparently, they were somewhat bewildered by the name of my trust, which is "In God We Trust." Ron had to explain to them that, although the name might be unusual, it was the legitimate name of my trust and not a joke. You can name your trust just about anything. My wife loves carousel horses, so she named her trust the "Carousel Trust."

Loophole

If you buy an insurance policy and then transfer it into an Irrevocable Life Insurance Trust, a quirk in the tax laws prevents the trust from sheltering the insurance from estate taxes for three years. However, if you first set up the trust and then have the trust purchase the life-insurance policy, your protection from estate taxes is immediate.

Charitable Remainder Trust

Talk about your win-win situations. A Charitable Remainder Trust is one you set up that generally provides you income for your lifetime; at your death, whatever is in the trust passes to a charity that you have previously picked. When you set up the trust by contributing assets to it, you will get a charitable deduction that you can use on your income tax return for the year in which you set up the trust. The amount of the deduction is based on the estimated value of the assets expected to pass to the charity at your death. So, by using this kind of a trust, you provide yourself with a source of income, reduce your income taxes, and make a charitable donation—all at the same time.

But, what if you want to leave money to your children or anyone else at your death? In that case, you take the money that you save on your income taxes by the use of the deduction, set up an Irrevocable Life Insurance Trust, and have the trust buy a life-insurance policy on your life to replace the money you are giving to the charity. Now, it's a win-win-win situation.

Defective Trusts

Generally, when you think of something as being defective, you think that is a bad thing. However, when it comes to estate planning, a Defective Trust just might be a good thing and save you a great deal of money that might otherwise be lost to estate and gift taxes.

For example, suppose you have some stock you want to give to your children or grandchildren. If you wait to give them that stock until you are old or bequeath it to them, the stock may have highly appreciated, and the corresponding gift tax or estate tax could be large. Instead, you could set up a particular kind of trust called a Defective Trust. You could put the stock into the trust and name your children, grandchildren, or whomever you wish as the beneficiaries of the trust. You would continue to pay the income taxes on any dividends earned by the stock rather than have the trust pay the income taxes at its higher rates. Then, at a specific time that you choose or at your death, the assets in the trust are distributed without any further gift tax or estate tax to the beneficiaries you named.

The trust is called a Defective Trust because it transfers property to a trust, but does so in a manner that, for income tax purposes only, the property is treated as still being owned by the creator of the trust. This is a particularly good technique for stock or other assets that may grow significantly in value but not result in large amounts of taxable income. Thus, a Defective Trust removes the assets and their increasing value from your taxable estate while costing you little, if anything, in gift tax.

Qualified Personal Residence Trust

A Qualified Personal Residence Trust (QPRT) is a type of trust that permits a senior to give away his or her home, which may be appreciating in value, at a low gift tax basis. A QPRT may be used for a person's primary residence or even a vacation home. It is a way of taking out of one's future estate subject to estate taxes an appreciating asset so as to reduce the amount of any possible future estate tax. In fact, the gift of the home through a QPRT is valued for gift tax purposes not at the value of the home at the time of the making of the gift into the trust, but rather at a discounted value based on a formula that considers the amount of years that the home will be in the trust before it is transferred out of the trust to the ultimate beneficiaries.

For example, if I had a summer home on Nantucket (if I say it enough, maybe it will happen), I could put the home into a QPRT under the terms of which I would be the beneficiary of the trust and could use the home for any period of time that I designate in the trust, such as seven years. At the end of the seven years, the home would be conveyed out of the trust to the ultimate beneficiaries, who in my example would be my children. The value of the home for purposes of ascertaining any possible gift tax on the gift (or how much of the lifetime 5 million dollar gift tax exemption to use to cover the value of any gift tax) is discounted according to a complicated formula that includes life expectancy IRS charts that reduce the value of the gift such that the longer that the trust continues before the home is transferred to the ultimate beneficiaries, the less the home is valued for purposes of gift tax. The longer the period of the trust, the greater is the discount for gift tax purposes. However, there's one important caveat to remember: If the person setting up the trust (me in my example) dies prior to the termination of the trust period, the value of the home comes back into the deceased trust owner's estate for estate taxes at the full fair market value of the home at the time of the death of the trust maker.

A home, the value of which is $500,000 at the time that a 60-year old person put it into a 15-year QPRT, would be considered to have made a gift of only $233,180.

Section 529 Plans

Putting away money for your children's or grandchildren's college education can be as simple as one, two, three if you use a plan known simply as five, two, nine (529). It also can provide some interesting estate planning opportunities for you as well.

Section 529 refers to a section of the Internal Revenue Code that first became part of the law in 1997. Under a 529 Plan, family members, such as parents or grandparents, can set up an investment account to be used for a child's or grandchild's college education costs.

Under the original 1997 law, taxes on the earnings of the account were deferred and were subject to tax when the student withdrew the funds for college expenses. Since 2002, the earnings are now tax free at withdrawal, and in some states, you can even get a tax deduction for contributing to a 529 Plan. In the back of this book is a chart that lists the states that allow income tax deductions for contributions to a 529 Plan.

Contributions to a 529 Plan are considered gifts for federal gift tax purposes, although as many people are aware, you can make gifts of up to $13,000 (in 2012) per calendar year without incurring a gift tax or even having to file a federal gift tax return.

The laws regarding 529 Plans are still evolving. Before choosing a 529 Plan, make sure that you have the most current information on the 529 Plan for any state that you may be considering.

Loophole

Annual nontaxable contributions in a calendar year from a husband and wife can be combined for a total of up to $26,000, regardless of whether all the money came from only one of the spouses.

Loophole

Section 529 further provides for a gift of as much as $65,000 in a single year without incurring a gift tax when that amount is considered to be five years worth of annual gifts. So, a married couple could actually give up to $130,000 to a Section 529 Plan in a single year without having to pay a gift tax.

Among the many advantages to Section 529 Plans is the fact that the person creating the account still controls the money even after the child reaches the age of majority, unlike the case of money contained in a Uniform Transfers to Minors Act Account, which passes to the child at the age of majority. In addition, if the child does not go to college, the creator of the account can use the money for the education expenses of any other family member.

Loophole

If you set up a Section 529 Plan for your children or grandchildren, you can still take out the money for your own use. So, if you needed the money, for example, to pay for a nursing home, you could withdraw the money whenever you choose. There would be a 10 percent penalty on the earnings. However, potentially the tax-deferred increase in value of the 529 Plan might make the 10 percent penalty of relatively little consequence, in which case you might find people using the plans as elaborate tax shelters.

Planning for Your Pets

It may be a dog's life, but if that dog, cat (or as in the case of my wife and me, horse and llama), is yours, its life is pretty important to you. So, how do you provide for your pets in your estate plan? Forty-six states now have laws, all of fairly recent origin, that allow pet owners to establish specific trusts for the ongoing care of their animals following the death of the pet's owner. Only Kentucky, Louisiana, Minnesota, and Mississippi do not have laws that permit such trusts. These laws permit trusts that specifically name animals as trust beneficiaries. Although these laws differ somewhat from state to state, most states permit money to be set aside in a trust for the benefit of the pet. The animal's owner and creator of the trust can make specific provisions for care and housing of the animal if he or she wishes. Upon the death of the pet, if there are any funds remaining, the trust will provide for a secondary beneficiary, which can be a person or even a charity if the pet owner so chooses. These laws also permit judges to reduce the amount contained in the trust if they believe it exceeds what is required to take care of the animal. When hotel magnate Leona Helmsley died in 2007, she left 12 million dollars to her dog "Trouble." A judge later reduced this amount to a mere two million dollars, a figure one would think that would hardly keep one in dog food, but which the judge apparently thought was sufficient to meet Trouble's needs.

Regardless of how you choose to provide for your pet, the most important choice you will make is that of whom you pick to care for your pet in the future. The whole subject may seem frivolous to some, but to those of us who have animals that play a significant part in our lives, this is an important issue. By the way, just for your information, llamas generally do not spit at humans, just at each other, and my advice is not to get in the way when that happens.

Digital Estate Planning

Many senior citizens are active on their computers storing documents, photographs, or other material, as well as being active online doing online banking, online purchasing, or other online activities. Without proper planning for these assets, they can be lost forever. Composer Leonard Bernstein left an inaccessible memoir on his computer, which no one has been able to have access to, because he died without letting anyone know his computer password.

It is important for seniors to inventory their digital assets and indicate how to access them, including passwords. The most efficient way to deal with this is through a separate trust that can be kept confidential.

Presently, only five states have laws that specifically deal with digital assets, but even in those states that do not have laws that deal with digital assets, a trust can be established to take care of these important matters.

POD Accounts

Stay out of expensive joints, as mentioned before, was the advice of one of my professors at Boston College Law School, and that good advice has many layers. Certainly, it may serve as an admonition to avoid places, such as restaurants, that may be a bit overpriced, but it was also intended to warn us of the perils of joint tenancies.

A joint tenancy is a way for more than one person to own property, such as a bank account, a home, or a stock. By law, under the terms of a joint tenancy, if one joint owner dies, the surviving joint owners inherit the share of the deceased owner without having to go through probate. Thus, the transfer of the deceased owner's interest in the property occurs quickly and with privacy. Note that it does not, however, provide any protection of the assets from estate taxes. Also, note that when you have jointly owned assets, the property may, for example, become subject to claims against any of the joint owners regardless of who provided the money to purchase the stock or set up the bank account. In addition, the person you name as a joint owner also has access to the joint asset. So, a joint owner may legally empty your joint bank account.

One way of achieving probate avoidance without the risks of a joint account is through the use of a Living Revocable Trust, but an easier, less expensive alternative, available in 44 states at least as to stocks, bonds, and brokerage accounts, is the use of a POD registration. POD stands for Payable on Death, and it is a simple way by which you can add the name of a person or persons to the ownership of stocks, bonds, or brokerage accounts without the risks of joint ownership. Upon the death of the owner of the account, ownership of the asset passes automatically and outside of probate to whomever you name to receive it. Meanwhile, until your death, you are free to deal with the stocks or assets in the brokerage account without limitation.

Loophole

If you live in one of the six states that does not have POD laws, you still may be able to use a POD designation if the mutual fund or stocks you own are companies that are based in states that permit POD designation.

Second Marriages

According to the old Frank Sinatra song, "Love is better the second time around." And he should have known. After all, he was married four times. Many older couples face numerous issues that should be considered before remarrying after a death or divorce. A prenuptial agreement to determine division of property in the event of a death or divorce is particularly important when either new spouse has children from a previous marriage. Prenuptial agreements are explained in detail in Chapter 1, "Asset Protection."

Marriage itself automatically invalidates a will in most states, so anyone marrying or remarrying will want to have his or her will reviewed and revised. Beyond a simple will, important documents, such as Durable Powers of Attorney and HealthCare Proxies should also be redone. Some couples want to take advantage of the estate-tax-saving provisions of the marital deduction while still ensuring that funds are preserved for surviving children after the surviving spouse has died. For such couples, a special type of marital deduction trust, called a Qualified Terminable Interest Trust (QTIP), will shelter from estate taxes funds left in the trust for the benefit of a surviving spouse while preventing those assets from being squandered by the surviving spouse.

It is also important to update the names of your beneficiaries on any insurance policies or retirement accounts. In regard to a 401(k) retirement plan, a surviving spouse has an automatic claim to the assets, regardless of who is listed as a beneficiary unless the spouse has waived all rights to that account. So, if you want your 401(k) to go to your children, for example, you must arrange for your spouse to execute the appropriate waiver with your plan administrator.

Estate Planning for Unmarried Couples

For a myriad of reasons, many couples live together without marrying. For these people, be they gay or straight, estate planning is of a heightened importance because the law will not generally provide for the surviving partner when one of them dies. Many seniors, in particular, may choose to live together without being married so as not to lose pension benefits they may have from a previous marriage.

A living-together agreement, similar to a prenuptial agreement, is a good way to provide a measure of protection for couples in the event of the death of one of them or their separation. But, such an agreement is most certainly not enough. A properly prepared will is even more important for unmarried people living together; without a will, assets would, through the laws of intestacy, automatically pass to relatives the deceased partner most likely would not have intended to receive those assets. Health Care Proxies and Durable Powers of Attorney also become of paramount importance. Some retirement plans have benefits that will automatically pass to a spouse, but do not automatically provide for payment of benefits to a domestic partner. Unmarried couples should make sure that the beneficiary designations on all of their retirement plans and life-insurance policies specify those to whom they wish to have these benefits pass in the event of death.

Now That You Have a Plan

Estate planning is not static. Review your documents whenever there is a major change in the law or a major change in your own personal or financial circumstances. Some of the changes in personal circumstances that would warrant a reconsideration of your estate plan include the death of a named beneficiary or the divorce of you or a named beneficiary. As a rule of thumb, it also is a good idea to revisit your estate plan every five years.

Having all of your documents in order is of little help to your family if they do not know where the operative documents are located. It is important to have a document location list that provides a precise indication of the whereabouts of your estate planning documents, such as your will, Durable Power of Attorney, Health Care Proxy, life-insurance policies, and retirement beneficiary designations. Just preparing such a document (see the Document Location form in the back of this book) will go a long way toward helping you organize your plan for yourself. Once this has been done, make sure that the appropriate people know where these documents are located and how to access them.

Banks and other financial institutions get taken over and lose things. Make sure that you have a copy of the beneficiary designations to any retirement plans, IRAs, life-insurance policies, or any other document that has a beneficiary. Have the beneficiary designation acknowledged by the bank or other institution and keep it with your other important documents. In some states, a safe deposit box is sealed and generally unavailable upon the death of anyone whose name is on the box. This is not the case in other states in which a safe deposit box would be an ideal place to keep important documents safe and secure. The important thing to remember is that you should have your executor or other agents listed on the safe deposit box as people who are allowed access to the box.

You should also have a form that lists the names and contact numbers for the important financial and legal advisors with whom you do business—for example, your lawyer, insurance agent, accountant, and financial planner. Again, you will find a form you can use in the back of this book (see "Procedures to Follow Upon the Death of ___" in the "Forms" section).

Your Health Care Proxy should be executed as duplicate originals. Keep one with your important papers, and give the other to your primary care physician (PCP) so that you can be sure that your wishes will be acknowledged and followed.

5

Investments

"October. This is one of the peculiarly dangerous months to speculate in stocks.

The others are July, January, September, April, November, May, March, June, December, August, and February."

—Mark Twain

In recent years, people have become more aware of just how difficult it can be to invest successfully. Yet, the need of older people to make their money work for them has never been greater. Truly, these are the times that try men's wallets (apologies to Charles Dickens). Knowledge of the vast array of investments available is important. This chapter helps you better understand investments, so that you can choose the most appropriate financial strategy for you.

Mutual Funds

Particularly for people who do not have a great deal of money to invest, a mutual fund can provide many benefits. Perhaps paramount of the benefits of mutual fund investing is the built-in diversification. Mutual funds may contain anywhere from 30 to more than 100 stocks. To get that important investment diversification on your own, you would have to invest much more money than the cost of buying into a mutual fund. Diversification is important, because it spreads out your risk. With all of your money in one basket (or stock), if that basket springs a leak (what a mixed metaphor) or that company has problems, you are in trouble.

Also, with a mutual fund, you get professional management: a team of people who are experienced in stock purchases who spend their entire time gathering investment information, analyzing it, and making investment decisions.

You may remember the old cigarette commercial (which is not a commercial for old cigarettes, but rather a commercial of long ago for cigarettes) in which the actors in the commercial, replete with black eyes, said that they would rather fight than switch cigarette brands. Well, sometimes switching is a good thing. When you invest with a mutual fund company, such as Fidelity, Vanguard, or any of the other major investment management companies, you are permitted to switch your investment from one mutual fund to any other within, what they refer to as, the family of funds the company offers, often at no charge. In this way, if you want to move your investment dollars from a growth mutual fund to a value fund or even to a money market fund, for example, you can do so quickly, easily, and economically.

Although it is not much fun to think about it, taxes play a significant role in investments. Mutual funds provide detailed year-end statements with all the important information you need to prepare your income tax returns and evaluate your investments.

No load mutual funds can be bought directly from the mutual funds themselves through toll-free phone numbers or websites, which can be found in magazine or newspaper advertisements. Another easy way for a little one-stop shopping is to buy mutual funds through a discount broker; frequently, you don't even have to pay transaction fees.

Fees and Charges

In sports, it is not whether you win or lose that is important, it's the point spread; when it comes to investing, it is not what you make that counts, it is what you keep. Mutual funds contain an abundance of fees and charges that, over time, can significantly reduce your earnings. Since 1988, the Securities and Exchange Commission (SEC) has required that all mutual funds clearly disclose in their prospectuses all of their fees and charges, along with a chart that shows the effect of the various fees and charges on a $1,000 investment over one, three, five, and ten years. I know that reading a prospectus is something people want to do about as much as give themselves a root canal, but skipping to the section on fee disclosure is a quick step that is relatively painless. So, let's look at the fees you will find.

Front-End Load Fees

First off are front-end load fees, which are not regulated by the SEC, but are limited by the Financial Industry Regulatory Authority (FINRA), the largest non-governmental organization that regulates security sales in America, to 8.5 percent of your investment just for the privilege of investing with a particular mutual fund company. Before you have even started, you are already 8.5 percent behind. That makes for a lot of catch up. These front-end loads are only found in funds designated as "load funds," which are funds generally sold through a broker or financial planner and which carry a sales commission. Unfortunately, the fact that a fund is a load fund is not always readily seen unless you look in the prospectus. You might assume that if you are charged a fee for merely purchasing shares in a load mutual fund, these funds would provide better returns than no load funds that do not charge sales fees. You would be wrong, however. Load funds do not, as a group, do any better than the no load mutual funds you can buy on your own, without a salesman and without having to pay a commission.

Why, then, do people continue to buy load funds? Load funds are sold by salespeople with whom investors have a personal relationship. These salespeople tell you that the fees are not that large when you think of your investment as a long-term one. But, the bottom line is that unless you need the salesperson's help in choosing the funds in which to invest, the cost does not seem to be worth it.

Mutual Fund Marketing Fees: 12b-1

12b-1 fees represent mutual fund-marketing fees. They were first approved by the SEC in 1980 as a marketing fee originally intended to aid the mutual fund industry, which at the time was suffering from a bear market, share redemption, and resulting shrinking assets. The intention was to allow the mutual-fund companies to recover their marketing costs, such as advertising and mailing costs, while they tried to stem the tide of redemptions and encourage growth.

Since 1984, the average 12b-1 fee has gone up 500 percent, costing investors a considerable amount of money. In fact, according to an article in the June 10, 2002, edition of *Business Week* online,[1] if fund expenses are calculated as a percent of the return on your investment, rather than a percent of the assets in the fund, many mutual funds are taking anywhere from 10 to 15 percent of investors' profits. The Vanguard Group of mutual funds, for example, has total fees of only a little over 4 percent of investors' returns; meanwhile, if you add up all the fees of some other mutual fund families, loads and charges take almost 16 percent of your profits.

Somewhat disturbing is the fact that you are charged 12b-1 fees year after year, although they are considered a marketing fee. Think about it. Why should you be charged a fee for the marketing of a mutual fund that you already own? In reality, a 12b-1 fee truly represents just another hidden charge in a business that is filled with fine print.

Management Fees

All funds, whether they are load funds or no load funds, charge management fees, which range from 0.5 percent to 1 percent of the total assets of the mutual fund.

Redemption Fees

Redemption fees, or back-end loads, represent fees that some mutual funds charge you when you sell any of your shares. Again, no load funds do not charge these fees that can eat into your profit.

Cost Comparison

So, how do you compare the costs of specific funds in which you may be interested to determine which ones will be best for you? Thankfully, the process is easier than you might imagine. FINRA has a simple-to-use, interactive Mutual Fund Analyzer that can help you compare the total costs of various mutual funds and the effects on your investments. Just go to the FINRA's website (www.finra.org) and follow the directions to get to the Mutual Fund Analyzer.

Types of Mutual Funds

Mutual funds come in more varieties than you can shake a stick at, which, considering the way the market sometimes performs, is exactly what people feel like doing from time to time. Some of the larger classes of funds include the following:

- **Aggressive growth funds.** These funds are highly speculative. They invest in companies that are expected to expand and grow rapidly.
- **Growth funds.** These funds are also speculative. They invest in companies that are anticipated to grow faster than the average stock (if there is such a thing).
- **Growth and income funds.** These funds contain a mix of the stock of companies, some of which would be characterized as "growth" whereas others are less growth-oriented companies that emphasize the payment of dividends.
- **Small-cap, mid-cap, and large-cap funds.** These designations refer to the total value of all the stock in a particular company, which is the company's capitalization. In essence, these are small, medium, or large companies.
- **Value funds.** These funds follow the strategy, popularized by Warren Buffet, of buying companies that have a low stock price when compared to their inherent worth or value.
- **International funds.** There is a whole world of investments beyond our borders. These types of funds are a simple way to invest in companies in foreign countries.
- **Bond funds.** These funds hold various kinds of bonds, from corporate to municipal to U.S. government bonds. Buying bonds through a mutual fund will provide you with a diversified portfolio of bonds and regular income payments.
- **Balanced funds.** These funds contain a combination of stocks and bonds.

- **Money market funds.** These funds consist of fairly secure money market instruments and commercial paper that provide a better interest rate than bank savings accounts and still allow you immediate access to your money through checks you can write against the account.

- **Ginnie Mae funds.** Ginnie Mae (GNMA) stands for Government National Mortgage Association, which is an agency of the federal government that insures payment of FHA and VA mortgages. By investing in a Ginnie Mae fund, you can effectively invest in real estate without the complications of owning real estate. It is a good way to diversify your portfolio. Ginnie Mae securities are guaranteed by the federal government. These are also a good investment for income rather than growth.

- **Fannie Mae funds.** Fannie Mae was the way the abbreviation for the Federal National Mortgage Association (FNMA) was pronounced. It sure sounds like a government agency, but it is not. For this reason, the company officially changed its name to Fannie Mae in 1997. Thanks to Mark Oliphant formerly of Fannie Mae for that piece of trivia. Fannie Mae issues mortgage-backed securities that are pooled in Fannie Mae mutual funds.

- **Freddie Mac funds.** Freddie Mac, the common name for the Federal Home Loan Mortgage Corporation, often abbreviated as FHLMC, also issues mortgage-backed securities that are pooled in a Freddie Mac mutual fund. Again, it is not a government agency, and as with Fannie Mae funds, its securities are not guaranteed by the federal government. Despite the fact that they are not guaranteed by the U.S. government, Fannie Mae and Freddie Mac securities are considered to be safer than other high-paying corporate bonds or municipal bonds. The return on Freddie Mac securities is usually higher than those of Fannie Maes and Ginnie Maes (sort of sounds like investments that should be managed by Jed Clampett).

- **Junk bond funds.** One person's junk is another person's treasure, and nowhere is this more apparent than with junk bonds, the rather pejorative name by which high-yield corporate bonds are often called. Junk bond funds invest in a portfolio of junk bonds issued by companies that, for whatever reason, are rated low by the various bond rating services and, therefore, must provide a higher interest rate to lure investors. Sometimes, junk bonds are a bad investment in a company that is not financially healthy; other times, they are a good investment in newer companies whose low bond rating is more reflective of a lack of a track record rather than economic instability.

- **REITs.** Real Estate Investment Trusts, or REITs, are mutual funds that invest in real estate. A fully diversified portfolio that will help buttress you against fluctuations in the economy should contain some real estate investments. A simple alternative to individual real estate ownership and its attendant aggravations is investing in a REIT that may contain residential or commercial properties.

- **Sector funds.** If, as Dirty Harry used to say, you "feel lucky," you can consider investing in sector funds, which is the investment equivalent of putting all of your eggs in one basket. Sector funds invest in a number of different companies in a single area of business, such as health care (if you think that with all those baby boomers getting older and older, someone is going to be meeting their medical needs), Internet, or biotechnology funds. With sector funds, you stand to make tremendous gains if you guess right as to what industries will be hot. Unfortunately, if you guess wrong with a sector fund, you stand to lose more than with a diversified mutual fund.

- **Index funds.** When it comes to mutual funds, the simplest way to invest—index funds—may very well be the best way to invest. Index funds are made up of all the stocks in a particular index, such as the S&P 500, which is made up of—you guessed it—500 of the most prominent companies in America. You will not do better than the general market with an index fund, because you are investing in the general market. On the other hand, because it takes no investment acumen for the managers of an index fund to pick stocks, the management fees are low, so more of your money is working for you rather than going to pay for high-priced investment management. In addition, the tax ramifications of an index fund can be less of a concern. Because the fund maintains a portfolio of the stocks in a particular index, sales of stock are reduced, which means less capital gains distributions for you to declare on your income tax return.

Investment guru Warren Buffet thinks so highly of Index Funds for the average investor that he has bet a million dollars against asset management firm Protégé Partners that an S&P Index fund will provide greater returns over ten years than the average returns of five hedge funds picked by Protégé Partners. The bet is for a period of ten years beginning in 2008, and it will be interesting to see who the ultimate winner is.

Mutual Funds and Taxes

Taxes are always a concern with mutual funds. Dividends, interest, and capital gains distributions are always passed on to the investors who must declare them on their income tax returns. In recent years, many people were startled and upset to find that, although the value of their mutual fund had gone down drastically, they had taxable capital gains distributions to report on their income tax returns, because the mutual fund had sold stocks at a gain although the overall value of the fund still remained low.

If you are seeking to reduce the tax ramifications of your mutual funds, look for funds that are deemed "tax efficient." These funds are often less aggressive in their trading strategies and may hold on to the stocks in their portfolios longer. You can find information about the tax efficiency of a fund either in its prospectus or on its website.

Loophole

Timing is important in many things in life, including buying mutual funds. You will be taxed on capital-gains distributions from your mutual fund any time they occur after you have bought into the fund. Earnings distributions are declared annually. If you buy shares in the mutual fund just before the declaration of earnings, you will have to pay income tax on the distribution the same as if you had owned the fund for the entire year. Therefore, it makes the most sense to buy your shares just after the mutual fund has made its capital gains distribution for the year; that way you avoid the taxes for that year. The easy way to find out when the distribution is declared is by just asking a representative of the fund.

DRIPs

Dividend Reinvestment Plans (DRIPs) are a good way to invest with no sales charges and only the most minor administration fees. With DRIPs, you can buy your stocks directly from the companies in which you are investing, and you can use your dividends to purchase more stock automatically. To make things even easier, more than a thousand companies actually allow you to buy shares of stock in their company right over the Internet. Although not every company has a DRIP program, many excellent companies with which you are familiar, such as General Electric, IBM, and Wal-Mart, have DRIP programs. If you are wondering why you may not have heard of DRIPs before, it's because the companies themselves do not advertise their DRIP programs, and you will never hear a broker tell you about them because there are no commissions.

Certificates of Deposit

Ask a teenager what a CD is and the answer will be a compact disc, which is how music is played today. But ask the parent or grand-parent of that teenager the same question and most likely the answer you will get is *Certificate of Deposit* (CD).

CDs are issued by banks and have penalties for early withdrawals of your money. At any one time, the longer you tie your money up in a CD, the higher the interest rate. A good strategy is to have a step approach to your CDs. Using this strategy, you could, for example, purchase five CDs, one maturing after one year, one maturing after two years and so on. When each CD matures, you replace it with a new CD that matures in five years. In this way, you will have the liquidity of a CD maturing every year while overall you will be getting returns of close to the five-year rate.

Treasuries

Many senior citizens are wary of investments that may seem too risky or that they do not understand. One investment that lets many senior citizens sleep at night is U.S. Government bonds and notes. No investment is safer than U.S. Government bonds and notes. These U.S. Treasury obligations are backed by, as they say, the full faith and credit of the United States Government, which means that, unlike corporate bonds, where if the company fails, your investment is in trouble, with Treasury notes, bills, and bonds, if the U.S. Government goes under, we all have bigger problems than our investments.

Taxes on Treasuries

U.S. Treasury bonds and notes are not subject to state and local taxes although they are subject to federal income taxes. A common axiom is that if interest rates go up after you have bought a Treasury note or bond, the value of your investment goes down. There is a kernel of truth in this, but only a kernel. It is accurate to say that, as interest rates rise and new notes and bonds are issued at the then current higher interest rates, the amount that you will pay for your lower interest bonds and notes if you sell them will be discounted to compensate for the interest rate differential. However, if you do not intend to sell your notes or bonds, but keep them until maturity, any change in value is irrelevant to you and you will receive the full value of your note or bond.

Purchase of Treasuries

You can purchase Treasury notes and bonds through a broker, but if you do, you will have to pay a commission of anywhere from $25 to $100. However, if you buy notes and bonds directly by phone, through the mail, or over the Internet, you can avoid commissions entirely. To order through the Internet, go to the Treasury's website (www.treasurydirect.gov).

Comparison of Treasury Notes and Bills

Many of you have heard of Treasury notes and Treasury bills without knowing what the difference is. Essentially, a Treasury bill is a government obligation that comes in three-month, six-month, or one-year durations. The minimum face values for T-bills are $1,000. They are sold at a discount that reflects the interest rate of the T-bill. If, for example, you were to buy a $1,000 bond, you would pay $1,000 for the T-bill, but shortly thereafter, you would receive a refund or discount representing the interest on the bond. At the T-bills maturity date, you receive the full $1,000 face value of the bond.

Treasury notes have durations of two, five, and ten years. They also are issued in $1,000 multiples. Unlike Treasury bills, Treasury notes are not issued at a discount and the interest is paid twice a year.

Treasury bonds are the granddaddy of Treasury obligations. Their durations range from 10 to 30 years with interest paid twice a year.

Treasury Inflation-Indexed Securities

Want a hot tip? Well, TIPS might be your answer. The actual name of these securities is Treasury Inflation-Indexed Securities, but they are more commonly known as Treasury Inflation-Protection Securities, or TIPS (TIIS apparently doesn't have much of ring to it). With the bite of inflation always a concern, TIPS have their principal adjusted in accordance with changes in the Consumer Price Index inflation measure. Interest is paid at maturity on the greater of the principal amount of the original purchase price or the inflation-adjusted principal amount at the time of maturity.

U.S. Savings Bonds

Perhaps the investment with which the most people are familiar is U.S. Savings Bonds. Series EE bonds are sold for half of their face value in denominations of $50, $75, $100, $200, $500, $1,000, $5,000, and $10,000. The interest on these bonds is exempt from both state and local income taxation. Federal income tax is not paid until either the bonds are cashed in or they stop earning interest, which is 30 years from issuance of the bond.

I bonds are inflation-indexed savings bonds that are a recent addition to the U.S. savings bonds offerings. Like the TIPS, their interest rate tracks the inflation rate. I bonds differ from EE savings bonds in that they are not sold at a discount. They come in denominations ranging from $50 to $10,000.

HH bonds are only issued in exchange for already existing E or EE bonds. People exchange their E or EE bonds to further put off the maturity of their investment and to delay the payment of federal income taxes on the interest earned.

Although many older Americans are still interested in savings bonds, many of them, unbeknownst to them, may be losing the interest in their bonds. According to the Bureau of the Public Debt, more than $9 billion in savings bonds that were issued 30 to 40 years ago have matured, ceasing to earn interest. Yet, the bonds remain unredeemed, losing their holders an estimated $300 million a year in interest. If you have savings bonds, be sure to check that they are still earning interest. If they have matured, cash them in. Otherwise, you are just losing money. The government is under no obligation to notify savings-bond holders that their bonds have matured, so do not expect to be notified when your bonds mature. The government tells us that it is concerned about people, many of them senior citizens losing money by holding these matured bonds, but the fact is that when people do not redeem their bonds, the government gets to use the money for free. The government even instituted a program a few years ago to publicize this issue and inform the public, although I didn't see the results of their efforts until I went to the savings-bond website on my own. And that is just what you should do to see if you are affected. Go to www.savingsbonds.gov and click Treasury Hunt. You can also find other helpful interactive calculators on the website that can help you determine the present value of your savings bonds and that also calculate what you can earn by investing in savings bonds as compared to other investments.

Annuities

Annuities are a controversial form of investment. Annuities are contracts, generally with insurance companies, that are either immediate or deferred. With an immediate annuity, the investor pays the insurance company a sum of money and within a year receives regular payments for life or a fixed period. With a deferred annuity, the investor makes payments to the insurance company over an extended period of time and then at a later date converts into an immediate annuity with regular payments for life or a fixed period.

Annuities also may be either fixed annuities with specific payment amounts or variable annuities where the payment amount depends on the performance of the underlying investments. Many seniors, looking for a safe source of income, pick fixed annuities that will pay them a specific amount for life regardless of how long they live. At first look, annuities might appear to be a good investment for seniors, but if you consider the exceedingly high charges, commissions, and tax ramifications of them, they may not be an appropriate investment for many people.

Tax deferral is often a good thing when it comes to investing, and annuities are often sold as a good way of deferring income taxes. However, withdrawals from variable annuities are taxed at higher ordinary income rates rather than lower capital gains rates even though the investments within the annuity might have been capital gains investments.

Surrender charges are another negative factor in annuities. A typical annuity might have a 7 percent surrender charge that will usually go down 1 percent per year in the fifth through the tenth year of the annuity, making annuities a less attractive investment for older investors.

Older investors in particular are well advised to consider and compare annuities to other investments, such as mutual funds or Treasury bills.

Bulls and Bears

One of the goals of this book is not only to provide you with important information that you can use, but also to provide you with information that is almost totally useless, but interesting, trivia that you can drop on your friends to make yourself look really smart. In keeping with that goal, we look at the derivation of the terms "bear" and "bull" for bad markets and good markets, respectively.

These terms have been used at least since the 1700s, although little is written that definitively explains how these terms came to be used. The most commonly accepted explanation for the terms start with "bearskin jobbers" who were people who sold bearskins before the bears actually parted with them. There was even an old proverb that has not withstood the test of time that referred to "selling the skin before you have caught the bear." After a while, this term was used to describe someone who contracted to sell, at an agreed-upon price, shares of stock that he did not yet own, counting on the stock price to fall. Then, he could then buy the stock at the lower price and sell it at the contract price to the people who had signed a contract. It goes without saying (another useless phrase because it always precedes someone saying what they just told you they would not be saying) that these "bearskin jobbers" were planning on the price of the stock going down precipitously. Eventually, "bearskin jobbers" became "bears."

But, what about "bulls?" Apparently, bull and bear baiting was once a popular sport and since bulls were the opposite of bears, bulls became those who were identified with the stock market going up in direct contrast to the bears, who were identified with the stock market going down.[2]

Your Stock Portfolio

Many investors with the time and the inclination desire to choose the stocks that make up their own portfolio either by themselves or with the help of an investment advisor. Investing in individual stocks provides you with more control over your investments than you would have if you were to merely purchase a mutual fund where the stocks were chosen for you, but buying individual stocks also requires greater attention to your investments on a regular basis. Other investors prefer to use the built-in management and diversification that is found in a mutual fund.

Dow Jones Industrial Average

We hear much about the Dow Jones Industrial Average. Every day, people find their mood rising or falling based upon whether the Dow, which to many people is synonymous with the overall economy, is doing well or poorly. But, how many people actually know what the Dow Jones Industrial Average is? After you read this section, you will know this fascinating trivia so you can toss it out at an opportune moment and look really, really smart, or be ready when Alex Trebek asks, during Final Jeopardy, a question about the number of stocks that make up the Dow Jones Industrial Average. Remember to make your answer in the form of a question. He is very picky about that.

In any event, the Dow Jones Industrial Average is an average of only 30 stocks that are deemed by many people to reflect the stock market in general. The first Dow Jones Industrial Average began in 1896 and was made up of 12 companies, most of which have faded from the scene: American Cotton Oil, American Sugar, American Tobacco, Chicago Gas, Distilling & Cattle Feeding, General Electric, Laclede Gas, National Lead, North American, Tennessee Coal & Iron, U.S. Leather pfd., and U.S. Rubber. Over the years, companies have come and gone, although General Electric still appears to have plenty of electricity left in it. The Dow now comprises 30 stocks. The most recent adding and dropping of companies came in 1999 when Microsoft, Intel, SBC Communications, and Home Depot replaced Chevron, Goodyear Tire and Rubber, Union Carbide, and Sears.

So, why do we give such credence to this one list of just 30 stocks? For the most part, it appears the answer is just because it has been around so long. Maybe that should tell us something about how we make investment decisions.

What Should Be in Your Portfolio?

Asset allocation is an important part of investing. At one time, retirees felt confident having all of their eggs, usually Certificates of Deposit (CDs), in one basket. But, with inflation often at a rate somewhat higher than the rate of return on CDs, keeping all of your money in CDs might just be a way of going broke slowly. Today, with people living longer lives, it is a fact of life that a proper mix of different kinds of investments is advisable for everyone's portfolio, but particularly the portfolios of senior citizens who just cannot depend on fixed income investments, such as CDs. They need the growth that can best be provided by stocks. But, with stocks comes risk. In recent years, we have all seen the devastating effect of the stock market decline on the portfolios of people who were too heavily invested in that one basket of stocks. Spreading the risk around through an assortment of stocks and fixed income investments makes the most sense.

But, just how much of your portfolio should be in stocks and how much in bonds or other more conservative fixed income investments? The ratio between the two certainly depends on your individual tolerance for risk, with people willing to take a greater risk for potentially greater rewards holding greater percentages of stock. A number of rules of thumb can be used as guides to help you determine the appropriate percentages of the various asset classes for you.

Rules of Thumb

One formula determines the amount of bonds in your portfolio by multiplying your age by 80 percent, with the remainder of your portfolio to be held in stocks. For example, according to this formula, 65-year olds should have 52 percent of their assets in bonds and 48 percent in stocks.

Another common formula takes your age and subtracts it from 100 with the resulting figure being the percentage of your assets that should be in stocks with the rest in bonds. According to this formula, if you are 65 years old, you should have 35 percent in stocks and 65 percent in bonds.

Which formula is correct? Neither; both represent only suggested general rules. The makeup of your own portfolio depends on many factors, including your own risk tolerance and your investment objectives.

Regardless of your age, it is important to rebalance your portfolio each year. Frequent trading is expensive and rarely, in the long run, adds to the profitability of your portfolio. But, regardless of whether you have individual stocks and bonds or various mutual funds, it is important to rebalance your portfolio to the proper percentages you have determined for your mix of stocks and fixed income investments, to avoid the risk of the market changing your allocation for you.

More Rules

Start with the premise that the stock market cannot be consistently predicted by anyone. If history has taught us anything, it is that this is true. A study of the 120 biggest up and down days in the stock market between 1801 and 2001 concluded that only 25 percent had a rational explanation. Therefore, diversification and asset allocation produces the best return over time. Spreading your investments across broad asset classes still gives you the greatest change of continual success. By diversifying your investment portfolio with assets that do not move in tandem, you minimize your risk, which should be a goal for all senior investors. A well-diversified portfolio of between 3 and 11 low cost, no load index funds will prove to be a long-term winner over the long haul.

The Stocks Portion of Your Portfolio

Purchasing individual stocks to make up the equity portion of your investment portfolio requires attention to many details and a sound investment strategy.

A Good Day to Buy Stocks

Once you determine that you are going to invest in the stock market either by purchasing individual stocks or mutual funds, when is the best time to buy? How about a bright, sunny day? Research shows that the stock market performs much better on sunny days than cloudy days. And it is not just in this country. According to a study by Professor David Hirshleifer of Ohio State University's Fisher College of Business and Assistant Professor Tyler Shumway of the University of Michigan,[3] there is a significant correlation between bright days and a better performing stock market in the 26 countries from which they gathered data for the years 1982 through 1997. The reason for this may lie in the fact that the stock market is truly a place where perceptions become reality. Facts are not as important to the stock market's rising or falling as people's perceptions of what they believe to be facts. It is a fact that people just feel more upbeat and positive on sunny days, and this may be reflected in the stock market.

Correspondingly, Seasonal Affective Disorder, which goes by the cloyingly cute acronym SAD, is the name for the medical condition from which so many people suffer wherein they become depressed during times of decreased daylight, such as winter. A study of the relationship between SAD and stock market performance by Mark Kamstra, an economist with the Federal Reserve Bank of Atlanta, along with Professor Lisa Kramer of the University of Toronto and Professor Maurice Levi of the University of British Columbia, seems to confirm this relationship.[4] Who should know better about winter than two professors from Canada?

What does this mean to you and me? Does it mean we should wait for a run of sunny days to buy stocks? I do not think so. Rather, I think, the lesson to be taken from all of this is that the stock market is, and always will be, irrational; and applying logical thinking and systems to an illogical institution will only take you so far. Perhaps this explains why the best stock analysts and mutual fund managers rarely do any better than the general stock market.

Dollar Cost Averaging

A popular plan for investing in either stocks or mutual funds is dollar cost averaging. This means that you invest the same amount regularly, be it weekly, monthly, or whatever time period you choose. The idea behind this plan is that you will get more shares at lower prices when the market is low and fewer shares bought at higher cost when the market is high. Because no one can consistently time the market—that is, know when stock prices will be low—using dollar-cost averaging ensures that you will be buying more shares when stocks are cheaper. If you are investing regularly, this is a good way to invest.

Discount Brokers

Because what counts is what you keep, a discount broker is a good choice for people who want to buy stocks and who are willing to give up the research and advice provided by full-service brokers. Sales charges can take a quick and substantial bite out of your available investment funds. Full-service broker commissions vary tremendously from brokerage house to brokerage house based upon a host of factors, including how many shares you are trading and which stock exchange is being used. Commissions with a discount broker also vary, but can often be as much as two-thirds less than what you would pay to a full-service broker. Then, there are the charges that many brokers levy for doing nothing at all. Full-service brokers generally have an inactivity fee, which is an annual charge assessed to your account if you fail to trade what they consider an appropriate number of times.

Online brokerage companies offer tremendous discounts and ease of use, so long as you do not want all the bells and whistles of handholding and research analysis that you can get at a full-service broker. When you think about it, if the research and stock-analysis services provided by the full-service brokers is so great, why aren't the brokers all rich and retired?

Services provided by so-called discount brokers, however, can vary significantly. Some discount brokers provide large amounts of investment information, while others merely execute trades for you. Just like the full-service brokers, some discount brokers charge inactivity fees if you do not trade a sufficient number of times throughout the year. They often call it an account maintenance fee, but the fee is only assessed if you do not make a certain number of trades over a set period of time, so we know what it really is.

How to Pick a Stock

Rather than reinvent the wheel, it makes sense to look toward the stock-picking strategies of successful investors in deciding how to pick a stock in which to invest.

The Dogs of the Dow is the name for a system for profitable investing.[5] The system, developed by Money Manager Michael O'Higgins, derives its name from the strategy of annually investing in the ten highest dividend-paying stocks of the Dow Jones Industrial Average, holding those stocks for a year, and then repeating the process by buying at the start of the next year the then ten highest-dividend-paying stocks of the Dow.

But, why would those stocks be classified as dogs? Often, a relatively high dividend is a compensation for a low-valued stock. At times, a stock paying a high dividend can indicate that the company is not in particularly good financial shape. However, in general, the stocks that make up the Dow are relatively stable companies.

The benchmark for just about any investment plan is how it compares to no-brainer index investing. In the case of the Dogs of the Dow, investing in those stocks has been marginally more profitable than the S&P 500 Index for 31 of the past 52 years. Over the past 10 years, the average annual return has been 1.6 percent better than investing in the S&P 500. So, it may appear that the Dogs of the Dow, an investment strategy that follows the KISS rule (keep it simple, stupid), might just be a Westminster Kennel Club winner rather than a mutt.

Warren Buffet is one of the legendary investors of our time and one of the richest men in the world, which should go together. Buffet is a champion of value investing—that is, looking for bargains. Buffet looks for solid companies that for whatever reason are underpriced. He has liked companies that dominate the market, like Coca-Cola or Gillette, which also make products that people need to buy over and over again. Then comes the hard work. Whenever you hear experts talk about investing in stocks, they always emphasize doing your homework, which often means reviewing and analyzing the hard figures and Byzantine accounting that characterize corporate assets, liabilities, and earnings.

The investment world's little old lady from Pasadena just might be Geraldine Weiss, the publisher of the *Investment Quality Trends Newsletter*[6] that analyzes and recommends dividend-paying stocks. She may not be from Pasadena, but as Jan and Dean said in the 1964 hit song *Little Old Lady from Pasadena*, "Go Granny, go Granny, go

Granny, go." This Granny has gone after profitable investments by restricting her picks to companies that pay good dividends. Using this strategy between 1988 and 2003, she has averaged a 12 percent return annually, putting her newsletter among the leaders of all newsletters for that period and beating the benchmark S&P 500. Her theory makes sense. Generally, the best dividend and earnings growth companies are better positioned to weather difficult financial times. They represent more stable companies, not flashy, but stable.

Peter Lynch is an investor with a great track record established when he managed Fidelity's Magellan Fund during its heyday. Once again, with trivial information that I think is important, the origin of the word "heyday" is unclear, although it is thought to be derived from an alteration of the ancient word "heyda," which was an exclamation of pleasure. I just thought you should know. In any event, Lynch not only knew how to invest, he knew when to leave, which is a tremendous skill in and of itself. He retired as the manager of the Magellan Fund in 1990 at the top of his game and with his reputation as an expert stock picker unsullied. Like Buffet, he likes companies that dominate the market. He bought them during their inevitable dips and sold after reaching his profit goal. Lynch generally liked companies with little debt and high net cash per share. He also generally preferred smaller companies with room to grow. Once again, he too stresses doing your homework, which brings me to my advice.

Few of us liked doing homework when we were in school, and we still do not like doing our homework now. The tedious research that is required to rationally and logically make reasonable stock purchases is both complex and exceptionally time consuming. There is much detailed information available, particularly online at websites such as the Securities and Exchange Commission's EDGAR database, which allows you to access corporate filings with the SEC at no cost. However, it is important to remember that the experts hardly seem able to consistently beat the market, as typified by the S&P 500. So, why should we delude ourselves to think that we can do better? Except for a fling with some "mad money," mutual funds, particularly Index funds, seem the best way to go.

A Few Words on Gold

Gold has been used in minted coins for more than 2,500 years. It is a scarce metal. All the gold ever discovered could fit into an 82-foot cube. At one time, there were restrictions on private citizens owning gold, but these restrictions were lifted by 1975 and gold became a market commodity. In times of fear or great inflation, the price of gold goes up. But, what do you have when you invest in gold? It does not earn interest? What is its real value? However, if you believe you must have gold as a part of your portfolio, you might want to consider buying the gold through gold-mining stocks or gold mutual funds.

Final Thoughts

Lurking in your attic may be some of your most valuable investments of all. Old comic books and baseball cards can bring in big bucks. In good condition, a 1914 Shoeless Joe Jackson (of *Field of Dreams* fame) can bring in up to $9,000; a 1933 Babe Ruth up to $5,000; a 1949 Leroy "Satchel" Paige up to $6,000; a 1951 Willie Mays up to $3,000; and a 1952 Mickey Mantle up to $18,000. The grand-daddy of all baseball cards, a 1909 Honus Wagner, of which there are said to be only 10 in good condition, sold for more than $1 million at an auction in 2000.[7] An interesting sidelight is that Wagner, a Hall of Fame second baseman for the Pittsburgh Pirates, protested when a tobacco company included his card with its product.

The baseball cards with which we are most familiar are the cards created more than 50 years ago by the Topps Company as a way of marketing bubble gum. The cards were so successful that for the last 10 years, the cards have been sold without the gum because collectors complained that the bubble gum was damaging the cards. By the way, if many of your cards and comic books fell victim to your mother's spring cleaning, you are not alone. The Topps Company, during the 1950s, got rid of hundreds of cases of now rare and expensive cards, including the 1952 Mickey Mantle cards, to clear warehouse space, dumping into the Atlantic Ocean a veritable treasure trove of collectables.[8]

For you comic-book collectors, the Detective Comics in which Batman first appeared sells for about $300,000 now. The first Action Comics in which Superman was introduced sold not long ago for more than $86,000, while a more recent comic book, a Marvel Comics Fantastic Four first edition, went for over $111,000.[9] Speaking of Superman, did any of you ever find it odd that no one ever put it together that Clark Kent, who was never seen in the same room as Superman, looked exactly like Superman from his face to his build except for the glasses? Do you think Lois Lane, investigative reporter that she was, ever pondered how much Superman and Clark Kent resembled each other and then dismissed her thoughts by saying to herself, "What was I thinking? Clark Kent wears glasses. Of course, he can't be Superman."

Endnotes

1. www.businessweek.com.

2. Sources of this information are "The Fool FAQ-Bulls and Bears," The Motley Fool (www.foll.com/FoolFAQ/foolfaq0047. htm), and "The History of Bull and Bear," by Don Luskin, www.thestreet.com/comment/openbook/1428176.html.

3. www.acs.ohiostate.edu/units/research/archive/goodinvs.htm.

4. Federal Reserve Bank of Atlanta Working Paper No. 2002-13, "Winter Blues: A SAD Stock Market Cycle."

5. www.dogsofthedow.com.

6. www.iqtrends.com.

7. "Top Ten Baseball Cards of All Times" by Ari Weinberg (www.forbes.com).

8. "Baseball Cards Hold Timeless Memories" by Mike Dodd (www.usatoday.com/sports/baseball/stories/2001-03-27-cover-cards.htm).

9. "Comic Relief: A Starter's Guide to Vintage Comic-Book Collecting" by Shawn Langlois (CBSMarketWatch.com).

6

Income Taxes

"The hardest thing in the world to understand is the income tax."

—Albert Einstein

The source of our tax laws is the Internal Revenue Code, which truly is aptly named because it often appears to be written in code. Fortunately, many tax laws and loopholes have been written specifically to help older Americans. Apparently, even Congressmen have parents.

Throughout this chapter, I refer to the tax laws in existence in the year 2012, which is when this book was written. It is important to remember that tax laws change every year with the speed of a Congressman's tongue. For the most up-to-date versions of the tax laws referred to in this chapter, go to the tax websites cited in "Favorite Websites."

Marital Status

When it comes to filing an income tax return, everyone is status conscious. Your filing status is an important factor in determining the income tax you must pay. The availability of some tax deductions and tax credits is based on your filing status. The filing status for most seniors falls into one of four categories: single; married, filing jointly; married, filing separately; and head of household.

"Single" Category

The first category is "Single." As the name implies, a single person is a person who is unmarried. The date for determination as to whether you are single for the entire tax year is the last day of the year, December 31. Some clever taxpayers trying to avoid the marriage penalty in past years planned Caribbean vacations around Christmas time, getting a quickie divorce in the Dominican Republic or some other country that provided easy divorces and then remarrying after the first of the next year. The IRS disapproved of this practice and was successful in court in having these divorces declared to be shams, thereby subjecting the participants to adverse tax consequences.

Love springs eternal, but so do taxes. Although the concept is not terribly romantic (or maybe it is just that—terribly romantic), seniors considering marriage or remarriage should consider how marriage will affect their income tax liability. The so-called marriage penalty may, and I should emphasize may, put a married couple in a higher tax bracket, which could cause them to pay more income taxes than if they had remained single. Although we hear much about the marriage penalty, the fact is that not all couples pay more income taxes than if they were single. Particularly where one spouse has significantly less earnings, the chances are that the couple will actually be better off as married, filing jointly.

Caution

Divorcing for income tax purposes may be penny-wise and pound-foolish, because unmarried couples are not eligible for each other's survivor's Social Security benefits.

"Married, Filing Jointly" Category

The second filing status is that of "married, filing jointly." This is common, and again, your marital status is determined by looking at whether you were married as of December 31 of the tax year. A sad exception to that rule is that in the year in which a spouse dies, the surviving spouse is considered married for the entire year for income tax filing purposes and can file a "married, filing jointly" return. When so doing, you should write "Deceased" along with the deceased spouse's name and the date of death at the top of the income tax return form. If the surviving spouse has been appointed as executor or personal representative of the deceased spouse's estate, he or she should sign as the representative of the deceased spouse's estate. If the surviving spouse has not yet been officially appointed as executor or personal representative for the deceased spouse at the time of the filing of the income tax return, he or she should sign and indicate "filing as surviving spouse."

For some married people, filing jointly might increase the total tax burden for the couple by putting them into a higher tax bracket and thereby limiting their itemized deductions through the itemized deduction phaseout. However, this phaseout of itemized deductions once your income reaches a certain level was repealed, but only through the year 2012. It is set to return in 2013. In addition, the higher joint income could result in incurring the much-feared and little-understood Alternative Minimum Tax, a provision of the tax code that was enacted to obtain greater tax payments from wealthy people whose use of various deductions and legitimate tax avoidance methods enabled them to avoid much income tax liability. Unfortunately, this difficult-to-compute tax was never indexed for inflation and presently affects many people to whom it was never intended to apply. "Married, filing jointly" status also could subject more of a couple's Social Security retirement benefits to being taxed.

For those people who paid more income tax due to the marriage penalty, the 2001 Tax Act provided some help. However, unlike the cavalry that always arrived in the nick of time, tax help for those affected by the marriage penalty was not exactly on the way. That help was not scheduled to even leave the fort until the year 2005, and it was not until the year 2009 that the marriage penalty was fully eased, thanks to the doubling of the standard deduction of single taxpayers for married couples filing jointly.

Fortunately, the major tax law revision of 2003, which goes by the rather unwieldy name of the Jobs and Growth Tax Relief Reconciliation Act of 2003 (JGTRRA, and just try and pronounce that; it sounds like the name of a character in *Star Wars*), provides some quicker, albeit temporary, relief. Under the provisions of JGTRRA, the standard deduction for married couples increased to double the standard deduction of single taxpayers for the years 2003 and 2004. In the year 2005, it was reduced by 36 percent and then, over the next four years, returned to the doubling of the standard deduction in 2009, where it was to remain for two years before it falls back again to the levels of the standard deduction for married couples existing in 2002. If any of that makes sense to you, you must be a Congressman. However, just in the nick of time, Congress came to the rescue (albeit again on a temporary basis) with the passage of the Tax Relief Act of 2010, which extended for the next two years the 15 percent income tax bracket for married couples filing a joint return and extended the doubling of the basic standard deduction of unmarried people for a married couple.

Note, however, that the marriage penalty has never been as serious a problem as many have made it out to be. Even before the marriage penalty was first eased, 51 percent of married couples paid less total income taxes jointly than if they had not been married with an average benefit of $1,300, while 42 percent of married taxpayers paid more total income taxes than if they had each been unmarried, with an average penalty of $1,380.

Married couples do reach higher tax brackets sooner, because their incomes are tacked on to each other in the computing of their joint income taxes so people with approximately the same income are hit hardest by the marriage penalty. Generally, couples with one spouse earning all or most of the income will make out better by filing jointly as a married couple.

Of course, there still are benefits to being married (as my wife has been known to remind me), with many of them being of a financial nature, such as health and pension benefits, Social Security retirement, and survivor benefits, preferential gift tax and estate tax treatments, and lower premiums for many types of insurance.

Although generally, for most tax purposes in regard to marital status, you are what you were on December 31 for that year's income tax return, a couple can still file a joint income tax return for the year in which one of them dies.

"Married, Filing Separately" Category

The third filing status is that of "married, filing separately," which almost sounds like the title of a country song if country songs were ever written about income taxes. Generally, married people are better off filing as "married, filing jointly." Non-working spouses cannot contribute to a tax-deductible traditional IRA if married and filing separately. The income limits that would permit a contribution to a Roth IRA are much lower for married couples filing separately than filing jointly, thereby limiting the availability to Roth IRAs for married people who file separately. Moreover, a non-working spouse would be unable to contribute to a tax deductible traditional IRA if the couple filed as "married, filing separately." Additionally, married people filing separately can now convert a traditional IRA to a Roth IRA, which can be advantageous. I discuss this in detail later in this book.

Loophole

Although most often "married, filing jointly" makes the most sense for the greatest number of seniors, if one of the couple has a large number of medical expenses, it may be advantageous to file as "married, filing separately." As always, the best way to determine which way is most advantageous to file for you is to actually prepare hypothetical returns both ways and compare the difference.

"Head of Household" Category

The fourth filing status is that of "head of household." This status can be claimed by taxpayers who are unmarried but have paid for more than half of the cost of maintaining a home for themselves and another qualifying family member. Most often, the tax rates for people who qualify for this status are better (meaning lower) than those for people filing as either single or as married, filing separately.

Parents and Children

Just as parents are able to claim their minor children as dependents on the parents' income tax return, turnabout is fair play; adult children who may now be paying the medical bills or other living expenses of their parents can, in some circumstances, take their parents as dependents for income tax purposes. Being able to deduct a parent's or grandparent's medical bills or nursing-home costs can be a great advantage to younger family members in a high income tax bracket. In addition, the bill-paying younger family member will get the advantage of an additional dependency exemption.

To qualify as a dependent in these circumstances, you must rely on your child to pay for more than half of your living expenses. In addition, your taxable gross income must be less than the $3,800 personal exemption amount. Tax-exempt amounts of income from Social Security retirement benefits as well as other tax-exempt income, such as tax-free municipal bond income, are not counted in determining your gross income for this purpose.

Loophole

If your children find it difficult to make the payments to reach half of your support expenses, you may choose not to use your own income and assets for your own support to make reaching that required level of payment by the child easier.

Loophole

If your gross income level is more than the $3,800 personal exemption amount, you can reduce the amount of taxable income by giving your children income-earning assets or by changing investments to those that earn tax-exempt, non-countable income, such as tax-free municipal bonds.

Loophole

A child seeking to take his or her parent as a dependent for income tax purposes who is caring for the parent in the adult child's home can count the fair market rental value of the space in the home being provided to the parent as if the child had paid that amount in support of the parent.

Caution

For a parent or grandparent to be claimed as a dependent for tax purposes, the parent or grandparent may not file a joint income tax return.

Often, children will join together to support a parent. According to *Consumer Reports*, more than 22 million American households assist in the care and expenses for an older family member.[1] If more than one child contributes to the support of a parent and together the children provide more than 50 percent of their parent's support, but no one child alone accounts for more than 50 percent of the parent's support, the children may allocate the dependency exemption and medical deduction among themselves by way of a multiple support agreement. Children who each separately provide more than 10 percent of the parent's support and more than 50 percent together can agree among themselves as to who will take the exemption and deductions. It is important to remember that only one person can claim the exemption and take the deductions each year. However, the same person does not have to claim the tax exemption and take the deductions every year. It can be allocated annually to the child who can make the best use of the exemption and deductions in that particular year. A Form 2120 Multiple Support Declaration must be attached to the income tax return of the child taking the exemption for the parent. Each participant in the multiple-support agreement who are not claiming the exemption must waive the exemption on the Form 2120.

Caution

A taxpayer is not permitted to file as head of household if the parent is a dependent under a multiple support agreement among several family members.

Domestic Partners

Loophole

Dependency exemptions are not restricted to family members. One member of an unmarried couple living together may be able to get the tax benefits of claiming his or her domestic partner as a dependent if the income of the partner claimed as a dependent does not exceed $3,800.

Whether domestic partners can be claimed as dependents by their live-in companion is a matter of state law. According to the U.S. Court of Appeals in a famous North Carolina case, regulation of marriage and domestic affairs is left to the individual states to determine. Therefore, in applying the tax laws, the IRS defers to applicable state laws in domestic matters. For domestic partners to take advantage of the dependency exemption for a domestic partner, the relationship must not violate the laws of the state in which the domestic partners live. In the North Carolina case, the U.S. Appeals Court interpreted the North Carolina lewd and lascivious cohabitation law as prohibiting people from living together outside of marriage. The lawyers for the North Carolina taxpayer who was trying to take his 21-year-old domestic partner as a dependent argued that the North Carolina law was unconstitutionally vague and therefore could not be applied to the taxpayer. In its decision denying the exemption and upholding the lewd and lascivious cohabitation law, the U.S. Court of Appeals said that what the statute prohibited was "more or less habitual intercourse." It did not, the judges said, prohibit "a single or occasional sex act." The judges went on to say, however, that "repeated sex acts within a period of several weeks may be found to be the habitual intercourse" that violates the statute. Although precise guidelines were not set by the Court, perhaps someday they will let the people of North Carolina know precisely how often they can make love without being lewd and lascivious.

In a case presenting a similar set of facts, a court in Missouri ruled that the couple living together did not violate the state's lewd and lascivious cohabitation law. It is also interesting to note that, throughout the country, in those states that still have laws prohibiting lewd and lascivious cohabitation, the laws refer to lewd *and* lascivious cohabitation, which would seem to imply that if you were either lewd *or* lascivious, you would not be in violation of the law. These laws apparently only make it illegal if you are both lewd and lascivious. Exactly what this means is also difficult to know because the definitions of both of these terms are imprecise.

The Over-65 Crowd

Unmarried taxpayers who are at least 65 years old got an initial break on their 2011 federal income tax returns by not even having to file a tax return unless their gross income was $10,950, which is $1,000 more than younger taxpayers. Married couples who are both over 65 years old filing a joint return did not have to file a 2011 return until their gross income reached $21,300. When both husband and wife were under 65 years old in 2011, the threshold for having to file a tax return was $19,000. Married couples with only one spouse 65 or older had to file a 2011 federal income tax return once their joint income reached $21,150. These amounts are adjusted each year by the IRS for inflation.

Being over 65 will not only get you a free cup of coffee at some hamburger joints, but will also get you an additional standard deduction allowance if you do not itemize your deductions. By the way, if you do get that cup of coffee, either make sure you do not spill it or if you do, get a good lawyer. Single taxpayers over 65 in 2012 get an additional $1,450 deduction, and married taxpayers an additional $1,150 each. The standard deduction for singles over 65 in 2012 is

$7,400. For those married and filing jointly, the standard deduction is $13,050 if both are over 65 or $11,900 if only one admits to being over 65.

In addition to the increased standard deduction for taxpayers over 65, if a single taxpayer over 65 is blind, his or her standard deduction rose to $8,850 for 2012 federal income tax returns. For those married people filing jointly who are both blind, the figure was $16,500 for 2012 federal income tax returns. If only one of the couple is blind, it was $15,350 for the 2012 federal income tax return.

Loophole

You do not have to be completely blind to get the increased standard deduction for blindness. If you are partially blind, you must file with your income tax return a letter from your physician certifying to the fact that your vision is not better than 20/200 in your better eye (the minimum standard for an American League umpire—just kidding) or that your field of vision (not to be confused with your Field of Dreams, to continue the baseball metaphor) is twenty degrees or less. If the letter from your physician states that you are not expected to improve beyond these levels, you do not have to file a new certification in future years. All you need to do is attach a statement referring to the earlier certification.

Untaxed Income

Some of the income you receive is not counted for tax purposes. In 2012, the year in which this is being written, payments you receive from a qualified long-term care insurance policy are not taxable so long as any amounts you receive more than $310 a day are not more than the actual cost of your care. In a rare instance of Congressional wisdom, this figure is automatically adjusted for inflation annually. A qualified long-term-care insurance policy is one that is guaranteed to be renewable, does not have any cash surrender value, limits the use of any refunds and dividends to reducing future premiums or increasing benefits, and does not pay for services that would be reimbursed by Medicare.

Life insurance proceeds that you receive are also not taxable, as are accelerated death benefits from a viatical company purchasing your life insurance policy if you are terminally or chronically ill as certified by your physician. Chronic illness is defined by the IRS for these purposes as being unable to perform at least two activities of daily living for 90 days or more because of incapacity. Activities of daily living include eating, personal hygiene, bathing, dressing, and mobility or requiring substantial supervision due to severe cognitive impairment.

In addition, payments you receive from a disability insurance policy may not be countable for tax purposes. As usual, the code splits hairs in a way that would make a hairdresser proud. If the premiums on your disability insurance were paid by you, the amounts you receive from the policy are not counted at all. But, if premiums were paid by your employer and not included in your taxable income when paid, the money you receive from your disability insurance is countable income. If you paid some of the premium, well, you know the drill, the IRS will calculate the amount of your disability benefit that relates to the amount of the premium you did not pay and will tax you on it. Obviously, the IRS never heard of Henry David Thoreau's motto of "Simplify, simplify, simplify!"

Tax Credits

Tax credits are even more attractive than tax deductions because a credit comes right off the amount you would otherwise have to pay in taxes, whereas a deduction merely reduces the amount of your income that is subject to tax. The good news is that the Internal Revenue Code provides a special tax credit for the elderly or disabled. The bad news is that hardly anyone qualifies for this tax credit. Maybe those Congressmen do not have parents after all.

The amount of the credit for income taxes starts at $5,000 for single taxpayers or those filing as head of household; $5,000 if you are filing a joint return and only one of you is over 65 years old; $7,500 if you file a joint return and both of you are over 65 or permanently and totally disabled, and $3,750 if you are married and filing separately. These amounts, by the way, were set in 1983 and have, unlike Congressional pay raises, never been indexed for inflation, thus making them much less helpful than they originally were so many years ago.

This base credit amount is reduced by all nontaxable pensions you receive and any Social Security payments you receive; so if, for example, you are married and both of you are over 65 years old, you will get no credit whatsoever if your annual Social Security payments exceed the princely sum of $7,500.

Social Security Taxes

A recurring theme in this book is the Government giveth and the Government taketh away. So, although the government does pay seniors Social Security benefits (with our own money), it also taxes that money sometimes.

How much of your Social Security benefits are taxed depends on what is referred to as your "provisional income" as well as your filing status. Your "provisional income" is computed by adding to your "taxable income" amounts of your income that are nontaxable along with half of your net Social Security benefits before subtracting adjustments to income, except for student loan interest, which I am sure affects so many senior citizens. An example of a type of income that is not taxable but that is used to determine the provisional income is tax-exempt interest, such as municipal bond interest as reported on line 8b of your income tax return Form 1040. Logical? No, but remember that it is the Internal Revenue Code. It is not supposed to make sense.

If you are married and filing jointly, none of your net Social Security benefits are taxable if your provisional income does not exceed $32,000. If you are single or married but filing separately, you may have up to $25,000 of provisional income without having any of your Social Security benefits taxable.

Under the Senior Citizens' Freedom to Work Act in 2000, or as I refer to it, the "Do You Want Fries With That? Act," people who work after reaching their full Social Security Retirement Age do not have their Social Security benefit payments reduced. However, in 2012, people taking early retirement benefits who had earned income of more than $14,640 would lose $1 of benefits for every $2 of earned income over $14,640. Unearned income, such as investment income, does not affect the amount of Social Security Retirement benefits received regardless of whether you take early retirement benefits or not. The rules for married and filing separately are particularly confusing. Married people who file separately and live together at any time during the year may not shelter any of their Social Security benefits from income taxes.

Loophole

You can reduce your income to limit taxation of Social Security benefits through investments, such as stocks and mutual funds, that are primarily growth oriented rather than investments that pay interest or dividends. Series EE savings bonds are also a good choice because the interest they earn is not taxed until the bonds are redeemed.

Everyone who receives Social Security benefits gets a Form SSA 1099 by January 31 of each year. This form will indicate not just the total benefits you were paid during the year, but also the net benefit. Shown in box 5 of the form is the figure used to determine the taxable portion of your income.

Loophole

Supplemental Security Income (SSI) benefits are not subject to tax, nor are they considered in determining your provisional income.

People born before 1938 who have reached the full retirement age of 65 and who are receiving Social Security benefits are permitted to work and have as much earned income as they can without that earned income affecting the taxation of their Social Security benefits. Full retirement age increased starting in 2003. It went up in two-month increments for various age ranges, starting with people born in 1938 whose full retirement age is 65; then, it continued to go up in two-month increments until it reached people born in 1960 and later whose retirement age for receiving full Social Security benefits is age 67. See the chart in Chapter 11, "Social Security."

Caution

If you are under 65 years old, receiving Social Security benefits, and considering working to get a little extra income, you should first figure out how much of your wages you will get to keep. To do this, prepare two tax returns: one with the wages and one without. The difference in your taxes between the two hypothetical tax returns will be the additional income tax costs to you. Also consider additional state and local taxes that you will incur as a result of the new job, as well as FICA taxes that are levied on your earnings despite the fact that you are receiving Social Security benefits. With today's tax-preparation software, doing two hypothetical tax returns should be a task so simple that a 5-year-old child could do it, which brings to mind the advice of Groucho Marx when confronted with a task that was also supposedly so simple a 5-year-old child could accomplish it. Upon being totally baffled, Groucho proclaimed, "Go out and find me a 5-year-old child." For most of us, a child or grandchild who is computer literate is a resource waiting to be exploited.

Tax Deductions

Being able to deduct an expense on your income tax return can take a little bit of the sting out of some of the costs of everyday life.

Loan Interest

It was not that long ago that interest on consumer credit cards was deductible. But the Lord giveth and the IRS taketh away, so the situation today is that your credit-card interest as well as your car loan interest is no longer deductible on your income tax return. However, with a little planning, you can make both of those costs tax deductible, and you can do it without even having to leave your home. In fact, your home is the key to being able to deduct these expenses.

Loophole

Take out a home-equity loan to pay outstanding debt on your credit cards as well as the cost of financing your car. That way, you can deduct both of these expenses on your income tax return. The reason is that the interest on a home equity loan is fully tax deductible if the loan is secured by a mortgage on your home or vacation home and the amount borrowed is no more than $100,000 for married couples or $50,000 for married people filing separately. The interest rate that you pay on a home equity loan is usually significantly lower than the average credit-card rate or automobile loan interest rate. Of course, it is important to remember that when you use a home-equity loan, you are using your home as collateral to secure repayment of the loan. Failure to repay the loan can result in the loss of your home, so taking out a home-equity loan is not something you should do frivolously. But, if you exercise proper self-discipline, a home-equity loan can be a smart financial move.

"Normal" Medical Expenses

Tax deductions are an important part of anyone's tax planning, but senior citizens have some particular opportunities when it comes to preparing their income tax returns. Medical expenses for the taxpayer, his or her spouse, and any dependents are deductible to the extent that they are more than 7.5 percent of the Adjusted Gross Income (AGI). Certainly, money spent for medical care would qualify for such treatment, but so would transportation costs of trips primarily for medical care.

Payments for premiums for qualified long-term care policies are treated as any other unreimbursed medical expense for purposes of income tax deductions, which means that they are not deductible until the total of your unreimbursed medical expenses is more than 7.5 percent of your AGI. The amount of the premium you may use for determining your deduction depends on your age. The limits for deductions in 2012, the year in which this book is written, are shown in Table 6.1.

Table 6.1 2012 Limits for Deductions

Age	Amount of Deduction
40 and younger	$350
41–50	$660
51–60	$1,310
61–70	$3,500
71 and older	$4,370

Nursing-home costs can also be deducted as medical expenses if the primary purpose for being in the nursing home is for medical care. If you are at the nursing home strictly for fun, the costs are not deductible. If, however, the reason for being in the nursing home is medical, the entire costs of the nursing home, including the costs of room and board, are deductible.

Off-Beat Medical Expenses

Relatively new is the deductibility as a medical expense of the cost of participating in a weight-loss program if it is for treatment of obesity as a disease or for other specific diseases, such as hypertension or heart disease, as noted by your physician. The IRS, unfortunately, is picky when it comes to allowing this deduction because it will not allow the deduction of the cost of buying diet foods if they are not supplements, but rather are dietary substitutions for less healthy food that you would otherwise consume. The cost of specific food supplements may possibly be deductible if the supplements do not, in the words of the IRS, "satisfy your normal nutritional needs." As if any of those supplements belong in the same sentence as the word "satisfy." In addition, the supplements must specifically treat your illness, and the need for them must be supported by your physician.

If your physician determines that you must join a health club or spa to treat a specific medical condition, such as obesity or heart disease, you may be able to deduct the cost as a medical expense. However, you may not deduct the cost of health club or spa memberships if you go either to maintain your health or to help reduce physical or mental discomfort that is not related to a specifically diagnosed medical condition. Apparently, in the eyes of the Spartan IRS, generally if something feels good, regardless of whether it is good for your health, it is not deductible.

The IRS continues its inconsistent rules when it comes to the deductibility of programs to help people stop smoking. The cost of programs to help people stop smoking is deductible as a medical expense. That seems logical. It certainly is related to people's healthcare. However, if through that program or on your own you use any non-prescription drugs, such as nicotine gum or patches, to help you kick the habit, the cost of those items is not deductible. A little less logical.

Although generally, the cost of dancing lessons is not deductible as a medical expense even if they help improve your general health, you may be able to take the cost of dancing lessons as a medical-expense deduction if you have a friendly physician who recommends dancing lessons for the specific treatment of a disease. Again, it appears that the IRS does not want to encourage people to do something that is good for their health in which they would actually find enjoyment.

As for cosmetic surgery, it should come as no surprise that the position of the IRS is to not permit the deduction of medical costs for what they refer to as "unnecessary" cosmetic surgery that is done to improve the taxpayer's appearance and is not done to treat a disease. Face lifts, hair transplants, and liposuction are just a few examples of the kinds of cosmetic surgery that the IRS frowns upon (which probably creates wrinkles in the face of the IRS examiner). However, if you need cosmetic surgery to fix a deformity that is either congenital or the result of an accident or disease, the IRS will allow the cost of cosmetic surgery to be deductible. Cosmetic surgery following breast cancer would be deductible. Again, your verbally gifted physician just might be able to come up with a reason why that face lift meaningfully promotes the proper function of the body, in which case the surgery could arguably be deductible.

The IRS does specifically allow as items that may qualify for tax deductibility as medical expenses, such items as acupuncture treatments, chiropractic care, dental work, hearing aids (as well as the cost of the batteries to operate them), and the cost of special telephone equipment that helps hearing impaired people communicate.

Home-Improvement Medical Expenses

Money spent for home improvements directly related to medical care or to make the home more accessible to the taxpayer with physical limitations may also be deductible. Air conditioners, whirlpools, or even swimming pools may be deductible. The deductible amount of the cost of the improvement is determined, according to IRS regulations, by subtracting from the actual cost of the improvement the increase in the value of the property as a result of the improvement. As an example, the IRS regulation cites an elevator installed in a home to assist a person whose heart disease made it difficult to climb stairs. According to the IRS, if the installation of the elevator cost $8,000 and the value of the home increased by $4,400, the deductible amount would be $3,600.

The IRS specifically allows some home improvements as capital expenses that qualify for tax deductibility as medical expenses but does not consider them to increase the value of your home. These include the following:

- Building entrance ramps
- Widening doorways on the outside or inside of the house
- Installing railings in bathrooms
- Lowering kitchen cabinets and appliances
- Landscaping to provide easier access

Deduction Documentation

The example of the home elevator points out an important element of tax preparation. Supporting documentation and records are of critical importance to successfully backing up tax deductions. Make sure that you keep statements from your physicians and complete records of all bills for medical costs such as prescriptions and medical procedures. In addition, keep detailed records of all transportation costs related to medical care.

Keeping good records is only a good thing if you are completely honest in your deductions. An owner of a furniture store in Pittsburgh retained the services of an arsonist in order to collect on his insurance policy. Following the burning of his building, the insurance company paid off to the tune of $500,000, which is quite a tune. The business owner properly claimed the insurance proceeds on his income tax return and took the customary deductions for the building and his business. However, he also claimed a deduction of $10,000 as a "consulting fee" for the services of the arsonist. Following an IRS audit, the business owner had the consulting fee disallowed, was assessed additional taxes, penalties, and interest of $6,500 and, along with the arsonist, was sent, as they say in the game Monopoly, to jail, to jail, directly to jail. They did not get to pass go and not only did they not collect $200, but the store owner also forfeited the insurance proceeds.

Loophole

Generally, to take a deduction of any kind on the income tax return for a particular year, you must have paid that bill during that year. Makes sense. However, with certain deductions, such as medical expenses, if you pay for your medical expenses by credit card, you may take the deduction in the year you charged the expense to your credit card rather than when the credit-card company is actually paid by you or even when the charge appears on your bill.

Often, someone entering a continuing care facility is required to pay a significant initial fee, sometimes called a "founders fee," in return for future lifetime care along with regular monthly fees for room, board and medical care. The part of the fee that relates to medical care is deductible, subject of course to the 7.5 percent AGI base. The amount of your bill that relates to medical care is easy to determine from your monthly bill because the facilities provide you with specific allocations on your bill.

Loophole

Again, although payments in advance for future services are usually not deductible, prepaid bills for future services, such as lump sum initial "founders fees" are allowed to be deducted in the year when paid when they relate to future care to be provided in a nursing home or retirement home that provides medical services. However, the amount you can deduct is limited to the amount of your retirement home payment that relates to medical care.

Loophole

The initial big upfront entrance fee usually does not specifically designate a portion of it that relates to medical expenses. However, the IRS will accept a deduction based upon what the particular facility usually allocates toward medical expenses.

Tax Relief as Big as a House

The home is most often the most valuable asset that an individual or a married couple owns. The sale of that home, which in many circumstances was bought years earlier for a very low price, could have dire tax consequences. Fortunately, over the years, a number of tax laws have reduced the problem of taxation of the profit on a home sale. Since 1997 individual taxpayers have been able to exclude $250,000 from capital gains taxes, and married couples have been able to exclude $500,000 from capital gains taxes otherwise incurred on the sale of their primary home in which they have lived for at least two of the five years before the sale.

Loophole

If you have put your home into a living revocable trust with yourself as both trustee and beneficiary of the trust, you can still take advantage of the $250,000 or $500,000 exclusion from capital gains taxes.

Loophole

For married couples, even if only one spouse owns the home, they can take the full $500,000 exclusion on their joint income tax return.

Loophole

Each of the unmarried owners of a shared primary residence would qualify for the $250,000 exclusion if they met the other qualifications. If Adam and Eve were unmarried but jointly owned the home in which they lived together, each would be able to take a $250,000 exclusion from capital gains tax if they had lived in the home for two of the five years immediately before the sale.

Reduced Exclusion

When the 1997 exclusion law was passed, in addition to allowing the exclusion of $250,000 for individuals and $500,000 for married couples from capital gains taxes on the sale of their primary residence, it also provided for a reduced exclusion for taxpayers who sold their home because of "unforeseen circumstances," too early to qualify for the full exclusion. Five years later, the IRS issued regulations to guide people in determining what particular "unforeseen circumstances" would qualify for a reduced exclusion. The amount of the reduced exclusion for which a home-selling taxpayer will be eligible is based on how long the homeowner or homeowners lived in the home. For example, if you were single and lived in the home for one of the previous five years before the sale, you would be eligible for an exclusion of $125,000; if you were married, you would be eligible for an exclusion of $250,000. The new regulations list a number of specific "unforeseen circumstances" that would qualify for the partial exclusion, including death and divorce.

The IRS list of "unforeseen circumstances" also includes multiple births from the same pregnancy, which for senior citizens would most likely truly be an "unforeseen circumstance."

The list of "unforeseen circumstances" foreseeable by the IRS is not intended to be exclusive. Other "unforeseen circumstances" considered legitimate by the IRS, which is interpreting the regulation liberally, will also serve to help homeowners to be eligible for the partial exclusion if they did not live in the home for a long enough period to qualify for the full exclusion.

In addition to the "unforeseen circumstances" provided for in the regulations, the regulations also provide for partial exclusions when the homeowner sells the home for health reasons such as going into a nursing home or assisted living.

Basis for Exclusion

It is important to remember that the exclusion from capital gains taxes is based upon the otherwise taxable gain, not the sales price. If a home that was bought for $50,000 was sold for $200,000, the taxable amount of the sales price would be $150,000, which represents the difference between the sales price and the original purchase price. In reality, a number of other adjustments can be used to raise the basis of the home's original purchase price for purposes of calculating the taxable gain to which the exclusion would be applied, for example, the cost of certain home improvements like a new kitchen. These adjustments to the purchase price will further reduce the amount of the sales price that is subject to capital gains tax.

I Get By with a Little Help from My Friends

Income tax preparation is a daunting experience for anyone, but can be particularly overwhelming for seniors. Fortunately, in an effort to make income tax preparation merely "whelming" (which, if it is not a word, should be), the IRS provides free help for taxpayers over 60 through the Volunteer Income Tax Assistance and Tax Counseling for the Elderly program.

Now That You Have Prepared Your Taxes, What Documents Do You Keep?

The starting point for determining which records you should keep and which you can throw away is three years, which is the period of time after you have filed your income tax return during which the IRS can audit that return. However, packrats like myself would point out that the IRS actually has up to six years in which to audit your return if they say that you underreported your income by at least 25 percent.

All those pesky receipts from credit cards, bank statements, and canceled checks can probably be safely tossed out after three years. Records and receipts for home improvements, however, should be kept until you sell your home since they affect the tax basis of your home and help with the later computations of possible capital gains taxes.

As for mutual funds, each year you should keep the first monthly statement that shows what you paid for how many shares. Also, keep your year-end reports, which will have important dividend and capital gains information.

As for the rest of those monthly statements for the year, rip them and pitch them. But, receipts for expensive items, such as jewelry or computers or even jewelry-encrusted computers, should be kept forever just in case you need to prove their purchase costs for insurance claims.

Final Words from Deep in the Heart of Taxes

For years, the IRS has been plagued by a number of people, some merely deluded, others downright frauds, who try to avoid paying taxes by citing various frivolous purported legal arguments. Now, the IRS has announced that it is changing its internal auditing procedures to speed up the prosecution of people who file frivolous claims to avoid paying federal income taxes.

A common tactic used in the past by tax protestors to postpone the inevitable has been to request a technical advice ruling that can tie up an audit for months or even years. The IRS will no longer honor such requests when the legal status of the questions presented has been established as being frivolous. Note that, despite what you may have heard from self-proclaimed tax experts, the IRS has never lost a single court case on the issue of whether income is subject to tax or the federal tax system itself is constitutional. One of the arguments used by tax protestors is that filing a tax return is an unreasonable search and seizure in violation of the Fourth Amendment to the Constitution. It has also been unsuccessfully argued that the income tax violates the Thirteenth Amendment that prohibits involuntary servitude. Some people will even go so far as to say that the Sixteenth Amendment that created the income tax does not permit non-apportioned direct taxes. None of these arguments has ever been successful.

Another favorite tax avoidance position is that the payment of income taxes is purely voluntary and that, in any event, the term "income" is not defined in the tax code. What it all comes down to is this: Not paying taxes is serious business that can result in civil or even criminal penalties.

> *"Now, the truth of the matter is that there are a lot of things people don't understand. Take the Einstein theory. Take Taxes. Take Love. Do you understand them? Neither do I. But, they exist. They happen."*

—Dalton Trumbo, *The Remarkable Andrew*

Endnote

1. www.consumerreports.org, "Family Matters: When an Older Parent Needs Help," September 2000.

7

Individual Retirement Accounts and 401(k)s

Retirement is a goal that we all have, yet many of us fail to adequately plan for it. One way of determining how prominent considerations of retirement are to a person is to see what they conjure up when you mention "IRA." This acronym has different meanings to different people. For example, a collegiate crew team was in London a few years ago for the Head of the Thames regatta. One of the American rowers was perplexed by the odd stares he received as he walked around London wearing his baseball cap with the logo for the Intercollegiate Rowing Association. Finally, someone pointed out to him that it was not particularly good form to traverse the streets of London wearing a cap with the letters "IRA" emblazoned on it, because in England, IRA is more commonly associated with the Irish Republican Army. Regardless of whether the acronym "IRA" means Irish Republican Army or Intercollegiate Rowing Association or even Individual Retirement Account, it would certainly behoove everyone to become more aware of the various forms of retirement accounts and how they work.

Individual Retirement Accounts (IRAs) come in the traditional vanilla IRA and the new, improved Roth IRA. With a traditional IRA, contributions to the IRA are generally tax deductible and accumulate income on a tax-deferred basis. With a Roth IRA, you pay income tax on the money you put into the IRA. However, it not only continues to grow untaxed, but in addition, you will be able to take it out without paying any income tax on the withdrawals. Retirement planning in general and IRA planning specifically can be a confusing maze of regulations, but the prize at the end of the maze makes the trip definitely worthwhile.

Loophole

When you retire, if you had a retirement plan at work, such as a 401(k), you generally have the option of leaving your retirement assets with your employer's plan or rolling over your retirement funds into your own IRA. When you roll over your retirement funds from work into your own IRA, you suffer no income tax on the transfer, can pick the investments for your IRA (you can even have multiple IRAs), and can stretch the payments out into the next generation. So, roll over your benefits into your own IRA.

Traditional IRA

A traditional IRA is a retirement account into which the law permits you to make, in many cases, tax deductible contributions on an annual basis of as much as $5,000 a year for the year 2012 ($1,000 more if you are over 50). To qualify for a traditional IRA, you must have earned income and be under the age of 70-and-a-half. The amount of earned income you have must equal or be more than the amount of your IRA contribution. If your spouse is not working outside of the home, you may also make an IRA contribution for your non-working spouse if you have sufficient earned income to cover both IRA contributions. If you are married and neither you nor your spouse has a retirement plan at work, your contributions will be fully deductible. Even if you have a retirement plan at work, you may be able to deduct some or even all of your IRA contribution if your taxable income meets certain guidelines.

If you have a company-sponsored retirement plan, such as a 401(k) plan, your IRA contribution may not be deductible. For single people in 2012 who are covered by a company retirement plan, the IRA deduction is phased out between $58,000 and $68,000 of adjusted gross income. For married people filing jointly, if both of you are covered by a company-retirement plan in 2012, the IRA deduction is phased out between $92,000 and $100,000 of adjusted gross income. Finally, in 2012, married people filing jointly where only one is covered by a company retirement plan, the deduction for an IRA contribution is phased out between $173,000 and $183,000 of adjusted gross income. However, even if you cannot make a deductible IRA contribution, you can still make an IRA contribution up to the statutory amount, and the funds within the account will grow on a tax-deferred basis until you withdraw the funds.

One thing that has always puzzled me is the recurring numbers 59-and-a-half and 70-and-a-half when it comes to federal laws pertaining to retirement. Many people are familiar with the laws that penalize withdrawals from retirement accounts before a person has reached the age of 59-and-a-half years and the laws that require the owner of the retirement account to start withdrawing from the account upon attaining the age of 70-and-a-half years. But, why those ages? And why half years? I do not know anyone over the age of 6 who refers to half years when giving his age. (The temptation to posit that Congressmen think at the level of 6 year olds is one that is somewhat compelling, but one that I will resist.)

For many years, I tried unsuccessfully to find an answer to this question. Then, a graduate student, Daniel Tilton, in a class I teach at Bentley University, provided the answer in an extra credit paper. When legislation to create the self-employed retirement plan that has come to be known as the Keogh Plan (named after New York Congressman Eugene Keogh) was being debated in Congress, there was considerable discussion about imposing penalties for early withdrawals before a designated "normal" retirement age and about the maximum age at which withdrawals would be mandatory. House and Senate committee reports show that the age of 60, a common retirement age in 1962, as determined by insurance company actuaries, was actually 59-and-a-half years. There was some concern that the new retirement plans, which Congress was authorizing, conform to the existing policy structures then used by the insurance companies, including the half year "insurance age" designations. Interestingly, 70-and-a-half is not "insurance age" for 70, although a report of the Social Security Administration done in 1960 found that the average life expectancy of men who would be contributing to self-employed retirement plans was 70.45 years. I suppose it could be worse. Congress could have used dog years.

Roth IRA

The Roth IRA is a great technique for retirement saving. To be eligible for the full annual $5,000 per person contribution to a Roth IRA in 2012, the year in which this book is being written, married couples may have no more than $183,000 adjusted gross annual income and single people may have no more than $125,000 of adjusted gross annual income. Smaller contributions are allowed for couples with income between $173,000 and $183,000 and singles with income of between $110,000 and $125,000. I could give you a fancy explanation of "adjusted gross income," but the easiest way to identify it is by just looking at the figure on line 33 of your Form 1040. These figures change from time to time. For current figures, consult the various tax websites found in "Favorite Websites."

Loophole

To let us aging baby boomers play a little catch-up when it comes to saving for retirement, taxpayers who are at least 50 years old can contribute in 2012, for example, an extra $1,000 for a maximum annual contribution of up to $6,000. Speaking of making that contribution, although you can make a contribution to an IRA for the previous year up until the April 15 tax-filing deadline, you are obviously better off if you make your contribution earlier in the year. The reason is that the sooner you get the money in the account, the sooner it starts growing, either tax deferred or tax free depending on which kind of IRA you choose.

Unlike the traditional IRA, which is so bland that it does not even have a name, your contribution to a Roth IRA is not tax deductible. However, the Roth IRA overcomes this disadvantage by having its earnings accumulate totally free of taxes, so you can withdraw money from the account without paying any income taxes. In addition, unlike the case with a traditional IRA, with a Roth IRA, you are never required to take any money out of the account. So, if you choose to let the money accumulate throughout your lifetime, you can leave the Roth IRA to your children, your grandchildren, or whomever you choose and they can take out the money income tax free as well.

As always, a few conditions must be met. With a few exceptions, you may not take out the earnings of your Roth IRA without paying a 10 percent penalty for the first five years of the account's existence. There is a common misconception that you may not take out any money from a Roth IRA account without paying a penalty unless it has been in the account for at least five years. This is incorrect. You may withdraw the money you put into the Roth IRA at any time without any penalty. It is only the account's *earnings* that are subject to the five-year rule.

You can convert a regular IRA to a Roth IRA. If you do this, you must pay income tax on the amount converted. For this reason, many older Americans think that it does not make sense to convert to a Roth IRA. However, some older Americans might find it useful to convert their traditional IRAs to Roth IRAs. If you do not need the money in your traditional IRA, it may make sense to convert it so that you do not have to take the mandatory distributions after reaching the age of 70-and-a-half, as you would have to do in the case of a traditional IRA.

Decisions, Decisions

A number of factors go into deciding whether a traditional IRA or a Roth IRA is a better choice for you. These factors include your present tax rate, your projected tax rate when you retire, how long you expect to keep the money in the IRA account, and what you expect to earn on your investments. Projecting your tax rate when you retire is particularly tricky because future tax rates are always subject to the slings and arrows of outrageous Congresses and their whims as to tax legislation. If you have a relatively long period of time before you expect to retire, such as 15 years or more, you may be better off with a Roth IRA. The more time the assets grow tax free, the better.

If you do not expect to need much of the IRA money in retirement, a Roth IRA account is also better because it will pass to your heirs without any income tax liability. A Roth IRA has no beginning date after which you must start taking withdrawals. In that way, I suppose, a Roth IRA is much like love, which was described in the song "Love Is All Around Us," by the Troggs during the 1960s, as having no beginning and having no end. There is no love in the traditional IRA. The latest date by which you must start taking your money out of a traditional IRA is April 1 of the calendar year following the year in which you turn 70-and-a-half. Apparently, some senator remembered the old adage that "a fool and his money are soon parted" and figured April Fools' Day would be a good time to make everyone start taking out their traditional IRA money.

Choosing the investments for your IRA is as difficult as choosing any other investments, but there are some basic rules. Because the account is already tax advantaged, you do not want to invest in things like annuities or municipal bonds that provide tax advantages that you do not need. Particularly if you are investing for the long run, a mix of stocks and bonds through mutual funds with small fees makes sense. Fees can add up over time and really reduce your return. Check your account about every six months to see if it if needs rebalancing. Once you have determined the ratio of stocks to bonds that is most appropriate for you, be aware that market conditions may often change that ratio without your doing anything. So, to maintain a safe and effective balancing of your investments between stocks and bonds, you should rebalance, but remember that frequent trades will increase your costs and reduce your return.

The Different Path

That great financial sage Yogi Berra once allegedly said, "When you come to a fork in the road, take it." For some people, choosing a different path has, as Robert Frost said, made all the difference in the world. When it comes to IRA investments, most people seem to put their money into the tried and sometimes true stocks, bonds, CDs or mutual funds. But, other people want to take Yogi's fork in the road, confident that indeed it just might make all the difference in the world.

Although the law does permit many forms of nontraditional IRA investments, few people take advantage of the law. Nontraditional investments are generally held in what are called self-directed IRAs. Not all forms of investments are allowed to be part of an IRA. Collectibles such as coins, stamps, or works of art are examples of prohibited IRA investments. However, the law will allow you to put into an IRA such less common investments as real estate, gold bullion, palladium bullion (whatever that is), limited partnerships, private mortgages, foreign securities, futures contracts, equipment leases, oil wells, private jet leasing, race horses, stock options, or even bull semen (I kid you not). You cannot invest in life insurance policies, art, rugs, antiques, stamps, coins, or alcoholic beverages. Nor can you invest in a company that you or a family member owns, buy a home for you or a family member, lease assets to you or a family member, or loan money to you or a family member. Yet, although it is legal to have your IRA invested in those vehicles, you may find it difficult to find an IRA custodian willing to hold them for you. IRA custodians must meet IRS guidelines or risk losing their certification to act as an IRA custodian. The average bank or brokerage house, neither familiar with the IRA rules pertaining to those types of investments nor wishing to take the risks associated with those investments, is unlikely to act as your IRA custodian in those instances. If you buy a vacation home as an IRA investment, you must run it as a business and cannot use it personally.

Loophole

Once you reach retirement age, if you want to live in the property held in your IRA, you can take the property out of the IRA as a distribution, pay the tax on the distribution, unless it was in a Roth IRA, and get to use the property as your own.

401(k)

Although it may seem like it has always been around, Section 401(k) of the Internal Revenue Code was passed in 1978. For one of the most powerful retirement savings vehicles available today, it does not have a very fancy name. It did not even have a sponsor in Congress eager to have his name associated with it, as in the case of Delaware Senator William Roth, the primary sponsor of the Roth IRA. It is just the 401(k).

If the 401(k) did have a name associated with it, it would be that of Ted Benna, a man of incredible vision who was able to crack the Internal Revenue Code and turn an innocuous provision, 401(k), into the basis of a retirement revolution. In 1980, he used the law to set up the first pretax salary reduction, employee contribution, company match, retirement plan using provisions of IRC section 401(k) that had been missed by the rest of the financial planning world. The use of employee pretax contributions to fund a retirement account was entirely unforeseen when Congress passed the initial 401(k) law. Even the IRS was unprepared for Benna's innovation, but to the surprise of many, the IRS approved Benna's interpretation of the law, thereby setting the stage for a dramatic change in how American retirement plans are funded.

With the traditional defined benefit pension plan going the way of the dinosaur (who, by the way, had an awful retirement plan), the 401(k) has become the retirement plan of choice for most companies. The most common type of 401(k) plan is the traditional 401(k) plan, which is set up by the employer and permits individual employees to contribute a portion of their wages to a retirement plan before those wages have been subjected to income taxes. The money you contribute to your 401(k) account is neither subject to federal income tax withholding nor subject to income tax in the year that you contribute to your 401(k) account.

Once in your 401(k) account, your money grows in the investments of your choice from an array of investment options made available to you in your particular plan. These investments include stock mutual funds, bond funds, money market funds, and even stock in the company you work for. The growth of your investment is on a tax-deferred basis. No income tax is due until you withdraw the money from your 401(k). The money you contribute to your traditional 401(k) plan comes directly out of your paycheck as a payroll deduction so once you have enrolled in your company's traditional 401(k) plan, it requires no effort to regularly save for retirement.

There may be no free lunches, but there actually is free money in many traditional 401(k) accounts. In an effort to induce their employees to save for retirement and to reward them for their service to the company, many companies provide matching contributions of as little as 10 percent or as much as 100 percent of the employee's contribution depending on the terms of the particular company 401(k) plan. Some employers pay their matching contribution as either a specific percentage of the employee's wages or a method to make a profit sharing contribution. Employers are allowed to require a certain period of employment at the company before an employee is eligible for a matching contribution. In addition, as an inducement of employees to stay with their particular employer, the employer can provide in the particular terms of its company 401(k) plan that the matching contributions for the employer are not vested in the employee until after a particular period of time, commonly five years.

One of the major additional benefits of a 401(k) plan over an IRA is the considerably higher amount that an individual may contribute to his 401(k). While in 2012, the limit for contribution to an IRA was $5,000 for someone under the age of 50 and $6,000 for people 50 and over, the limit for contribution to a 401(k) was a much healthier $17,000 for those under 50. If you are 50 years old or older, you could contribute an additional $5,500, for a total maximum contribution of $22,500. The advantage is tremendous if you are able to put away that much more money to work for you on a tax-deferred basis.

When you leave your company, you have a number of decisions to make regarding your 401(k). You can do nothing and leave it with the company to continue growing, but without your being able to make additional contributions to the account. You also can choose to have your 401(k) plan transferred and rolled over into your 401(k) account with your new employer, if your new employer, as most do, offers a 401(k) plan. Another option available to you is to have the account rolled over into an IRA that you can self-direct. This option may not only provide you with a greater choice as to investment options for your retirement money, but also may be much less costly to you in regard to the maintenance fees related to your IRA as compared to your previous company's 401(k) plan fees. This is most likely your best option if you are retiring from work.

The last option available to you when you leave a company is the one that should be used only as a last resort: Take the money out of the 401(k) plan without putting it into another retirement account. Unless you have reached the magic age of 59-and-a-half, if you utilize this option, not only will you be assessed income taxes on the money you take out of your 401(k) account, but you also will be subject to an additional 10 percent excise tax penalty for an early withdrawal unless certain exceptions apply, such as using the money to buy a home, avoid foreclosure on a home you already own, pay for certain home repair expenses, or pay for funeral expenses for family members. Unfortunately, too many people just take the money from their 401(k) accounts and spend it. Not only will this subject you to immediate income taxes as well as the excise tax penalty If you are under 59-and-a-half, but it will also eliminate the future tax-deferred growth of your retirement investment.

Roth 401(k)

In 2006, employers were first able to offer Roth 401(k) accounts that permitted employees to put all or some of their 401(k) contributions into a Roth 401(k) account. The amount of the worker's salary that is contributed into a Roth 401(k) is part of the taxable wages of the worker in the year that the money is contributed to the Roth 401(k). However, once the money is deposited into the Roth 401(k) account, it grows tax free and may be withdrawn later without incurring income taxes. I'll let you in on a little secret: The Roth 401(k) shouldn't even be called a 401(k), because the law authorizing it is actually Internal Revenue Code Section 402A, but why quibble?

Similar to a regular 401(k) account, an employee could contribute as much as $17,000 in 2012 to his Roth 401(k), and if he or she was 50 years of age or older, he or she could contribute up to $22,500.

Although these are the amounts that federal law permits as a maximum contribution, employers may set a lesser limit for their own particular plans, such as a limit of an employee's contribution to a maximum of 10 percent of his or her salary, which in the case of a person earning $100,000 would be $10,000.

Only about one-third of large employers, including IBM, General Motors, and Johnson & Johnson, presently offer Roth 401(k)s for their employees, but more are expected to do so in the near future. Originally, the 2001 law that authorized the establishment of Roth 401(k)s was set to "sunset" in 2010, but in response to public interest, the law was made permanent in 2006 providing greater incentive for companies to provide them for their employees without the fear that they would be spending money setting up a retirement fund that would not be around for very long.

An employee whose employer offers both traditional 401(k) and Roth 401(k) accounts has the option of taking advantage of both types of retirement accounts so long as the total money contributed to the traditional 401(k) and the Roth 401(k) does not exceed the total amount that he can contribute under the terms of the plan. For example, a worker over the age of 50 who is eligible under federal law and the terms of the particular plan at his place of work to contribute $22.500 could choose to put half of that contribution or $11,250 in the traditional 401(k0 and another $11,250 in the Roth 401(k).

Bad News/Good News

The bad news is that although employers are permitted under federal law and many do choose to provide some amount of matching funds to the contributions of their workers to traditional 401(k) accounts, thereby giving free money to the retirement accounts of participating workers, no such matching contributions may be made by employers into the Roth 401(k) accounts of employees. However, the good news is that the employers can make matching contributions into the traditional 401(k) account of the employee so the employee will have both a Roth 401(k) account and a traditional 401(k) account with his employer and get the benefit of the matching contribution.

Choices

So, which is better: the traditional Roth 401(k) or the Roth 401(k)? For younger workers, the choice is clear. They will probably find that the advantages of years and years of the tax-free growth of a Roth 401(k) account to be of more value than the mere deferring of income taxes until retirement. In addition, younger, lower-paid workers may find that the present income tax deferral is not worth as much to them as totally tax-free growth. Older employees who may be better paid and not directly eligible for a Roth IRA due to their incomes being too high may find the opportunity to take advantage of the tax-free growth in a Roth 401(k) tempting. Those workers who are convinced that income tax rates are likely to go up in the future from their present historically low levels may also be more inclined to take the tax-free growth provided by a Roth 401(k) rather than the tax deferral offered by the traditional 401(k).

Devil in the Details

Unlike with a Roth IRA, an employee with a Roth 401(k) is required to start taking minimum distributions from the account upon reaching the age of 70. On the plus side, those minimum distributions will still be tax-free. On the negative side, those amounts taken as minimum distributions will reduce the amount of tax-free growth of the account that the employee may otherwise have chosen to leave in the account if not immediately needed.

How to Exorcise the Devil

You can avoid the minimum distribution problem altogether by rolling over the Roth 401(k) into a Roth IRA, which has no such requirement for required minimum distributions and which will also give you greater control over the investments and fees involved with your retirement savings.

Beneficiary Designation

Every IRA and 401(k) owner, regardless of whether the IRA or 401(k) is traditional or Roth, should have an up-to-date beneficiary designation form that indicates who will receive the funds remaining upon the death of the IRA owner. If there is no beneficiary designation form or if the form is lost, the IRA money will pass to the estate of the IRA owner.

Key

It is important to have both primary and contingent beneficiaries named in the beneficiary designation.

Keeping It Current

Many people fail to keep their beneficiary designations current. You should review these forms regularly, particularly as family circumstances change due to births, deaths, or divorces. If you neglect to remove a former spouse from your beneficiary statement, your ex-spouse could receive that money regardless of your divorce. If you do not list anyone as your beneficiary or if those people predecease you, the money will go to your estate. That means the money will have to come out over the next five years at a much greater income tax cost, rather than the IRA payments stretching out over the lifetimes of children or grandchildren whom you might have wished to name as your beneficiaries.

Keeping It Handy

Banks and other financial institutions that act as IRA custodians and administrators too often lose beneficiary designation forms. This is a particular problem when banks get taken over by other banks. The best protection from lost beneficiary forms is for you to keep a duplicate copy of the beneficiary designation form that has been acknowledged by the IRA custodian or administrator. The forms that are supplied by the IRA custodian or administrator often do not leave enough room for you to indicate who will be the primary beneficiary and contingent beneficiaries. If this happens to you, you can adapt the form supplied by the custodian or administrator to provide for all the beneficiaries you may wish to list. If you are naming children as beneficiaries, it is particularly important to also list who will get a deceased child's share. In the case of children or grandchildren, you may also want to name one or more trusts as a beneficiary. Doing so can stretch out the tax savings on an IRA by as much as 70 years or more.

Keeping It in the Family

The most common choice of a beneficiary of an IRA for a married person is that person's spouse. A surviving spouse is allowed to merely roll the inherited IRA into his or her own IRA without any tax consequences. Another sensible choice is to name children as contingent secondary beneficiaries. In this way, not only might the children inherit the IRA upon the death of the IRA account owner, but in addition, if the surviving spouse did not need some or all of the inherited account, some or all of the inherited IRA could be disclaimed and passed directly to the children, who would then withdraw the funds over their lifetimes. Providing additional flexibility is the fact that the law lets you decide to disclaim an interest in a retirement account up to nine months from the date of death of the retirement account holder.

You can achieve even more tax deferral by having a trust for grandchildren as a beneficiary. In this way, you could spread out the distributions over the lives of the grandchildren. For example, a 15 year old who inherits an IRA can spread out the payments over a life expectancy of 67 years and achieve significant tax deferral or, in the case of a Roth IRA, tax avoidance.

Roth IRA Accounts for Children and Grandchildren

Talk about a win-win situation. Setting up a Roth IRA for a young child or grandchild will allow you to pay the child or grandchild for doing work around the house and contribute in 2012 up to the maximum $5,000 a year into a Roth IRA on behalf of the child and watch that money grow tax free. With the magic of compound tax-free interest over a long period of time, even if the contributions occurred only between the ages of 7 and 18 years, the young person would have millions at age 65. And the IRS has already conceded that a child as young as the age of 7 can be paid for work actually performed. Moreover, if your child or grandchild has no other income during those years, no income taxes will be due on the wages you pay the youngster and you do not have to pay Social Security taxes on that money either.

A problem encountered by some people trying to set up Roth IRAs for children or grandchildren has been that some IRA administrators have refused to set them up for children because as minors they cannot be bound by contracts they make. Fortunately, many of the major brokerage firms and mutual fund families will open a custodial IRA for a minor as long as a parent or guardian cosigns the documents as the child's guardian. Some brokerage houses offer custodial IRAs for children, with no minimum balance requirements and no annual maintenance fees. Others require a small minimum balance of as little as $250, and still other brokerage houses provide custodial IRAs for children with no minimum balance, but with small annual maintenance fees.

Conversion to a Roth IRA

Until 2010, converting a traditional IRA to a Roth IRA was an option available only to people whose adjusted gross income was no more than $100,000. This $100,000 figure applied to both single people and married couples filing a joint tax return. But now anyone can convert some or all of their traditional IRA to a Roth IRA.

For many people, converting their traditional IRA account into a Roth IRA account presents a good news, bad news situation. The good news is that once you have converted your traditional IRA into a Roth IRA, all the money in that account will grow tax free and can be either taken out or passed to the next generation without taxes. But, the bad news is that if you convert a traditional IRA to a Roth IRA, you must pay income taxes on all the money you convert. And the worst news is that you may find that, after your conversion, the stock market heads for the porcelain receptacle (a nicer way of saying toilet), and you find yourself with a tax bill on a conversion of an account, for example, valued at $10,000, that by the time it comes to pay taxes, is only worth about $6,000. In this example, someone in the 28 percent tax bracket would pay an extra $1,128 in taxes.

Loophole

The best time to convert a traditional IRA to a Roth IRA is when the economy is down and the value of your traditional IRA is reduced. You will pay less income tax on the converted funds. If the market dropped drastically after you made your conversion, you should reverse the conversion and convert again later.

Key

If you are under the age of 59-and-a-half, you should convert a traditional IRA to a Roth IRA only if you have sufficient money outside your traditional IRA to pay the tax incurred. Any money taken from your traditional IRA used to pay the income taxes will be considered an early withdrawal and will be slapped with a 10 percent penalty in addition to the income tax.

IRS regulations permit people to nullify an IRA conversion from earlier in the year until their income taxes are due on April 15 (or as late as October 15 if they file for extensions) and thus save themselves some tax money. To undo the conversion, you must contact the custodian of your IRA and have the funds rolled back into a traditional IRA. Along with your income tax return, you must file a Form 8606. With this accomplished, and in the light of an ever-lower-priced stock market, you may well want to reconvert to a Roth IRA and pay less income tax because of the reduced value of the traditional IRA. IRS regulations permit the reconversion into a Roth IRA but prohibit you from doing so until the next tax year. If you are considering doing this double conversion at the end of the year, be aware that there is a minimum 30-day waiting period between the time you undo a Roth IRA conversion and the time you convert it back to a Roth IRA.

Key

If you do an IRA conversion, it is imperative that you do not personally take possession of the funds but rather have the funds passed from one IRA trustee to another.

When you convert to a Roth IRA from a traditional IRA, the amount that you choose to convert is added to your other income for that year. Plan ahead by converting no more than the ceiling of your present income tax rate bracket. By doing this, you can reduce your tax burden. IRA conversions do not have to be done all in one year. In fact, it can be prudent and advisable to spread out conversions over a number of years. You also may want to consider setting up a number of Roth IRA accounts with each invested in different types of investments, some conservative, such as bonds, and others more speculative, such as growth stocks, thereby making recharacterization into a traditional IRA simpler.

When you convert a traditional IRA to a Roth IRA, you will have significant taxable income in the year of the conversion, so you will be better off if you do your conversion before you start to take Social Security benefits. Otherwise, the income from the conversion could cause an increase in the amount of income taxes owed on your Social Security benefits received. See Chapter 6, "Income Taxes," for more details.

When Does It Make Sense to Convert a Traditional IRA to a Roth IRA?

Although it may seem that changing taxable income to non-taxable income would always be a good thing to do, converting a traditional IRA to a Roth IRA is not always a good idea.

Because you will have to pay income taxes on the amount of your IRA conversion, it makes sense to delay converting until you are in a lower tax bracket, such as you may find yourself in retirement, however, that also presupposes that income tax rates will not go up significantly. As Yogi Berra said, predicting is difficult, particularly about the future. Predicting income tax rates is almost impossible.

If your traditional IRA is large, it may make sense to convert some or all of it to a Roth because with a traditional IRA, you must start taking distributions once you attain the age of 70 and those distributions could push you into a higher tax bracket.

Converting to a Roth IRA will also give you the ability to pass it on to grandchildren as an income tax-free bequest at your death, which can result in double the tax savings of leaving them a traditional IRA.

Distribution

On April 16, 2002, the IRS issued final regulations for minimum distributions from retirement plans. Before that, we had been working under proposed regulations that had been around since 1987, without ever being finally accepted and a radically different set of proposed regulations enacted in 2001 that were clarified by the 2002 final regulations. The former "proposed" regulations might have been the longest on-going proposal since Captain Parmenter proposed to Wrangler Jane on the 1960s Western situation comedy *F Troop*. If you are not a baby boomer, there is no way you would remember that show—your loss.

The idea behind minimum distribution rules is that, except for Roth IRAs, a retirement plan owner must annually withdraw amounts from that retirement account, subject then to income taxes that had been deferred until the time of withdrawal. These required withdrawals are calculated to use up the retirement account over the life expectancy of the plan owner. However, people have a habit of not exactly following statistical models when it comes to things such as life expectancy, and that is where planning opportunities present themselves. In addition, depending on how much the IRA earns, there may well be more money in the account at the death of the owner than at the time of the first required withdrawals. It is also important to remember that the rules concerning minimum distributions are just that: rules as to the minimum you must take out. If you find you need the money, you can take out more at any time without penalty after age 59-and-a-half, although you must pay income taxes on any amounts you do withdraw from a traditional IRA.

These new regulations work much to the advantage of the taxpayer, which makes one wonder why the IRS issued them. The answer is a simple one. The former regulations were so complicated that many people did not follow them, not out of cheating hearts (apologies to Hank Williams), but because they just did not know better or understand the rules. This left the IRS in a position of receiving less tax revenue from retirement accounts. Under the new drastically simplified rules, the IRS will most likely receive more tax money because the rules are both easier to understand and to enforce, while people who do follow them will be in a position to fare better than under the old rules. A key to understanding the new rules is to note that people can use the new minimum distribution rules to shelter money from taxes for longer times.

Following the admonition of Henry David Thoreau to "simplify, simplify, simplify!," there are now just three life expectancy tables used to determine the minimum distribution amounts. The first is the Uniform Lifetime Distribution table, used during the owner's lifetime. The second is the Joint Life Table, used when the owner has a spouse who is the sole beneficiary and who is more than ten years younger than the owner. The third table is the Single Life Table, which is used for all beneficiaries who inherit the retirement plan. Calculating the amount of your minimum distribution amount is a simple task. All you need to do is go to the applicable life expectancy table and look up your age; this number corresponds to an "applicable divisor," which is the number you divide into your IRA account balance to determine the amount you must withdraw in that year.

Withdrawal Pains

Harry Houdini was the famous magician who more than once performed marvelous escapes from inside locked safes. In a moment of candor, he privately admitted that it was easy to get out of a locked safe because safes were constructed to be hard to break into, not out of. The same might be said for IRA accounts.

Early and Late Withdrawals

While it is not particularly complicated to get money into the account, getting the money out of the account before the magical age of 59-and-a-half can present problems. Withdrawals from a traditional IRA or 401(k) before age 59-and-a-half can result in not just income taxes on the withdrawn amount, but also a 10 percent excise tax as well.

People wishing to delay withdrawals also face obstacles. Failure to take required minimum distributions after age 70-and-a-half can result in a 50 percent tax on the amounts not distributed that should have been withdrawn. The IRS rules do, however, provide for a way of avoiding this 50 percent tax if your failure to take the minimum distribution was a "reasonable error," a term the IRS uses but does not define. When you file a Form 5329 to report the failure to take a minimum distribution, include a letter both explaining why you believe the failure was the result of a reasonable error and specifying the steps you are taking to remedy the situation. If the IRS accepts your explanation, they will refund the 50 percent tax you must include with your Form 5329.

Loophole

There are some exceptions to the early withdrawal penalties, including taking substantially equal yearly payments made over the life expectancy of the IRA owner. Once again, using its gift for language, when the IRS says that the payments must be made over the life expectancy of the IRA owner, what it really means is that the yearly payments have to be made either until the person reaches the age of 59-and-a-half years or until five years have gone by, whichever event occurs later. So, if you use this exception to get penalty-free access to some of the money in your traditional IRA, you will also be able to defer taking further withdrawals if you desire.

Other exceptions include paying for certain unreimbursed medical expenses and paying for some educational expenses for the IRA's owner or some family members, but perhaps the most used exception for avoiding the penalty for early withdrawal is the exception for a first-time home buyer.

A Painless Withdrawal

If you are doing something now that you had done two years earlier, when are you doing it for the first time? This may sound like a Zen riddle, but in fact, it is a relevant question when applied to a person who is looking to take a penalty-free distribution from his or her IRA before the age of 59-and-a-half years. The reason for its relevance is that the IRS has rules that permit you to take as much as a $10,000 early distribution from your IRA, without penalty, to help buy a home. To qualify as a first-time home buyer and avoid the 10 percent early distribution penalty, you must meet certain requirements.

First, the home being purchased must be used as your principal residence. Second, if it will be your home, you must be the owner of the IRA or the IRA owner's spouse, child, grandchild, parent, or grandparent.

Third, and the condition with which as a former English major (at least one of my majors, along with journalism, sociology, and finally philosophy) I have the most difficulty, you must be a first-time home buyer, which according to the IRS means that you have not owned a home during the preceding two years. Does that make much sense? Not really, but it is the Internal Revenue Code. It was never intended to make sense.

Fourth, you must use the money for the cost of buying, building, or rebuilding a home along with whatever usual financing and settlement costs there might be.

Fifth, you are subject to a lifetime limitation of $10,000 being withdrawn from your IRA for first-time home buying. This is significant. Remember, according to the IRS, you can be a first-time home buyer any number of times, so long as the purchases are at least two years apart.

Finally, you must use the money withdrawn from your IRA for a first-time home purchase within 120 days of taking out the money.

By the way, the IRS is not the only government agency that fractures logic as well as the English language. Federal laws pertaining to student loans permit the consolidation of a single loan.

> "When I use a word," Humpty Dumpty said, in rather a scornful tone, "it means just what I choose it to mean—neither more nor less." "The question is," said Alice, "whether you can make words mean so many different things." "The question is," said Humpty Dumpty, "which is to be master—that's all."
>
> —Lewis Carroll, *Through the Looking-Glass and What Alice Found There*

Loophole

If, for some reason, you take the money out and the closing on the home is delayed, you can put the money back into your IRA within the 120-day limit and consider the distribution and contribution as a rollover and thus avoid any penalties.

Survivors

The new minimum distribution rules provide great new opportunities for estate planning actually done after death that can potentially save huge amounts of taxes. The key is that the proper beneficiary designation must be in place prior to death before these tax-saving decisions can be made after death. Two essential dates to remember are September 30 and October 31. Following the death of the owner of the IRA, a beneficiary does not have to be officially designated until September 30 of the year after the death of the IRA owner. October 31 is the date by which documentation pertaining to individual beneficiaries of a trust must be provided to the custodian of the IRA.

If you are a surviving spouse named as the beneficiary, you can roll the IRA into your own IRA and prolong the payout of the IRA with tax deferral over your lifetime. At your death, your children or grandchildren, if they are listed as beneficiaries, can then spread out the payments from the IRA over their individual lifetimes for further compounded tax savings. The money gets to either continue growing tax deferred or, in the case of a Roth IRA, tax free for potentially many more years.

Disclaimers

If you determine that you do not need the money from your deceased spouse's IRA or are concerned that the money will increase your estate up to a level where it will incur estate taxes, you can disclaim the right to receive the money as the primary listed beneficiary. The money can then go to children if they are named as secondary beneficiaries; or it can even go to grandchildren if they are named as tertiary beneficiaries and the children disclaim the money.

A disclaimer is just the legal process by which someone who has a right to something waives that right, causing the right to go to the next in line to receive that property. The law provides for a period of nine months from the date of death of the IRA owner for a beneficiary to disclaim his or her interest. Some people (even some lawyers) originally misinterpreted the regulations to mean that a new beneficiary could be named after death. This is incorrect. However, the law does allow through the proper use of disclaimers for beneficiaries to be chosen from among the people already named as primary, secondary, or further contingent beneficiaries.

Loophole

If a surviving spouse, children, and grandchildren are all listed in that order on the beneficiary designation form, disclaimers made by the surviving spouse and children can possibly result in significant income tax savings. Since the grandchildren receive the payments from a traditional IRA over their lifetimes, it is likely that the amounts distributed to them annually will be taxed less because their tax rate will probably be less than their parent's or grandparent's. In addition, the amount of the yearly required distribution will be smaller than that required for the surviving spouse and children because it is based on life expectancy tables. Thus, the money is able to compound longer on a tax-deferred basis. And note that, if the IRA is a Roth IRA, no income taxes will be due because the money is distributed over the life of a surviving spouse, child, or grand-child.

Key

A properly executed beneficiary designation form is absolute-ly essential to any after-death estate planning. If beneficiaries are not specifically provided for, the law says that the IRA must be distributed to the estate of the deceased owner and distrib-uted to the heirs according to the terms of the will or, if there is no will, according to the laws of intestacy. In either event, the money must come out of the IRA over the next five years, so the opportunity for long-time tax deferral is lost.

Key

A Durable Power of Attorney is a most important estate and financial planning document that everyone should have. It is particularly important that a surviving spouse have one that specifically provides the authority to be able to execute spou-sal rollovers, disclaimers, and distribution elections if the sur-viving spouse becomes disabled and unable to make these decisions on his or her own behalf.

Opportunities

The laws regarding the treatment of IRAs after death provide tre-mendous tax savings opportunities, but there are also a number of picky little details with which you must comply in order to be eligible for those savings.

Picky Little Detail One

Following the death of an IRA owner, a beneficiary other than a surviving spouse must actually maintain the IRA in the decedent's name or have a 6 percent excise tax tacked on. So, for example, the titling might appear as "Fred Flintstone, deceased, IRA for the benefit of Pebbles Flintstone."

Picky Little Detail Two

Trusts can be particularly effective beneficiaries of IRAs for managing money on behalf of children or grandchildren whom you may not wish to empower to control their receipt of IRA money. To be recognized for IRA purposes, a trust must meet four conditions. First, it must be valid under applicable state law. Second, it must be irrevocable at the death of the IRA owner. Third, the beneficiaries of the trust must be readily identifiable. And fourth, a copy of the trust must be provided in a timely fashion to the IRA administrator.

8

Planning for the Home

According to Dorothy, from *The Wizard of Oz*, "There is no place like home. There is no place like home." Apparently, Dorothy was fond of repeating herself. But, the question of housing options for senior citizens is one worth repeated examination. There are many things to consider in proper planning for housing for seniors, including Reverse Mortgages, paying off a mortgage, private mortgage insurance, refinancing, life estates, and selling your home to your children and then renting it back.

Many senior citizens want to stay in the homes they have lived in for so many years. Their homes are familiar places with which they have an emotional attachment. According to figures supplied by the Department of Housing and Urban Development's Office of Policy Development and Research (HUD), approximately 80 percent of older Americans own their own homes and many of these people have no present mortgage. Some seniors find themselves cash poor, but house rich as the value of the home, which they may have purchased for a relatively small amount of money many years ago, has now increased in value tremendously. A number of options can help people stay in their homes and tap into its equity as a source of funds. A *Reverse Mortgage* is one option that will help people remain in their homes and convert some of its equity into ready cash.

Loophole

With a Reverse Mortgage, the bank pays you on a regular basis instead of the other way around.

Reverse Mortgages

A Reverse Mortgage is the name for a loan that uses your home as security for the loan, just like the conventional mortgage arrangement with which you are familiar. However, with a Reverse Mortgage, you do not have to pay back the loan for as long as you live in the home. This allows people to take the equity out of their home and turn it into cash to meet their daily needs without having to be concerned about monthly payments. Repayment of the loan with interest is generally done at the earliest of the following: the borrower selling the home, moving out of the home, or dying. With some Reverse Mortgages, however, the total loan with interest is due after a specific number of years.

Perhaps the greatest advantage to a Reverse Mortgage is that you, the homeowner, continue to control your home while gaining access to the home's equity. If you had sold your home to get at the equity, you would have faced the difficult decision of how to invest the proceeds of the sale and would have had to find a new place to live. In addition, by using a Reverse Mortgage, you bypass capital gains tax issues.

Although many people are unfamiliar with the concept of Reverse Mortgages, they have been with us for a long time. They became much more available after Congress passed the Alternative Mortgage Transaction Parity Act in 1982, which permitted the making of Reverse Mortgages despite state laws to the contrary. In 1987, more federal laws authorized FHA-insured Reverse Mortgages without a predefined maturity date. These mortgage loans can be made only by FHA-approved lenders.

Loophole

FHA-insured Reverse Mortgage rules require that repayment be absolutely limited to the value of the mortgage property. The bank cannot look to your other assets for repayment. This is important because, with a Reverse Mortgage, you are not making payments on the loan to your bank, so the interest continues to compound and the amount you owe increases significantly over the years. This is of particular importance if the value of your property goes down and you end up owing more than your home is worth.

Before the development of Reverse Mortgages, there were two main ways by which older Americans whose homes had greatly increased in value could get access to that value. First, they could sell the home. This is good, because it would provide the senior with a lot of money. I am a firm believer of the principle that generally something that legally provides you with a lot of money is a good thing. However, in this case, although you get a lot of money, you also have just lost your home and have to find a new place to live at a cost that could well be greater than the cost of staying in your old home. The second option is that you could get a conventional mortgage loan or a home equity loan to be able to use the equity in your home. (Equity is the value of your ownership interest in your home; it is calculated by subtracting any mortgage debt you owe from your home's fair market value.) This also is a good thing, but with the drawback that you have to make monthly payments on the loan to the bank or mortgage company. Reverse Mortgages present a third, and for many people, more attractive alternative.

With a Reverse Mortgage, you give the bank a mortgage on your home to secure a loan to you, but you do not have to pay back the loan for as long as you live in the home. A Reverse Mortgage loan can be constructed so that you get the money either in a lump sum, through regular monthly payments to you from the bank, or as a credit line you can access whenever you wish. As with other lines of credit, no interest is charged on the unused portion of the line of credit. A Reverse Mortgage will provide you with a loan of percentage of your home's appraised value, which can range from between 50 percent to 80 percent. As a rule of thumb, the older the borrower, the larger the percentage of the home's value that can be borrowed.

Speaking of the rule of thumb, I'd like to dispel the commonly held notion that the rule of thumb was based on old English law according to which it was legal to beat your wife with a rod, so long as that rod was no thicker than the husband's thumb. Although this notion was incorrect, it was cited as fact, albeit critically, in three cases from the 1800s from Mississippi and North Carolina. According to the Oxford English Dictionary, the term "rule of thumb" has been used for at least three hundred years and refers to any method of measurement or technique of estimation derived from experience rather than science.

Meanwhile, back at the Reverse Mortgage, the money borrowed is paid back to the bank with all the accumulated interest when you die, sell your home, or permanently move out of the home.

Reverse Mortgages must be first mortgages on the home, which means that if you presently are still carrying a mortgage on the home, that mortgage must be paid off through the money you are borrowing through the Reverse Mortgage as a condition of receiving the Reverse Mortgage.

Even people with poor credit can be eligible for a Reverse Mortgage. The lender's decision to offer a Reverse Mortgage is based exclusively on the age of the borrower or borrowers and the value of the home. Your credit score and income are irrelevant.

Keep It in the Family

Quite often, seniors will abstain from getting a Reverse Mortgage in order to protect the home as a legacy that they can pass on to their children, but the adult children can step up and assist their aging parents as well as protect their legacy by either buying the home from their parents or doing a private Reverse Mortgage with their parents personally. This can be a win-win situation, where the children protect their legacy while the parents are able to get a Reverse Mortgage without the high costs of a commercial Reverse Mortgage.

Uncle Sam Likes Reverse Mortgages

The National Council on Aging received a $295,000 grant from the Federal Centers for Medicare and Medicaid Services to encourage Reverse Mortgages. The motivation for the grant was simple:

Nursing home costs paid by Medicaid are extremely costly to state and federal governments. If people could be encouraged to use their homes to finance their long-term care in nursing homes, it would be better for the government. But, would it be better for you? Not necessarily. Once you go into a nursing home, you must pay back the Reverse Mortgage, which could mean losing your home; if you utilize other forms of planning, you might be able to preserve that home as a legacy for your family.

Using Reverse Mortgages to Pay for Long-Term Care Insurance

Ham and eggs is a good match. Simon and Garfunkel was a good match. But, as desirable as it might seem to link long-term care insurance and Reverse Mortgages, there are some problems. Presently, the average age of a person buying long-term care insurance is 64, while the average age of a person getting a Reverse Mortgage is 75. The best time to get long-term care insurance is when people are in their 40s and 50s. However, the optimum time for getting a Reverse Mortgage is when homeowners are in their 70s. This discrepancy creates a potential problem because a person who waits until his or her 70s to buy long-term care insurance could have a more difficult time passing the medical tests necessary to qualify for long-term care insurance.

Another potential problem with tying long-term care insurance to Reverse Mortgages was indicated in a study done by the Department of Housing and Urban Development (HUD), which indicated homeowners using Reverse Mortgages were most often unmarried people with little income and few assets other than their homes. These people still might not be able to afford long-term care insurance with the money they would get from their Reverse Mortgages, and they might also be less inclined to bother with long-term care insurance than a person concerned about the needs of a spouse. The people could well be more inclined to merely depend on Medicaid to meet their long-term care needs with little concern about protecting other assets.

It is important to remember that when you get a Reverse Mortgage, you are still the owner of the home and, as such, are fully responsible for paying the real estate taxes, homeowner's insurance, and repair costs required to maintain the property.

There are three types of Reverse Mortgage plans: FHA insured, lender insured, and uninsured. Each of these types of loans will impose origination fees and closing costs. The insured plans also will charge you for the premiums for the insurance while some lenders even impose mortgage servicing charges.

Loophole

You may be able to add these closing costs to the amount you are borrowing and avoid having to pay them up front.

Creative Uses of Reverse Mortgages

For some seniors with little in the way of retirement funds, taking out a Reverse Mortgage in their mid-60s can provide funds that not only can be used to help fund retirement, but also can enable these seniors to postpone taking their Social Security retirement benefits until they are age 70, which can provide a benefit of raising the senior's Social Security retirement benefits by an additional 8 percent per year for each year after full retirement age until age 70 that the senior defers taking Social Security retirement benefits.

Seniors who plan to sell their home and move to a smaller and less costly home can get a Reverse Mortgage to help cover their living expenses until they sell the home, at which time, they can repay the Reverse Mortgage and pocket the rest of the money for their future retirement needs.

FHA-Insured Reverse Mortgage

FHA-insured Reverse Mortgages have a number of different payment options from which you can choose. You can receive regular monthly payments for a specific set period of time, or for as long you live in the home, you can receive a line of credit, or you can receive monthly loan payments plus a line of credit. Using the line of credit provides the greatest flexibility by allowing you to take whatever amounts you need as you determine you need the money. The interest on an FHA-insured Reverse Mortgage is an adjustable rate, which means that over time the rate may go up or it may go down. The interest rate of the loan will not affect the amount you receive as a monthly payment, but it will affect how fast the loan balance grows over time.

Loophole

For a small fee, you can change the payment option of your FHA-insured Reverse Mortgage.

FHA-insured Reverse Mortgages, also known as HECMs (Home Equity Conversion Mortgages), are available to homeowners who are at least 62 years old, regardless of income level. To qualify for the program, you, the owner, must use the home as your primary residence. Single-family homes, multiple-family homes of up to four units, and condominiums are all eligible for the program. In addition, even if the maximum amount of the limit of the loan has been paid out to you, you can stay in the home for the rest of your life or you can choose to move out. HECMs can be obtained directly through banks or mortgage companies.

The insurance provision of the FHA-insured Reverse Mortgage protects you if the lending institution that is providing you funds in the Reverse Mortgage transaction finds itself in financial difficulties. Two major drawbacks to FHA Reverse Mortgages are these: amounts you are able to borrow are often less than the amounts you would be able to borrow through a lender-insured Reverse Mortgage; and the loan costs are usually higher than the costs of uninsured Reverse Mortgage plans. In the past, it was not unusual for the total closing costs to be as much as 4 percent or 5 percent of the loan amount; however, the FHA and private lenders have reduced some of these immediate closing costs in an effort to make the loans more attractive although in some instances they just roll them into the loan amount which just means that you have less money available to you. In an effort to make Reverse Mortgages more affordable in 2010, HUD started the HECM Saver Program in addition to their Standard HECM Program. The HECM Saver Program does not offer as much money through its Reverse Mortgage, but in return for offering less money to borrowers, the equity in the home is greater, which provides less risk to HUD which in turn permitted them to reduce the Mortgage Insurance Premium which traditionally has been 2 percent of the appraised value or the HUD lending limit, whichever was less. This fee was generally the largest fee involved in a homeowner obtaining a Reverse Mortgage. Through the HECM Saver Program, this fee is reduced to .01 percent. For someone obtaining a Reverse Mortgage on a home valued at $300,000, this could result in a reduction of the fee from $6,000 to $30 which is a significant reduction in cost. However, a 75 year old homeowner of a home valued at $500,000 would only be able to receive $262,000 through the HECM Saver Program Reverse Mortgage as compared to $331,500 with the more traditional Reverse Mortgage.

An advantage of a FHA insured loan is that the federal government backs the loan. A disadvantage is that the amount available for an FHA-insured loan is less than that available through lender-insured plans.

Borrowers using HECMs are able to lock in their interest rate at the time they apply for a HECM Reverse Mortgage. For anyone concerned with the cost of borrowing money in an environment where interest rates may change dramatically, being able to lock in an interest rate is important. However, for someone borrowing money through a Reverse Mortgage, the ability to lock an interest rate is even more critical because the interest rate has a direct effect on the amount of money that can be borrowed. An applicant for a HECM receives a guaranteed interest rate for 60 days from the time of application.

Of further benefit to HECM borrowers is the fact that if interest rates decline between the time of the HECM Reverse Mortgage application and the closing of the loan, the borrower gets the new lower rate; this means that he or she will be able to borrow more money.

HECMs are the most popular Reverse Mortgages and undoubtedly will increase. With the declines in home equity in recent years, a number of former providers of private Reverse Mortgages have stopped making these loans. In the last year alone, MetLife, Bank of America, and Wells Fargo all got out of the Reverse Mortgage business.

Counseling

Because of the complexity of these loans, FHA rules require mandatory counseling before an FHA-insured Reverse Mortgage may be issued. However, the counseling may consist of nothing more than a phone call from a HUD-approved agency that involves a discussion of alternative methods the homeowner might use to obtain necessary funds. The counseling session also will include consideration of the tax consequences of a Reverse Mortgage and the effect of a Reverse Mortgage on the ability to pass the home to heirs.

Lender-Insured Reverse Mortgage

Lender-insured Reverse Mortgages provide monthly loan payments to you or monthly loan payments to you along with a line of credit for as long as you live in your home. The interest rate may be either a fixed rate or an adjustable rate. As with the FHA-insured Reverse Mortgage, there are additional costs to the borrower, which include mortgage insurance premiums and other loan fees. An advantage of the lender-insured Reverse Mortgage is that the amount of the loan may be for a larger amount than you could get from the FHA-insured Reverse Mortgage plan. A disadvantage is that these loans usually include higher loan costs, that when added to the borrowed amount to which your loan interest rate is applied, add significantly to your debt.

Closing costs can include such things as appraisal fees, credit report fees, monthly service fees, and "points" that go under a number of different names such as origination fees. Each point is equal to 1 percent of the loan. So, a loan of $200,000 with two points would carry $4,000 of points as a closing cost. In real estate, like betting on football games, it is often not whether you win or lose, but the point spread that counts. Points can significantly add to the cost of borrowing money. And what do you get for these points? Nothing except the privilege of doing business with the particular bank.

Another advantage to you is that some lenders providing insured Reverse Mortgages also include an annuity that will continue to make regular monthly payments to you even if you move out of your home and sell it. Before taking this option, you should consider the financial strength of the company paying the annuity as well as the income tax consequences of the payments. You should also be clear as to how such annuity payments might affect your eligibility for SSI or Medicaid.

Bells and Whistles

Some private lender-insured Reverse Mortgage programs tie in with annuities that make regular monthly payments to the homeowner even if he or she has to move out of the home. In other instances, Reverse Mortgage borrowers may use a lump-sum payment from a Reverse Mortgage to purchase an annuity, however it is absolutely critical that you understand all the costs involved and that you don't end up paying more in interest through a Reverse Mortgage to pay for an annuity that pays you less interest.

Uninsured Reverse Mortgage

The third type of Reverse Mortgage is the uninsured Reverse Mortgage. It, too, is available to homeowners who are at least 62 years old, regardless of income level. In other respects, however, it differs significantly from the other two loan programs. An uninsured Reverse Mortgage plan provides a monthly payment to you for a specific fixed period of time you choose when you take out the loan. The entire unpaid balance of the loan becomes due and payable when that period of time has ended. Interest on this type of Reverse Mortgage loan is usually at a fixed rate, and because no mortgage insurance is involved, there is no mortgage insurance premium. If you are considering this type of loan, it is of critical importance for you to consider how long you will need the money and how you will repay it when it is due. If you are not able to repay the loan when it is due, your home will have to be sold to get the money to pay your debt.

An advantage of the uninsured Reverse Mortgage is that it offers more bang for the buck. You can receive a larger loan through an uninsured Reverse Mortgage than you would with other forms of Reverse Mortgages. More money sounds good, but before you leap, it is important to remember that with more money comes more risk. If you are receiving monthly Reverse Mortgage payments from a lender that declares bankruptcy, your payments are in serious jeopardy (as in I'll take Financial Ruin for $500, Alex).

The law requires that anyone who applies for a Reverse Mortgage be informed of the tax consequences of such loans and that a Reverse Mortgage may affect eligibility for various state and federal programs, as well as being informed of the serious effect on the ability of the homeowner to leave an inheritance to the homeowner's heirs.

Loophole

The money you obtain through a Reverse Mortgage is not taxable by the IRS.

Loophole

If you are already receiving SSI payments or Medicaid benefits, the money you get through a Reverse Mortgage is only countable for determining your continued eligibility for these programs if you keep them in an account past the end of the month in which you receive the payments.

Shared Equity and Appreciation Fees

One of the great lessons in the book, *All I Really Need to Know I Learned in Kindergarten* (Random House, 2003), by Robert Fulghum, is the benefit of sharing. However, with all respect to Mr.

Fulghum, sharing is not always a good thing. When it comes to Reverse Mortgages, sharing could be more akin to being financially taken advantage of.

With a shared equity fee, the fine print in the Reverse Mortgage (and you will never find anything fine in fine print) indicates that at the time the loan becomes due, you are required to pay an additional amount that is equal to a specified percentage of the value of your home at the time of the loan's maturity. One particular Reverse Mortgage offers somewhat higher monthly payments to Reverse Mortgage borrowers who choose this option, but they must pay an additional fee equal to 10 percent of the home's value at the time of maturity. This could be a steep price to pay. If your home is worth $300,000, this provision will cost you an additional $30,000 on top of the interest you are paying on your loan.

In the case of a shared appreciation fee, a share of the home's appreciation in value from the time of the origination of the loan to the time the loan becomes due is payable to the lender. This fee can reach 50 percent. Even Tony Soprano didn't charge loan fees that high. An increase in the value of a home by $75,000 would result in an extra fee of $37,500 at the time of the loan's maturity when the Reverse Mortgage loan carries a 50 percent shared appreciation fee. The danger of both shared equity fees and shared appreciation fees is that if a borrower dies or must leave his or her home because of health reasons or other circumstances within a few years of the loan being made, the fees could actually be larger than the Reverse Mortgage payments.

Odds and Ends

As when you conventionally refinance your home or take out an equity credit line, when you sign the papers to close on a Reverse Mortgage loan, you get three business days to change your mind and cancel the transaction. At the closing, you will receive forms to enable you to exercise that right if you so choose. There is nothing fine about the fine print of Reverse Mortgage documents. They can strain both your eyes and your wallet. Fortunately, Reverse Mortgages are subject to the Federal Truth in Lending Act, which requires lenders to provide you with a disclosure statement that clearly tells you (or at least as clearly as any form drafted by lawyers and bankers can) the highlights and the lowlights of the terms of your Reverse Mortgage. At the top of the form is a box that contains the Annual Percentage Rate (APR) of the loan. The APR represents the real cost of borrowing the money when you consider the closing costs. The form also tells you how much you will have to eventually pay back, which, when you are using compound interest, can be an astonishingly high figure. The disclosure statement will also inform you of all the other fees that go into closing the loan, such as attorney's fees and points.

Just as with conventional mortgages, the actual terms may vary considerably from lender to lender, so it is wise to do some comparison shopping. In addition, before even considering a Reverse Mortgage, think about other ways of getting the money you need. For example, if you need the money to pay real estate taxes, you may be able to take advantage of reduced property tax programs available to senior citizens in all states.

You should also be wary of scams involving Reverse Mortgages. One of these scams involves companies that say that in return for a small percentage of your loan, they will help you find a lender that offers Reverse Mortgages. This service is unnecessary. You can get a complete list of lenders that offer Reverse Mortgages from HUD free of charge by going online to http://portal.hud.gov/hudportal/HUD?src=/program_offices/housing/sfh/hecm/hecmlenders. HUD will also provide you with the names of HUD-approved counseling agencies to help you determine if indeed a Reverse Mortgage is a good choice for you. Reverse Mortgages are definitely more expensive and complicated than conventional financing, but in certain situations, they might be the best choice of all.

Reverse Mortgage Fees

It is not unusual for the fees associated with a Reverse Mortgage to reach between $6,000 and $12,000. Lenders are allowed to charge up to two points on each loan.

Origination fees (points in disguise) are limited by HUD to no more than $6,000 with a minimum of $2,500.

Mortgage insurance is another closing cost for which you are responsible. This works both to your benefit and to that of the lender. It guarantees that you will receive payments even if your lender declares bankruptcy, and it ensures that if you are unable to back the loan when it becomes due that the lender will get what it is owed. Unfortunately, although both you and the lender benefit from mortgage insurance, guess who pays the bill? Those of you who said, "We do," get a gold star. Remember, all financial institutions essentially follow their own version of the Golden Rule: They have the gold, so they make the rules. Unless you choose the HECM Saver Program, the Mortgage Insurance premium is another 2 percent of the property value or the mortgage lending limit, whichever is less.

The lender can also charge appraisal fees of between $450 and $500; Repair Administration Fees of 1.5 percent of the repair bid; credit report fees of up to $20; Flood Certification fees of up to $20; Courier fee for paying off a present mortgage of about $30; Counseling by HUD approved counselors of up to $125, Closing fees to the lawyer or title company of around $350; Title search fees of around $185; Title insurance based on the property value and recording fees of around $75.

For Whom the Reverse Mortgage Tolls

So, for whom are Reverse Mortgages advisable? Along with the instances I gave at the beginning of this chapter, Reverse Mortgages for a fixed period of time are useful for people who are particularly old, whose life expectancies are not long, and whose income needs are great. If you are on a fixed income and your primary asset is your home (which you do not plan to leave to your children), a Reverse Mortgage just might be for you. Closed-end Reverse Mortgages also make sense for "younger-oldsters" who may have serious and chronic medical problems that require continuing care, but who may be able to receive this care in their own home. Obviously, caretakers that provide this at-home care must be available either through professional healthcare agencies or through family members.

The high cost of Reverse Mortgages should be carefully considered before determining if a Reverse Mortgage is something you want to do. A homeowner in need of financial assistance might be eligible for various state or federal aid programs that can reduce or defer real estate taxes or pay for other costly expenses such as medical expenses. A simple, free, and confidential way to see what benefits you might be eligible for is to go to the website (www.benefitscheckup.org), sponsored by the National Council on Aging, and fill in their simple interactive questionnaire.

The Bottom Line

The bottom line is that rarely should a Reverse Mortgage be the first choice when it comes to obtaining necessary funds for elderly homeowners. However, in some circumstances, they could be the best option available.

Mortgage Prepayment

Many seniors believe that paying off a mortgage early is always a good idea. If your mortgage interest rate is, as many are, around 4 percent, you might see making extra mortgage payments as the equivalent of getting an investment return of 4 percent. But, you would be wrong. If you are in the 25 percent tax bracket, and you are deducting your mortgage interest on your income tax return, the true effective rate of interest you are paying is closer to 3 percent, which means that if you can get a return of better than 3 percent on an alternative investment, you would be better off.

But, perhaps more importantly, there are things you might do with that money that would be more to your benefit than paying down your mortgage. If you are under the magic age of 70-and-a-half, putting that money into a tax-advantaged retirement plan, such as an

IRA, is probably a better use of your money in the long run. And if you are intent on paying off a debt, you might look at what you are carrying as a balance on your high-interest credit cards. Not only is the interest rate on credit cards much higher than the interest rate of your mortgage, but in addition, the interest you pay on your credit cards, unlike your mortgage interest, is not tax deductible.

So, when does it make sense to pay down your mortgage? One situation in which it would be advisable is if you are paying private mortgage insurance. By reducing or eliminating your mortgage debt, you may be able to drop this charge and save yourself some money. Also, if your mortgage is almost paid off and the deduction is of little value, you may wish to consider paying it off. The bottom line, as almost always, is to do the math.

Private Mortgage Insurance

Private Mortgage Insurance (PMI) is often required by lenders when people buying a home put down a deposit of less than 20 percent of the purchase price. The cost of PMI shows up on your monthly mortgage bill and is used to pay for insurance that protects the lender if you default on your mortgage loan. Over the lifetime of a mortgage, the cost to you can be significant. For example, on a $100,000 loan with 10 percent down, PMI could cost you $40 a month ($480 a year). Multiply this by the life of your loan, and you are talking about a lot of money.

Loophole

A little known law entitled the Homeowners Protection Act, which went into effect in 1999, sets out rules for automatic termination and cancellation of PMI on home mortgages. The law applies to certain home mortgages since July 29, 1999, for the purchase or refinance of single-family homes. The law does not apply to FHA or VA loans. According to this law, once your equity in the home reaches 22 percent, based on the original property value, the PMI must be terminated and you will not be required to pay further premiums so long as you are up to date with your mortgage payments. In addition, once you reach 20 percent equity in your home, based on the original property value, you have the right to have your PMI canceled on request, again if your mortgage payments are current. The law now requires borrowers to be told at both the closing and annually about their rights to cancel PMI. Even if you signed your mortgage before 1999, you can still ask your lender to cancel your PMI when your equity exceeds 20 percent, although the law does not require them to cancel the insurance. Many lenders are willing to terminate the PMI in these circumstances, although the law does not require them to do so.

Loophole

Even if you have not made enough payments to have your PMI terminated, the value of your home may have gone up sufficiently so that your equity may be more than 20 percent of its present value, in which case you may be able to have your PMI eliminated. To do this, you must obtain an appraisal of the home and present it to the bank. Another time at which you would get an appraisal that might enable you to eliminate PMI is when you refinance, which makes sense if you wish to take advantage of lower interest rates.

Refinancing

When mortgage rates are low, many people refinance to take advantage of the lower rates and reduce their monthly mortgage payments. Many costs are involved in refinancing, and paramount among them is points.

When you apply for a loan, the bank or mortgage company is required by law to provide you with a document called a Good Faith Estimate Disclosure Statement. This disclosure statement will detail the various closing costs you will incur under the terms of the mortgage loan they are offering. There are many costs involved in closing a refinancing loan, including points, application fees, document preparation fees, title insurance, credit report costs, and survey fees.

Loophole

Although your bank will not tell you this, some of these fees are negotiable, and with competition among banks being particularly intense, you may be in a position to negotiate with your bank to lower some of these costs. In addition, if you have previously obtained title insurance when you first bought your home, the same title insurance company will reinsure the title for a lesser premium if you ask. The same goes for the cost of the required survey. If you use the same surveyor, the cost will be reduced. To see what average closing costs are, go to www.bankrate.com.

Life Estates

Placing their home into a life estate may be an advantageous course of action for many seniors. As the name implies, a life estate is an interest in property which lasts for the lifetime of the person called the life tenant. When the life tenant dies, his or her interest in the property ends and the ownership and possession of the property becomes fully vested in the remaindermen, the people identified in the life estate document as the people taking title upon the death of the life tenant. There can be any number of joint life estate holders, typically, a husband and wife and any number of remaindermen as well, often the children of the life tenants.

During the lifetime of the life tenant, he or she may live in the property and has control of the property. In most states, a life tenant's interest in a life estate is a noncountable asset for determination of Medicaid eligibility. In many states, upon the death of a life tenant whose home is held in a life estate, the state cannot seek to use the home for reimbursement for amounts paid by Medicaid. In other words, the home is protected from Medicaid claims.

There also may be income tax advantages to the use of the life estate. Children or others inheriting a home through a life estate as remaindermen receive title to the home at a stepped-up basis for income tax purposes. For example, if a home purchased for $18,000 was placed in a life estate and its fair market value was $200,000 at the time of the death of the life tenant, the basis for the remaindermen would be the $200,000 fair market value. So, if the remaindermen sold the home for $200,000 following the death of the life tenant, there would be no taxable gain.

Sell the Home to the Children

Another housing option is for seniors to sell their home to their children for its fair market value and rent it back from the children. In some instances, this can work to the benefit of everyone. The children get an asset that increases in value over time while getting the tax benefits of mortgage interest deductions, maintenance and upkeep as well as depreciation. The parents, who lease the property back from their children, get money they can invest as they choose. And with the capital gains exemption for the sale of a home at $250,000 for a single person and $500,000 for a married couple, most seniors will be able to avoid paying any income taxes on the proceeds of the sale. In addition, many seniors may want to receive payment for the sale of the property through an annuity, one that if properly done can provide them with regular monthly income for life while not being a countable asset for Medicaid eligibility.

9

Alternative Housing

At one time, the options available to aging people were few. They would stay in their own homes as long as they were capable of caring for themselves, and when they could no longer do so, they moved in with their children. If their children were not willing or able to care for their parents, the elders went to a nursing home, a process that prompted the dark humor one sees occasionally on bumper stickers which read: "Be kind to your kids, they pick your nursing home."

In recent years, there has developed a whole slew of housing and care alternatives for older people, which, of course, leads to the questions "Just what is a slew?" and "How much is a half a slew?" Unfortunately, I cannot help you there because the dictionary merely defined "slew" as meaning "a large number," without giving any interesting derivation or specifics. However, the dictionary did provide a number of more interesting and colorful synonyms that you might want to use to spice up your language, such as "mickle," "muckle," and "spate," which sounds like the name of a law firm. In any event, suffice it to say that there now are many alternative housing choices for seniors providing a range of services from little to quite extensive.

Unfortunately, there is little regulation pertaining to the identification of many particular types of housing, so self-proclaimed classifications of care such as "congregate care" may not tell you much. Three important housing options are Retirement Communities, Continuing Care Retirement Communities,[1] and Assisted Living.

Retirement Communities

Retirement Communities originated about 70 years ago as significant numbers of people reached retirement age and were looking for housing that would be low maintenance and that would provide services and amenities. They also were looking to avoid the cold of winter, so it is not surprising that most of these early Retirement Communities were located in Arizona, California, and Florida rather than in North Dakota. Retirement Communities vary a great deal in the kind of housing and services available, but the essential element of them all is that this is primarily independent living with recreational facilities, health services, and social programs made a part of the community. At the high end of Retirement Communities, you may even feel like you are staying in an upscale hotel and you might not be too far off—Hyatt Hotels has been in the Retirement Community business since 1987, operating 18 Retirement Communities as "Classic Residence by Hyatt."

Retirement Communities vary substantially from one to another. Some consist of a landscape of individual free-standing homes, while others may be high-rise apartment type buildings. Often, there is a central facility building that may provide exercise rooms, restaurants, and shopping. Some even have golf courses.

Retirement Communities will often contract with a medical care provider for their presence on the grounds. Medical services are not provided as a benefit of the Retirement Community, but availability of such services is made on an independent basis for residents by the providers of these services on the grounds. These services are provided on an "as needed" basis by the medical care provider such that the residents can tailor their own particular needs with the provider.

It is important to note that Retirement Communities are independent living, which is great if you are independent. If you grow frail while living in a Retirement Community, there is little or no monitoring of the residents to follow changes in needs.

So, how do you pay for housing in a Retirement Community? Many early Retirement Communities were constructed by religious groups or fraternal organizations that essentially required new residents to turn over their entire assets to the entity operating the Retirement

Community in return for lifetime care and services. Unfortunately, this was a recipe for financial disaster as unanticipated and prolonged expenses put many of these Retirement Communities out of business.

Another way of financing Retirement Communities is by way of an initial entrance fee and monthly fees that change over time with inflation or other cost-of-care adjustments.

A third way of paying for Retirement Community housing involves regular rental payments with payment for services done "as needed." This form of financing is also found commonly in Assisted Living and Continuing Care Retirement Communities.

The fourth way of paying for Retirement Community housing is through ownership of your home through a condominium or cooperative contract along with a Continuing Care Contract for additional services.

Continuing Care Retirement Communities

Continuing Care Retirement Communities is a term that also represents a broad spectrum of alternative housing arrangements. They formerly were referred to as Life Care Communities. A common thread among Continuing Care Retirement Communities is the providing of housing, meals, nursing home and other health services, as well as social and recreational facilities. A primary feature of a Continuing Care Retirement Community is the availability in one complex of independent living, assisted living, and nursing-home care arrangements. As an entity, Continuing Care Retirement Care Communities (CCRCs) are not regulated by the federal government although nursing home components of CCRCs are covered by federal regulations. In addition, state regulations vary tremendously from state to state with many states primarily concerned with financial disclosures rather than levels of care while 12 states do not have any CCRC regulations at all.

Generally, Continuing Care Retirement Communities provide a guarantee of a place to live for the rest of the resident's life, a guarantee that is not usually provided by nursing homes or assisted-living facilities. As a result of this guarantee, the CCRCs carefully screen applicants and usually require that applicants for residency provide detailed financial information including income tax records and financial statements so that the CCRC can predict that the applicant will be able to afford the costs of living at the particular CCRC for the rest of his or her life. CCRC's use actuarial studies coupled with financial analysis to determine likely inflow and outflow of income to the facility by its residents and the expected turnover of residents along with studying mortality tables for prospective residents. Consideration of Medicare and Medicaid reimbursement is also done by the CCRC.

Note, however, that if a room is not available within the particular Continuing Care Retirement Community's own nursing home component at the time that the resident needs such services, the CCRC can place the resident in another nursing home in the area.

Like the more fully independent living Retirement Community, the primary way of financing Continuing Care Retirement Communities is through an initial entrance fee supplemented by regular monthly fee payments. However, a significant number of Continuing Care Retirement Communities have eliminated the entrance fee requirement and are funded entirely through monthly fee payments. Some Continuing Care Retirement Community contracts have provisions for the refund of the entrance fee in full or in part, while others declare the entrance fee nonrefundable. When refunding of the entrance fee is allowed, the fee is generally refunded in full if the senior dies before coming to the Continuing Care Retirement Community, or a portion of the fee is refunded depending upon the amount of time that the elder lived in the particular Continuing Care Retirement Community.

Money Matters

A major concern of seniors entering a Continuing Care Retirement Community is whether their assets will be sufficient to pay for the cost of care throughout their lifetime. With Continuing Care Retirement Communities (CCRCs) that are sponsored by religious or charitable organizations, this is of less concern because the sponsoring organization often has special funds available or endowments to cover the continuing costs of seniors who have depleted their savings. Unfortunately, if the Continuing Care Retirement Community is operated by a for-profit company, the senior is in jeopardy of being evicted.

The bankruptcy of a Continuing Care Retirement Community can have a devastating effect on senior citizens who have poured their life savings into the new housing arrangement. As a result of this substantial financial risk, Continuing Care Retirement Communities are regulated in almost all of the individual states, although there is no federal regulation except for nursing home components. In addition, entrance fees that are held in escrow are protected if there is a bankruptcy. The industry itself has been engaged in self-regulating since 1985 through the efforts of the American Association of Homes and Services for the Aging, which set up the Continuing Care Accreditation Commission to manage a national program for the evaluation and accreditation of Continuing Care Retirement Communities. Under the Continuing Care Accreditation Commission, accreditation is awarded for five years, after which reaccreditation must be sought. You can find a list of accredited Continuing Care Retirement Communities by going to the website www.carf.org. Also, go to the website www.ccrcdata.org, where you can find information on individual CCRCs through a directory to the websites of individual CCRCs throughout the country.

Warning

Rainy days and Mondays may have always gotten Karen Carpenter down, but for me it is fine print. There is rarely anything very fine about fine print. Unfortunately, even though most of the individual states regulate Continuing Care Retirement Communities, those regulations most often only require the disclosure of detailed, fine print information rather than mandating particular standards. Fortunately, some states do set specific financial reserve requirements to help protect deposits and refund obligations.

Contracts

An essential element in the Continuing Care Retirement Community arrangement is the Continuing Care Contract, which supplies the details of the services to be provided, such as health care, food, and recreational services. There are three types of contracts. Extensive Contracts cover long-term nursing care for no significant increase in cost beyond the regular monthly payments. Modified Contracts provide for coverage of a specific period of long-term nursing care, after which time the elder is financially responsible for payment of the cost of long-term care; at that time, though, the senior may also be eligible for Medicaid coverage for the cost of long-term nursing home care at the nursing home facility of the Continuing Care Retirement Community. Fee For Service Contracts provide no benefits for long-term nursing care, but again, Medicaid may be available to pay for such costs.

Important Considerations in Evaluating a Continuing Care Retirement Community

Seniors value experience, and there is no substitute for experience in operating a Continuing Care Retirement Community. Make sure that the operator of any Continuing Care Retirement Community you may consider has a good and extensive track record. Some Retirement Communities may be affiliated with a charity, nonprofit organization, or religious group with which you may be familiar. It is important to know the full extent of the affiliation. The group you know may only be lending its name. Make sure you know the actual connection between familiar organizations and the day-to-day operation of the facility.

Make sure they are sufficiently funded. You may not be able to decipher the financial projections and balance sheets for the company, but you should have someone who can understand them review them for you. Have someone who understands these things evaluate a financial statement of the facility. Have the company provide this information for the past few years. If the facility is a new operation, obtain projections, but consider them for what they are: merely projections. An important financial consideration is how much money is allotted as a contingency fund to meet unanticipated needs.

Make sure that any entry fees are held in an escrow account that is not subject to the claims of any creditors of the company that owns the Continuing Care Retirement Community. If possible, you would want the funds in an interest-bearing escrow account with the interest credited to you. This is particularly important in the light of the fact that a significant number of Continuing Care Retirement Communities have gone bankrupt, in which case you would want any funds held by the CCRC to be secure. The Erickson Retirement Communities, was, until its bankruptcy in 2009, one of the largest developers of CCRCs. The downturn in the real estate market coupled with tighter credit and a reliance on borrowed money contributed to its financial failure and subsequent bankruptcy in 2009.

You may not like the place. See if there is a time during which you can cancel the contract and get a refund of your fees. This is regulated in some states and not in others, with the range from "no right to cancel the contract with a refund" to up to 90 days in California.

Even if you like the place, you may have to move for health or other reasons, so make sure there is a provision in the contract for the refund of your entry fee. It is reasonable for the amount of the refund to go down the longer you are there. Common refund provisions would reduce the amount of your entrance fee to which you would be entitled by 1 or 2 percent for each month you stay in the facility. So, for instance, with a 2 percent reduction per month, you would be eligible to get back half of your deposit if you left the facility after two years and one month.

Make sure you know what all the fees are and under what circumstances they can be increased. There are no laws that limit fee increases, but it is reasonable to expect that the facility be required to provide you with a sufficient notice of any fee increase and that the number of fee increases in a year be limited. It is wise to get a copy of the history of fee increases for the facility you are considering.

It can be helpful if you can deduct some of the entrance fee and monthly fees as prepaid medical costs. To do this, you need this amount to be itemized on your bill. See Chapter 6, "Income Taxes," for more details.

Particularly because you may not be eligible for Medicaid or Medicare to pay for the costs of a Continuing Care Retirement Community, it may be crucial to know the facility's policy if you become financially unable to afford the regular fees in the future. Some of the facilities operated by charities or nonprofit organizations may permit you to stay, while others, including for-profit facilities, have financial aid programs for which you may be eligible. If this applies to you, you should know how these programs operate.

By definition, Continuing Care Retirement Communities have independent living, assisted living and nursing home components. In reviewing the contract and other documents, you should note what the policy is for transferring residents from one type of housing to another. Make sure you know what your rights of appeal are as well.

Although no one enters a Continuing Care Retirement Community with the thought that they could be thrown out by the management of the facility, that is a possibility. Only a few states have laws or regulations requiring "just cause" for any termination of your rights to stay in the facility. Many facilities have their own rules, which could be more accurately classified as "just because," allowing them to terminate your right to continue to live in the facility for almost any reason. You should look for and understand what the written policy is for any facility you are considering.

The old commercial used to say "look for the union label," which was sung to such a catchy tune that I sometimes found myself involuntarily humming it. Rather than look for the union label, however, you should look in the Continuing Care Retirement Community's documents for any waivers of liability to which you may be asked to agree. Do not agree to give up your rights against the facility or any of its employees for any injuries you may suffer or damage to your property caused by their negligence. Some courts have found such waivers to be unfair and have refused to enforce them.

You should have a Durable Power of Attorney and a Healthcare Proxy to ensure that someone can make financial and health care decisions on your behalf if you are unable to do so. However, under no circumstances should you give the Continuing Care Retirement Community these rights. Make sure that such a provision is not contained in the contract.

Many facilities permit the residents to have representation on the Board of Directors, although not necessarily in a voting capacity. You will want to know what the rights of residents are regarding participation in the governing of the facility. You also will want to know what procedures are available for lodging and resolving complaints.

Assisted Living

Alf, the television comedy about a furry visitor from another planet (Melmac), used the acronym for Alien Life Form as the name of the main character. For the four years that it was broadcast (1986–1990), Alf was a cultural icon. People who remember little else from the series might remember his loud laugh—it was always good for a laugh. (Extra points for you if you remember that although he was referred to as Alf, his name on Melmac was Gordon Shumway.) It was always hard to determine just exactly what Alf was. So, it is only fitting that Alf is also an acronym for assisted-living facilities: As much as the term is bandied about, there is no precise universally accepted definition of what an assisted-living facility is. In a way, it is like Supreme Court Justice Potter Stewart's attempt at defining the term "hardcore pornography" by saying that although he could not define it, he knew it when he saw it.

Assisted-living facilities represent a fairly recent development in alternative housing for seniors. What distinguishes an assisted-living facility is its combination of housing with help with Activities of Daily Living (ADL). Once again, the cost of assisted-living facilities can vary greatly, depending on the level of healthcare and the level of housing and other services provided.

Legalities

One unfortunate result of the lack of precision in the term "assisted-living facility" is the lack of regulation. Even where there are regulations, they are not particularly vigorously enforced. This means that when it comes to choosing an assisted-living facility, the best place to find a helping hand is at the end of your own arm. The responsibility is yours. Although many of us are always a bit cynical when we hear the phrase, "I'm from the government and I am here to help you," at times, you would like to rely on government regulations for at least minimal protection of your interests.

So, what is an assisted-living facility? The generally understood meaning is that it is a facility that provides housing, some level of personal care, and some form of health center for people who need some assistance with ADLs, such as bathing, dressing, eating, mobility, and personal hygiene, but who do not require the level of services provided in a nursing home.

Assisted living is not regulated on a federal level, but is regulated in varying degree in all the states.

What's in a Name?

Exacerbating the problem of choosing an assisted-living facility is the fact that assisted living is so undefined. In fact, not only are there more than 17 different designations for what most often can be called assisted-living facilities, but in some states, such as New Hampshire, more than one term is used to refer to assisted living facilities. However, most states do refer to these facilities as assisted-living facilities while the second most used term is "residential care facilities."

According to a study commissioned by the Senate Special Committee on Aging, assisted-living facilities should have written disclosures of all costs, services provided, and facility policies, including a policy for minimum notice for evicting residents. The study also recommends that the facilities have rules that guarantee that "trained and awake staff are on duty" at all times. I find this recommendation particularly troublesome. James Martin, my high school social studies teacher, always said that society's strongest rules are the unwritten rules that everyone knows and accepts. The fact that the Senate's study found it actually necessary to say that the staff should be "awake" is something that Mr. Martin would have found amusing.

Presently, there are more than 31,100 facilities that could be called assisted-living facilities serving 733,400 residents according to the National Center for Health Statistics, yet the federal government does not provide any regulation of this large and expanding industry. State regulations vary tremendously from state to state. Some do not even require that a nurse be employed or independently contracted with the facility. Training regulations for direct-care workers are also lacking with some states requiring a mere twelve hours or less of training. However, on the plus side, the state of Washington in 2012 began re-requiring new direct-care workers (referred to as long-term care workers) in their state to take 75 hours of training within 120 days of being hired and also required them to become certified home-care aides within 150 days of being in hired.

Additionally, although only a nurse can administer medication in a nursing home, a majority of the estates permit assisted-living facility workers with little training to perform that function. Some states do not even have minimum staffing requirements while others may. Assisted-living facilities in states with minimum staffing requirements mislead families by including janitors, cooks, administrators, and even gardeners when computing the staff-to-resident ratio. Your concern should always be the ratio of people actually available to assist your family member entering the particular assisted-living facility.

Accreditation

Although the federal government does not regulate assisted-living facilities and the state regulations can be often lacking, some help is provided by the non-governmental Joint Commission on Accreditation of Healthcare Organizations (JCAHO), which evaluates and accredits assisted-living facilities as it does with nursing homes. Its website, www.jcaho.org, can be helpful.

Important Considerations in Evaluating an Assisted-Living Facility

Just about all the considerations for evaluating a Continuing Care Retirement Community also apply to assisted-living facilities. In addition, you should consider some other things.

Medicare generally does not apply to the costs of assisted living, although some states do provide in widely varying situations for Medicaid funds to be used for assisted living. Even in states that don't generally provide for the use of Medicare or Medicaid funds for assisted-living costs, there may be instances in which Medicare may provide for the cost of certain home care provided in the assisted-living environment, and there may be other public programs for which you may be eligible.

Also, everyone has to eat. You want to make sure you understand the arrangements for meals. If you have special dietary requirements, it is important to understand what the assisted-living facility provides.

Make sure their emergency response systems function around the clock. Also, check into just what on-site medical services are available, including assistance, if necessary, with medicines you take on your own.

Many assisted-living facilities provide an extensive range of other services, including housekeeping and recreational services. A good way to consider how a particular assisted-living facility might fit your needs is to consider both the present activities of your average day and your hobbies and interests. See how the particular facility you are considering matches your needs and expectations, how these services are provided and what the cost for those services will be.

Warning: Negotiated Risk

I have always believed that life would be much better if we had background music as it exists in the movies. Up-tempo, light music would enhance our enjoyment of happy times, and more intense music would alert us to impending danger. For this reason, I have little sympathy for anyone who was eaten by the shark in the movie *Jaws*. The shark consistently never attacked anyone until it had given ample warning through his theme music that built up to a crescendo just as it finally attacked.

If life had background music, we would be so much better off. Unfortunately, it does not. Therefore, I want you to imagine the theme from *Jaws* whenever you see a negotiated risk provision in an assisted-living contract. A negotiated risk provision releases the assisted-living facility from any legal responsibility if it fails to provide adequate care.

Because this provision might not be immediately apparent to you, it is important to employ your own shark, a lawyer, to review your contract with an assisted-living facility before signing anything.

Just How Much Assistance Does a Resident Get at an Assisted-Living Facility

Asking how many angels can fit on the head of a pin could be an easier question to answer. The true answer is a consistent one: It depends. Among the basic services generally provided at an assisted-living facility are light housekeeping, two or three meals per day, social activities, and some assistance with activities of daily living. According to a survey released by MetLife in 2012, the average cost of these basic services from state to state ranges from a low of $2,218 in Arkansas to a high of $4,812 in Connecticut. Troubling indeed is the fact that an assisted-living facility can raise its rates any time it wants, which makes it somewhat hard to plan for future costs. Most assisted-living facilities require an initial deposit as well as monthly fees that can vary considerably depending on the services available. Some measure of medical care might be provided through services sometimes managed by a nurse. However, many facilities have no on-site nursing staff; physicians are generally not a part of the package.

Things to Ponder When Choosing an Assisted-Living Facility

Although the federal government does not regulate assisted-living facilities, it does at least offer a good website, www.eldercare.gov, to help you compare and locate assisted-living facilities in your area.

You also can look for help from your state's long-term care ombudsman. Each state has one, and you don't even have to be able to pronounce the word to be able to avail yourself of this person's services. Your state's ombudsman might also be able to assist you in locating inspection reports and records of complaints that have been lodged against the facilities you are considering. An easy place to find your state's long-term care ombudsman is www.ltcombudsman.org.

Geriatric care managers also can help you in both gathering and analyzing information on particular assisted-living facilities. Geriatric care manager is the term for health and humans services professionals such as social workers, gerontologists or nurses who specialize in issues facing older people. They can be extremely helpful in helping gather information and constructing a plan for your older family members. A good place to start your search of a geriatric care manager is at the website of the national Association of Professional Geriatric Care Managers at www.caremanager.org.

A Word of Warning

When you are considering hiring a geriatric care manager, make sure that the person you are considering hiring has total allegiance to you and your family. The assisted-living facilities pay some geriatric care managers for placing people with them. Obviously, this is a conflict of interest that you want to avoid.

Location, Location, Location

Just as when buying a home or picking a nursing home, location is an important factor in choosing an assisted-living facility for a family member or yourself. If the location is inconvenient for family members and friends, visits that are so important might be lessened.

Check It Out

Go to facilities you are considering and check them out for your-self. Go beyond the fancy lobby in some facilities and look for the building adaptations that are so important to seniors, such as elevator access, ramps for wheelchairs, accessible bathrooms, and emergency call buttons.

Go right to the source. Talk to the residents and get their take on what life is like in the particular assisted-living facility. When you speak with them, pay attention to their grooming and manner of dress. These things will tell you much about the care they are receiving and how they are supervised.

Observe the buzz. What are the residents doing? Are they watching television every waking hour or are they involved in activities that stimulate their minds and bodies? Study after study has shown that combining physical and mental exercises helps preserve cognitive function. Check out the exercise room, the computer room, the craft facilities, and the library.

Security

How secure is the facility? This is particularly important if you have a parent or grandparent with a cognitive disorder, such as Alzheimer's Disease, which can result in wandering. Does the facility have employees who are responsible for the security of residents who could become confused while walking the hallways? Is the facility sufficiently locked to keep residents in and unauthorized people out.

Hospitals

Where is the closest hospital, and what is the facility's relationship with that hospital for handling emergencies?

The Smell Test

Too often, the first thing you notice when you enter a facility is the smell. If the place does not please your nose, turn around and leave.

Smoking

"That's our policy." This justification can be used for just about anything, so it is important to know the policy of the facility where you are placing your family member. For example, an assisted-living facility may not allow smoking, and although that is an understandable and laudable policy, it could have a significant effect on your decision. After all, dad could be a chain-smoker with good genes who has managed to avoid respiratory illnesses despite smoking for 65 years. If dad is happy smoking, as the Beatles would say, "Let it be"—in this case, find a facility that provides a convenient place for dad to smoke to his heart's (if not his lungs') content.

Pet Policy

Pets are important to many people because they provide companionship and affection. If your family member has a pet, find out the facility's policy regarding pets. Many are quite understanding, although I imagine few would be too thrilled to see my llama or horse coming through the front door.

Transportation

Transportation is a critical aspect of life in an assisted-living facility. Unlike in a nursing home, many routine medical services are not provided onsite, so the availability of transportation to and from medical appointments is of major importance. In addition, because assisted-living facility residents could be quite active and self-sufficient in many ways, transportation to shopping and social engagements (or the closest casino) is of major importance. Find out whether the transportation costs are included in the basic package at the assisted-living facility you are considering and, if not, what those costs are.

Do You Get Fries with That?

It is important to know precisely what services are included with your basic monthly payment. You also should have a complete fee schedule for services that are not included in your basic monthly payment.

You will want to know the facility's policy on changing its fees. How much advance notice will you receive? How much can it raise fees?

Is a security deposit or other fee required upon entering the assisted-living facility? If so, are any of those fees refundable, and under what circumstances? Preferably, the policy should state that if residents must leave the facility, for whatever reason, they can get a proportionate refund of any entrance fee depending upon who long they were there.

What Would Tim Russert Ask?

The late Tim Russert, the host of *Meet the Press*, always managed to ask probing questions without appearing to be hostile. You need to ask probing questions to evaluate the assisted-living facility. You need to know how long they have been in business, how strong the parent company is financially, whether complaints or lawsuits have been filed against the facility, and whether the facility is accredited by the Joint Commission on Accreditation of Healthcare Organizations.

The financial stability of the assisted-living facility is of supreme importance to you and it makes sense to have your attorney or accountant review the facility's financial statement to ensure that there are sufficient financial reserves to operate the facility in a secure manner.

The Fine Print

There is nothing particularly fine about fine print. Actually, fine print often should be described as "really small print containing confusing language that describes rules that work against you." However, that is quite a mouthful, so I guess we are stuck with "fine print."

A report titled, "Critical Issues in Assisted Living: Who's in, Who's Out, and Who's Providing the Care," by the National Senior Citizens Law Center in 2005 showed that not only may assisted-living facilities in 39 states evict residents when they no longer meet the residents' needs, but the determination of this is generally left up to the facility itself, with little right of appeal by residents. Many assisted-living facilities are aligned with nursing homes within the same complex and might be a good choice. If your family member is no longer able to function in the assisted-living facility setting, he or she may be able to merely transfer within the complex to the company's nursing home.

How Do You Pay?

How do most people pay for assisted living? Simple. They pay out of their pocket. According to the Assisted Living Federation of America, 86 percent of assisted-living residents pay from their private funds. A few long-term care policies cover the cost of assisted-living, making it very important to look into this when you consider purchasing a long-term care insurance policy. Medicaid, which is a joint federal-state program, does not generally pay for assisted-living, although 44 states do provide vastly varying financial support for people in assisted-living facilities. Payments for services, which notably do not include housing costs, are most often made through the Medicaid Home and Community-Based Services (HCBS) waiver plan of Medicaid or under Medicaid payments for personal care services. Complicating this is, as I have said before, the fact that the term "assisted-living" does not have a consistent definition from state to state. To see what the Medicaid assisted-living benefits are in your state, go to www.payingforseniorcare.com/medicaid-waivers/assisted-living.html, which is a website of the American Elder Care Research Organization.

Checklist of Important Issues in Considering an Assisted-Living Facility or Continuing Care Retirement Community

Choosing an assisted-living facility or a Continuing Care Retirement Community is a complicated decision. Here are some of the many issues that you should consider in making that decision:

1. What experience does the entity have? Does it operate other similar facilities or nursing homes?

2. What is the reputation of the facility?

3. Is the facility financially sound?

4. Is the facility licensed?

5. Is the facility accredited by any private accrediting organizations and, if so, by which ones?

6. Has it had violations of state law? If so, what was the nature of those violations?

7. Have any lawsuits been filed against the facility and what was the result of such lawsuits?

8. What is the entrance fee, if any?

9. Under what circumstances, if any, can the resident obtain a full or partial refund of the entrance fee?

10. What are the basic monthly charges and what services are included in those charges?

11. Under what circumstances can the charges be increased?

12. What are the procedures and internal resources available if the resident cannot afford increased charges?

13. Does the facility offer different payment options for different services at the option of the resident?

14. Are fees reduced if the resident does not utilize some services on a temporary basis, such as when the resident may be on vacation or spends part of the year elsewhere?

15. Are fees increased if the resident's level of care changes?

16. Do fees change if the resident's marital status changes?

17. Is there Medicare or Medicaid coverage available and, if so, for what services and in what amounts?

18. Does the facility accept long term-care insurance payments?

19. What do the living spaces consist of and what services, such as utilities, are provided as part of the basic services package?

20. What kind of assessment is done to ascertain the needs of the resident and how is a plan developed to meet those needs?

21. What medical services are provided on site?

22. What assistance with activities of daily living, such as eating, dressing, and personal hygiene, is provided and at what cost?

23. Does the facility have a security system?

24. Does the facility have an emergency call system?

25. How is the staff trained to handle emergencies?

26. What is the meal plan and is it adaptable to the specific needs of the resident?

27. What recreational, cultural, or religious activities are available?

28. Does the facility provide transportation and under what circumstances and at what cost for activities, events, and appointments off of the premises?

29. Do residents have any rights in decision making and management of the facility?

30. What procedures are in place for dealing with complaints and disputes?

31. What personal care services are available and at what cost?

32. Does the facility require a release of liability of the facility as a condition of living in the facility?

33. What are the grounds for eviction and what rights does a resident have to appeal such decision?

The Final Words

The lack of federal regulation and comprehensive state regulations places a great deal more responsibility on people who are considering moving to an assisted-living facility and their families. There is great variance in the cost and quality of entities calling themselves assisted-living facilities. The bad news is that it will take much more effort and questioning to ensure that you are making the best decision for your family member. The good news is that there are some wonderful assisted-living facilities that provide a life-enhancing experience. I am glad to say that my parents' final years were spent in an assisted-living facility that made their lives happy and safe.

Endnote

1. The Elder Law Portfolio Series, Portfolio 5, "Housing Options," by Stephanie Edelstein, Charles P. Sabatino, and Nancy M. Coleman, Aspen Law & Business, a division of Aspen Publishers, 1999.

10 ——————————————————

Long-Term Care

According to the final report of the Commission on Affordable Housing and Health Facility Needs for Seniors in the twenty-first century, almost 20 percent of people over the age of 65 have "significant long-term care needs." With an aging population, this number is expected to rise considerably. Also rising is the cost of long-term care. Statistics compiled by the Agency for Healthcare Research and Quality indicated that from 1987 to 1996, the total cost of nursing home care in the United States went up 150 percent to $70 billion. Those figures have continued to rise. According to a research report by Prudential Insurance in 2010, between 2004 and 2010, nursing-home costs for a private room have increased 47 percent. During this time, the Consumer Price Index only increased at an annual compound rate of 2.5 percent. With the baby boomers aging, it is expected that the number of Americans 65 years of age or older will more than double over the next 20 years, reaching 71. Many of these aging baby boomers will need long-term care as those baby boomers reaching age 65 can expect to live an average of 20 more years. In turn, approximately 70 percent of people over 65 can expect to require some form of long-term care, and more than 30 percent will end up receiving long-term care in a nursing home. Despite these staggering statistics, relatively few people plan for the cost of long-term care.

History[1]

In the 1700s, America's early days, the good news was that long-term care was not a major issue. The bad news was that this was because few people lived long term. Those who did require care in old age utilized their primary asset, their children, for support. It was expected that children would either take in and care for their parents, or they would pay for the cost of their parents going to live with another family.

During the late 1800s and early 1900s, "old age homes" came into being as a new alternative across the country operated as nonprofit institutions. They actually became elaborate, in that often farms and hospitals would be added to the facilities to meet the needs of their residents.

By the early 1900s, more and more people were living to old age. Life expectancy increased substantially, less because of better treatment of older people than because fewer people succumbed to childhood illnesses. In fact, those who made it to age 65 in 1900 statistically could expect to live well into their 80s, and someone who made it to age 85 could expect to just about make it to 90.

The Great Depression (which probably should have been called the "Awful Depression" since there was little that was great about it) devastated families and wiped out the savings of many Americans, although senior citizens, with less time to recover, were particularly hard hit. Depending on children was of little help, because the children had their own financial woes. By 1934, 28 of the 48 states enacted old-age assistance laws; however, they frankly provided little old-age assistance. In keeping with the tradition of children being responsible for the long-term care needs of their parents, older Americans who had children were denied benefits, the thinking being that it was the obligation of the children to provide for their parents' needs. In keeping with the morality of the time, benefits were denied to anyone who had ever been convicted of a crime or had been a tramp or beggar.

Following World War II, the federal Hospital Survey and Construction Act of 1946 provided federal funds for the construction of new hospitals in rural parts of the country and modernization of existing hospitals in the cities. In many parts of the country where older hospitals were being replaced by newly constructed hospitals, those former hospitals were often converted into long-term care facilities. Until the 1950s, nursing homes had gone largely unregulated, but with more and more people going to nursing homes, federal laws were enacted, requiring the states to initiate nursing home regulations in order to be eligible for federal funds. According to a national survey of nursing homes in 1954, there were almost 270,000 older Americans living in 9,000 nursing homes, nearly all of them for-profit facilities. As the 1950s progressed, Congress enacted a number of different programs providing funds that encouraged the construction of new nursing homes.

With the creation of Medicaid in 1965, a new era in long-term care began. Through Medicaid, a joint state and federal program, the state would provide long-term care in nursing homes for its financially neediest seniors. It was never anticipated, however, that the cost of nursing-home care would be so great or that so many people who might otherwise not be thought of as "needy" would through "Medicaid planning" make themselves eligible for long-term care through Medicaid while still preserving assets for their families.

The development of long-term care insurance has been rapid in order to meet the needs of an aging population. From 40 companies selling this product in 1986 to 137 companies at its peak, it is estimated that more than 8 million people own long-term care insurance, according to a survey by the Health Insurance Association of America. However, since its sales peak in 2000, when 600,000 individual policies were sold, the number of policies sold have consistently declined until 2011 when the number of new individual policies sales increase slightly. It is not expected, however, that this was the beginning of a new trend. In addition, many insurance companies have stopped selling long-term care insurance. In the last five years, 10 of the top 20 long-term care insurance issuers have dropped out of the market. Their numbers include such formerly major players as Prudential and MetLife. Part of the reason for their exiting the market is that the long-term care insurance companies used actuarial projections in pricing the policies that turned out to be wrong. In particular, they assumed that many people would follow the lead of many holders of life-insurance policies and let the policies lapse without ever making a claim. That has not been the case. Also contributing to the decline in the sales of long-term care insurance has been the hesitancy of consumers to purchase this insurance due both to present costs and the real prospect of their premiums increasing substantially in the future.

Cost of Long-Term Care

With the median cost of private room long-term care in a nursing home nationally averaging $81,030 per year (much more in some states, with Alaska being the most expensive at a median annual cost for a private room of $232,505), financing long-term care is a major family concern. Medicare only pays, at most, for 100 days of skilled nursing-home care following a three-day hospital stay. Medicare will pay the full cost for the first 20 days and then requires a daily deductible of $144.50 for days 21 through 100. This amount is subject to change. For the most current figures, go to the Medicare website listed in "Favorite Websites."

Future Cost of Long-Term Care

Studies predict the costs of nursing homes will approach $200,000 per year amount nationally that it already costs in Alaska by the year 2030 when the last of the baby boomers will be reaching age 65. Premiums for new long-term care insurance policies are soaring as insurers confront recent slumping sales, rising claims, and weak investment revenue, according to a *cbsmarketwatch.com* investigation. Substantial rate hikes are expected as companies learn that baby boomers are not particularly interested in rushing out to buy coverage. In addition, relatively few people who buy these policies stop paying the premiums and let the policies lapse before they would be eligible for benefit payments, which has caused the insurance companies to have to pay more claims than their actuaries had expected. Also, unanticipated by the insurance companies when they first created these policies was the number of single people without a spouse to care for them who would need longer nursing home stays.

Financing Long-Term Care

The simplest way to pay for long-term care is not quite as simple as it seems. Self-insure. Pay for the cost out of your own savings. But, for many people, paying the huge cost of long-term care in a nursing home for years is not a viable option.

Your Home

Use your home as a source of funds. Many older Americans inherited their homes or bought them for relatively small amounts of money (although it may not have seemed so at the time), and now find that the worth of the smallest of houses has grown tremendously. Sell it. Sell it to your children. Rent it out. Take out an equity credit line that will allow you to tap into the equity you have built up in the home throughout the years.

Life Insurance

If you have a whole life or universal life insurance policy, you probably have accumulated significant cash value in it. You can pull this money out of the policy either by canceling the policy outright or by taking a loan against it. If you cancel the policy, however, you may find that you are uninsurable if you want another policy. Desperate times call for desperate measures, and if you require the money now for your long-term care needs, isn't that more important than having a life insurance policy to leave money to your children? They will understand, and if they do not, get new kids.

You also can take out a loan from the insurance company, using the policy as collateral without having to pay it back until you die, at which point the loan would be deducted from the death benefit (an interesting combination of words: "death" and "benefit").

Your life insurance policy may also include a provision for living benefits or accelerated death benefits (now there is a really interesting combination of words: "accelerated death" and "benefit"). Accelerated death benefits, or the more euphemistic "living benefits," allow you to begin to receive life insurance payments while you are still alive, assuming that you meet the eligibility standards. These typically include having a year or less to live or being confined to a nursing home. Note that this option is not automatic. You must select it when you purchase your policy, although some insurers have provided accelerated death benefits as a no-cost policy enhancement.

Viatical settlements allow you to sell your life insurance policy to a company that then becomes the beneficiary of the policy. In return, the company sends you a lump sum payment while you are living and receives the insurance proceeds when you die. Generally, this option is available only to people with a two- to three-year life expectancy, and it is rare for viatical settlements to occur when the policy holder is expected to live for at least five years. For people expected to live no more than two years, the viatical company will generally pay about one-half of the policy's death benefit. The payments received from a viatical settlement are not subject to income tax if the money is used to pay for nursing-home care.

Loophole

An attractive insurance product that offers the most "bang for the buck" when it comes to financing long-term care is the single-premium life insurance policy, which has specific provisions for the payment of long-term care both in a nursing home and at home. The policy, as the name implies, is bought with a single payment that can be as little as $10,000, but more often is within the range of $50,000 to $100,000. The source of your single-premium payment can be from your regular savings or even from an IRA or another insurance policy. The policy, like all life insurance, will have a death benefit that is double— or even triple—the amount of your single payment. What is unique about this insurance policy is that monthly you can take out 2 percent of the death benefit for nursing-home care and 1 percent for home healthcare. This gives you money that can pay toward 50 months of nursing home care or 100 months of care in your own home. Like other insurance products, another attractive feature is that your money in the policy accumulates on a tax-deferred basis. You pay no income taxes until you take the money out, and even then you only pay tax on the policy's earnings. In addition, as time goes by, the value of your policy should increase as should the death benefit. And, if you never need the money during your lifetime, at your death, the substantial death benefit will be paid to the beneficiaries you name—totally income tax free. If you need the money for other purposes during your lifetime, you can always just cancel the policy and get back at a minimum what you paid for it. These policies are generally available to people no older than 80.

Life Insurance with Long-Term Care Riders

The insurance industry is always innovating to meet the needs of the public and although many of these insurance companies have pulled out of the stand-alone long-term care insurance policy business what they have developed is a new type of permanent life insurance that permits the policy holder to access the death benefit for long term care needs. Under the terms of these new policies, policyholders can access, some, all, or none of the death benefit to meet long-term care needs. The cost of the policy is less than buying a permanent life insurance policy and a long-term care insurance policy separately with the additional cost over a life insurance policy without such a rider averaging about 10 percent. In addition, and important to consumers, is the fact that many people who apply for stand-alone long-term care insurance policies are rejected for medical reasons. Although the decline rates vary from age group to age group with 17 percent of people within the ages of 50 and 59 being rejected for long-term care insurance for medical reasons, 45 percent of those between the ages of 70 and 79 are rejected for long-term care insurance. The acceptance rate for people applying for these new hybrid life insurance policies is 90 percent, which is attractive to consumers.

There are variations among the companies offering this type of hybrid policy, but generally, they will start with a universal life or variable universal life insurance policy as a base with an accelerated death benefit rider that permits you to take 2 percent of the death benefit per month. Some policies set a base below which the benefit may not be reduced. Some even include additional provisions that will extend the long-term care benefits after the policy limits have been met.

In addition, some of the policies will even have a significant guaranteed interest rate that grows tax deferred. As with conventional long-term care insurance, you can also purchase simple or compound inflation protection for the amount that you would access for long-term care benefits. Benefits for some policies can also include payment of expenses incurred while in an assisted living facility as well as home care benefits if you receive skilled nursing or other professional services from a home healthcare agency at home.

In today's world, where people who bought long-term care insurance policies many years ago are facing unanticipated premium rate increases, buying life insurance to meet the dual needs of long-term care insurance and life insurance involves a premium that you can depend on to not rise unexpectedly as time goes by. The cost for this extra protection is reasonable.

Finding the Money

People who have reached the magic age of 70-and-a-half when they are required to begin withdrawing from their retirement plans present an interesting possibility. In that instance, if the individual does not have an immediate need for those funds, he or she can use the funds that must be distributed to pay the premium for life insurance with a long-term care rider.

Another Thing to Think About

Less often stated, but a real-life consideration in the decision of whether to purchase long-term care insurance or life insurance with a long-term rider is the matter of whether the insurance company issuing the long-term care insurance policy might contest a claim made years later for long-term care benefits. This is of particular concern, because anyone who makes a claim for long-term care benefits is, by definition, not in great shape to fight the insurance company on this matter. It could be that the insurance company has determined as a matter of policy to try to keep its costs lower by making the claims process difficult, or the initial application could contain incorrect medical information that the insurance company still can contest years later. Regardless of the motivation, the potential problem is the same: the risk of paying the premiums on the long-term care insurance policy for many years, only to find that when the policy is needed, it is not available. However, when the basic vehicle for long-term care planning is life insurance, the insurance company might be more apt to pay the long-term care claim because the company understands that, ultimately, it will be paying on the policy somehow; thus, there would be no benefit to contesting it when it is tapped into for long-term care benefits.

Swap

What if you bought a life insurance policy many years ago without an accelerated death benefit rider? Instead of cashing in your policy and incurring potential income taxes on investment gains from years of accumulating significant cash value, you can choose to merely swap your policy for another insurance policy with the accelerated death benefit rider and avoid any income taxes when you acquire the new policy. Or maybe you have invested in conservative "let me sleep at night" investments, such as certificates of deposit that offer little in the way of interest in an economy of low interest rates. You, too, might find that you can be well served by purchasing a life insurance policy that can provide you with long-term care benefits, life insurance benefits, and investment benefits.

Other Considerations

Many considerations arise when buying a life insurance policy with the intention of making it available as a source of funds for long-term care needs. Does the policy restrict coverage to nursing homes or will it pay for assisted living or at-home care? How is the amount of the long-term care benefit calculated? Is an inflation rider available? These are important considerations when comparing policies and choosing one to best meet your needs.

Creative minds in the insurance industry have also come up with life insurance products that provide a life insurance policy coupled with a right to purchase long-term care insurance at specific time periods in the future. This gives you the opportunity to evaluate your situation at various stages of your life. Ultimately, conventional long-term care insurance, which provides no financial benefit unless you use it for long-term care despite the fact that you have been paying premiums for many years, may not be as advantageous or cost effective as the hybrid life insurance policy with a long-term care rider that provides long-term care benefits if you need them, but if you don't need long-term care, the death benefit of the policy can be accessed for a loan by the policyholder during his or her lifetime and provide a death benefit payments to the policyholder's beneficiaries at the policyholder's death.

Long-Term Care Insurance

Long-term care insurance is not for everyone. What is? If your assets, not including your home, are under $100,000, not only would it be relatively easy for you to become eligible for Medicaid to pay for the cost of long-term care in a nursing home, but in addition, the cost of the insurance would most likely not fit within your budget. People with assets of more than $2 million can probably afford to pay for the cost of long-term care themselves without the insurance. According to the Department of Health and Human Services, the average time that a person stays in a nursing home is 2.8 years. Of course, some people with millions of dollars may want to purchase long-term care insurance as a safeguard for those assets. For the rest of you with assets between $100,000 and $2 million, long-term care insurance may be a viable option for providing for long-term care if, and that is a big if, the premiums fit within your budget.

There are, however, choices you can make in selecting a policy that can reduce your premium. The younger you are when you purchase a long-term care insurance policy, the cheaper the premium will be. The best time to buy long-term care insurance is around age 55. Buying a policy between the ages of 50 and 60 will, over the long haul, cost you far less than if you waited until you were in your seventies to buy long-term care insurance. The average age of long-term care insurance purchasers is rapidly going down. In 1990, the average age of a person buying long-term care insurance was 72. By 2001, that number had dropped to 62 and, today, the average age at which a person purchases a long-term care insurance policy is 57.

Eligibility for Long-Term Care Insurance

Many people applying for long-term care insurance are concerned that they are not in perfect health, but who at age 55 and above is? Most of us have one or another of the aches, pains, and diseases that are our reward for having lived as long as we have. The companies that issue long-term care insurance are aware of this and do not expect applicants to be without health issues. The main concern of long-term care insurers is your ability to function in a normal daily routine because the inability to perform activities of daily life (ADLs) are what trigger payment from a long-term care insurance policy. ADLs are generally defined as bathing, dressing oneself, eating, toileting, and mobility. Mobility is commonly defined as the ability to move in and out of a chair or a bed. Most policies require that you demonstrate a disability to perform two or more ADLs to trigger benefit payments under your policy. In addition, cognitive impairment by itself will trigger benefit payments.

Cognitive impairment is also a critical element in the determination of whether or not you will be eligible for long-term care insurance when you initially apply for a policy. Cognitive impairment is generally defined as a "deficiency in a person's short- or long-term memory; orientation as to person, place, and time; deductive or abstract reasoning; or judgment as it relates to safety awareness." With so many people entering nursing homes as a result of cognitive impairment, insurance companies deem assessment of this risk to be of critical importance during the application process.

Although insurance companies expect and tolerate many medical conditions, certain specific medical conditions will automatically disqualify you from being eligible for a long-term care insurance policy. These include Alzheimer's disease, AIDs, dementia, Parkinson's disease, kidney disease, paraplegia, senility, and cirrhosis.

There is no one set of standards to determine your eligibility for a policy. Standards vary from company to company. In fact, one company may rate you as a high risk and have a higher premium than another company that, under its own underwriting criteria, may issue you a standard policy at a lesser premium. Even if, for whatever reason, your premium is higher because the insurance company considers you a greater risk, you may be able to apply for a premium reduction after you have paid for the policy for a certain period of time, which varies among insurance companies. You have nothing to lose, and during that time, it is possible that either the underwriting standards or your medical condition may have changed. Underwriting standards are always changing, as the actuaries who make these decisions for the insurance companies get better and more updated information regarding claims.

Trivia

Long-term care insurance policies all have exclusions according to the terms of which they will not pay for claims if they are caused by a person becoming disabled while committing a felony. Can you imagine that someone actually thought that this problem was significant enough to warrant such a provision in the standard policy?

Choosing a Company

Depending on your age when you purchase a long-term care insurance policy, you may expect, as Humphrey Bogart said to Claude Raines at the end of the movie *Casablanca*, "a beautiful friendship," or if not a beautiful friendship, at least a long-standing one with your insurance company. If you buy a policy while in your 60s, you may not need to make a claim for as long as 20 years or more. For this reason, it is paramount that you feel confident that the insurance company from which you will be buying the insurance is going to be around for a while. A number of companies, such as AM Best, Standard & Poor's, Moody's and Weiss Ratings, evaluate insurance companies. However, it is important to remember that the ratings are not consistent from company to company. A grade of B+ or A- might have been a good grade when you were in school, but not when it comes to insurance ratings, where an A- is only the fourth-highest rating by AM Best, the third-highest rating for Weiss, and, believe it or not, the seventh-highest rating for Standard & Poor's.

You should also contact your state insurance commissioner to inquire as to whether there have been complaints or investigations of the company from which you are considering buying a policy. How long a company has been around is a good indicator of financial health.

Don't buy a policy from a company just because it has the lowest premium. A low premium may, although not necessarily, be an indication that either the company will be raising rates soon or that their actuaries have not appropriately priced their product. Either of these scenarios can work to your ultimate disadvantage.

As more and more major companies, such as MetLife and Prudential, have stopped issuing new long-term care policies, it is more important than ever that you carefully choose your company. The company from which you purchase your policy today may be taken over by another company tomorrow or, in a worst-case scenario, be out of business when you need to access your policy's benefits. The individual states have specific funds set aside to compensate people in this situation; however, those funds have yet to be tested by a large scale default by an insurer.

You can access AM Best at www.ambest.com, Standard & Poor's at www.standardandpoors.com, Moody's at www.moodys.com, and Weiss Ratings at www.weissratings.com.

Agent or Independent Broker

Generally, insurance agents sell the products of the single company that employs them, whereas independent brokers can sell the policies of any number of insurance companies with which they may be affiliated. You would think that it would make little sense to go to an agent who only represents one company because the choices it can provide would be necessarily limited. However, in some instances, it may be advantageous to buy through an agent who represents just one company. That agent will have a closer relationship with his company than most independent brokers, and this can translate into the agent not only being more familiar with the company's policies, but also being in a better position to assess the likelihood that your application for a long-term care insurance policy will be approved. In addition, single-company agents usually have better contacts within the company.

On the other hand, independent brokers represent you rather than the insurance company. Your independent broker is more apt to shop around to find the company that provides the policy that is the best fit for you rather than try to fit you into the terms and conditions of the policy of a single company.

Tip

The commission on the sale of a long-term care insurance policy is generally between 40 percent and 70 percent of the first year's premium. Ask your agent or broker what the commission is for each company you are considering. It is good information to know.

Application Process

The entire application process should take anywhere from four to six weeks or even longer. The biggest source of delay is the time it takes to get copies of your medical records, which are required by the long-term care insurance company in order to evaluate your insurability.

Tip

Once you apply for a long-term care policy, the insurance company will obtain a copy of your medical records to evaluate your insurability. A random note on your medical record made by your physician, particularly one related to cognitive functioning, can have a significant effect on whether your application for long-term care insurance will be accepted. Your physician might not have even discussed the matter with you, but it can still come back to haunt you. Fortunately, under the Health Insurance Portability and Accountability Act (HIPAA), you have the right to see your medical records. So check out your medical records before you apply for a long-term care insurance policy. If you find mistaken or inappropriate notations on your record, you can bring these matters to your physician's attention and ask him or her to correct the record.

Also, check with your long-term care insurance agent about the possibility of the insurance company regarding any prescription drugs you are taking. The insurance company could consider an innocuous prescription to be a narcotic that can end up either disqualifying you for the policy or making the premiums much higher. When it comes to health conditions and prescriptions that concern the underwriters of long-term care insurance companies, the companies vary about what they consider important; you might want to evaluate policies from a number of long-term insurers to see which company matches you best.

Be completely honest and forthright about your medical history in your application. The failure to disclose your true medical history can be considered a fraudulent misrepresentation and constitute grounds for the insurance company to rescind your policy.

A critical moment in the application process is the medical exam, required by most companies for applicants who are at least 70 years old. It is usually done in your home by an examiner who will review your medical records and give you a perfunctory examination. The important determination of your cognitive abilities will be substantially made during this interview, which generally lasts anywhere from a half-hour to an hour. Remember that, during the examination, the examiner will also be observing how you move. If you have difficulty getting up from a particular chair or moving around the room, that will be noted in the examiner's report and could adversely affect your application. So, choose your chair accordingly.

Tip

At the beginning of the interview, it is common for the examiner to provide you with ten words and ask you to use them in a sentence. This is merely a ruse. The real purpose of giving you these words is to test your cognitive abilities. At the end of the interview, you will be asked to repeat those ten words that were given to you at the start of the interview. This "delayed word recall" test is very important.

Length of Coverage

The average stay in a nursing home is about 2-and-a-half years, although we are all familiar with people who have been there much longer. The most common period for long-term care insurance coverage is either three or four years.

When you apply for Medicaid to cover the cost of long-term care in a nursing home, Medicaid looks back five years from the time of your application and will disqualify you from Medicaid coverage for a period that does not begin until you are in the nursing home and your assets have been spent down to no more than $2,000. The duration of the disqualification period depends on the value of the assets you gave away. However, Medicaid does not even inquire as to gifts you may have made more than five years earlier. So, if you get a long-term care insurance policy that will cover the cost of five years of nursing-home care, you could give away your assets when you first go into the nursing home, have the policy pay for the cost of care during the next five years, and then apply for Medicaid at the end of five years.

But, what if the look-back period changes? This is not an idle question, because Congress has in the past increased the period from two years to three years and most recently to five years. Getting a policy that provides lifetime benefits may not be necessary, but a policy with six years of coverage may be a good call. And the cost of increasing coverage from four years to six years is less than you might expect if you logically did the math. The reason is that the actuaries at the insurance company are content to bet that you won't live long enough to use that sixth year of coverage.

Waiting Period

A waiting period is the provision of a long-term care policy that delays the paying of benefits for a specific period of time from the time you first go into the nursing home. During this waiting period, you are responsible for the cost of your own care. Or are you? If you are over 65 and covered by Medicare, you may well be eligible for Medicare to pay in full the cost of the first 20 days in a nursing home and all but a $144.50 per day deductible (in 2012) for the next 80 days. Therefore, a 100-day waiting period may not pose too great a financial burden for someone covered by Medicare. As you might imagine, the longer the period you choose for a waiting period, the lower your premium will be. The range of waiting periods from which you may choose are subject to state insurance regulations, but range from no waiting period at all to a year. Most people pick 90 to 100 days.

Inflation Protection

Inflation protection can be important. Because many people own long-term care policies for 20, 30, or more years, protection of the policy benefits from inflation is a significant consideration. Three primary alternative provisions for inflation can be made a part of a long-term care policy: 5 percent compound interest, 5 percent simple interest and benefits based on inflation as determined by the Consumer Price Index. When you first choose a policy, you can pick either the 5 percent compound interest provision or a 5 percent simple interest provision, which will be factored into your premium payments. The difference between a simple interest provision and a compound interest provision can be quite large. A daily benefit of $150 will rise to $300 in just about 20 years, using a 5 percent simple interest formula, while that same initial daily benefit amount of $150 will reach $300 after only about 15 years, using a 5 percent compound interest formula. The Consumer Price Index (CPI) inflation protection provision is offered to existing policyholders periodically by the insurance company for an added premium.

Inflation protection is of critical importance. The policy you buy today might serve you little at a time when you need the policy to start paying. But, inflation protection in a long-term care insurance policy can be costly. One possible solution to this problem is to put it off to another day. As Mark Twain said, "Never put off until tomorrow what you can put off until the day after tomorrow." You may want to get some coverage by buying a long-term care insurance policy now without inflation protection and then pay for inflation protection later. But, remember, you will eventually have to pay the piper and get the protection.

Waiver of Premium

A waiver of premium is a provision contained in a long-term care policy that eliminates the need to continue to pay the premiums for the policy during such time as you are in a nursing home and receiving benefit payments from the policy.

Home Care

Although many people refer to long-term care insurance policies as nursing home insurance, you can also choose to have your policy provide for home healthcare. Because most of us would prefer to stay in our homes as long as possible, a home healthcare benefit is a desirable benefit. Providing for home healthcare through long-term care insurance is even more important because, unlike care in a nursing home, Medicaid and Medicare coverage for at-home care is, to say the least, limited.

Nonforfeiture

Nonforfeiture is a provision within your long-term care policy that allows you to cancel the policy but still receive some amount of reduced benefits if you require long-term care in the future. This is an expensive form of coverage, because it greatly increases the potential payout by the insurance companies, who factor into their pricing a projected number of people who will initially purchase a policy and then let it lapse without receiving benefit payments. If you choose to have a nonforfeiture provision in your policy, it can tremendously raise the amount of your premium. However, it still may be a good choice if you are concerned about whether you will have enough money in the future to continue to pay the premiums necessary to maintain the policy.

Renewability

Guaranteed renewability is a standard provision of most policies. It means that the insurance company is not allowed to cancel your policy if you are late in the payment of your premium as long as you make your payment within a specified grace period. In addition, your premium will not automatically increase as you get older, although this is of small consolation since all that this means is that you will not be individually singled out for a premium increase. Increases in premiums may occur across the board for everyone so situated if the insurance company's actuaries are able to show that it is necessary.

Triggers for Benefits

There are a number of different situations that trigger benefit payments under a long-term care insurance policy.

Activities of Daily Life

Activities of daily life (ADLs) are the triggers for payment of benefits under a long-term care insurance policy. There are no standard definitions for ADLs. Rather, each insurance company defines them for itself. Generally, ADLs include eating, bathing, dressing oneself, personal hygiene, and mobility. Benefit payments from the policy occur when two or three ADLs are affected, depending on the policy. Obviously, the fewer ADLs necessary to trigger benefit payments, the more attractive the policy. Also, although it requires reading the fine print, you want a policy in which the definitions of ADLs are written as broadly as possible.

Cognitive Impairment

Cognitive impairment, which is a reduction in your mental faculties, is another trigger for the payment of benefits. Loss of short-term memory, long-term memory, or both may be serious enough to warrant the payment of benefits under the terms of the policy. Loss of the ability to use basic deductive reasoning and a lack of orientation to person, place, and time also may cause benefits to be payable under the terms of the policy. Orientation to person, place, and time is knowing who you are, where you are, and what day it is.

Very Important: Mental Impairment

Many states require that all long-term care policies sold in their states provide benefits for people who develop Alzheimer's disease or other forms of dementia. However, in other states, policies are sold that exclude benefits for people who develop Alzheimer's disease or dementia. Make sure your policy covers these mental diseases and disorders.

Creative Solutions

If you cannot presently afford a policy at the benefit level you would prefer, buy a policy with a small amount of coverage and an inflation rider; then, after a few years, get another policy to supplement that initial policy. Overall, you will save considerable money. If a 50-year old bought a policy with a $100 per day coverage for four years and then, ten years later, bought another policy with $100 per day coverage, his premium would be less than if he bought a $200 per day policy at age 60. He also would have had some coverage for all the years between 50 and 60.

Who Is in Jeopardy of a Premium Increase?

The owners of older policies in general and those with shorter waiting periods and lifetime coverage periods are most likely to find themselves facing premium increases. What do you do if you are notified of a policy premium increase and you do not want to lose your coverage, but you find it difficult to provide your budget for the additional premium? Work with your insurance agent to see if you can reduce the amount of your daily benefit, reduce the policy coverage period, or extend the waiting period before the policy starts paying as alternatives to either having to pay an increased premium or letting the policy lapse.

Good News

Just as some thought *Star Trek the Next Generation* was an improvement over the original *Star Trek* (think Captain Picard versus Captain Kirk), the more recent generation of long-term care insurance policies are an improvement when it comes to consistency of the premiums. The insurance companies have learned from their experience in this relatively new form of insurance and have priced them more accurately. Drastic premium increases for policyholders of the new policies are unlikely.

It Pays to Be Married

"When it comes to long-term care insurance and country club dues, it pays to be married."

—Ron Nathan, financial planner

It pays to be married in many instances. In fact, some would say that it pays and it pays and it pays. But, do not listen to those cynics. A recent development in long-term care insurance companies has been 10 to 15 percent reductions in premium costs when married couples buy long-term care insurance together. When you think about it, it makes sense. Married people are more likely to be in a position to care for each other at home for some period of time before a nursing home stay would be required. Single people without such a devoted caregiver are more likely to need the services of a nursing home earlier.

Another new development in policies for married couples is "shared benefits," a policy provision by which husbands and wives can share the total coverage years according to their needs. For example, if both the husband and wife purchased coverage for five years each, and one of them goes into the nursing home while the other remains healthy and in the community, the healthy spouse can share some of the years of coverage from his or her policy to cover the institutionalized spouse who has exhausted his or her own benefits.

Group Policies

It is always nice to be a member of a group. But, when it comes to purchasing a group long-term care insurance policy, it is important to note that, for some reason apparent only to the politicians writing these rules, some states do not apply the same regulations to sellers of group policies. In Massachusetts, for instance, an individual policy may not be sold that excludes coverage for Alzheimer's disease. Unfortunately, group policies excluding this important coverage may be legally sold in Massachusetts. Obviously, it is important to carefully scrutinize any group long-term care policy that you might consider buying.

It is also important to note that, unlike health insurance where employers often pay some of the premium on behalf of their employees, that is not generally the case when group long-term care insurance is offered as a benefit to employees. In addition, although group health insurance is generally at a lower premium than an individual policy, that is not generally the case with group long-term care insurance policies. Group policies, as a rule, are subject to reduced underwriting requirements. Therefore, they are riskier for the insurer who may charge a higher premium. However, if you have health issues that might prevent you from obtaining an individual policy, a group policy may be a great option.

Deferred Annuities

Another creative way to provide for the costs of possible long-term care is through a deferred annuity. Many people (including me) have been critical of annuities as an appropriate investment for older people, but it is probably better to think of annuities like carbohydrates: They are not bad in and of themselves, but if used inappropriately, they could be bad for you. One criticism of annuities as an investment for older people is the penalties that are attached to premature withdrawal. However, some deferred annuities are available with a provision for a penalty-free withdrawal amount if the proceeds are used for long-term care needs. Generally, a deferred annuity does not allow the surrender or withdrawal of amounts form the annuity without a "surrender charge," but in this instance, that charge would be waived to permit money from the annuity to be used for long-term care needs.

Just as a long-distance runner benefits from loading up on carbohydrates, an older person might benefit from buying an annuity to be available for long-term care needs. This is particularly true when age and health considerations might make the option of buying life insurance for those needs either unavailable or too costly. People within the ages of 65 and 85 might find that annuities offer a better buy than life insurance.

People in their 50s and early 60s who are in good health might find that life insurance offers more coverage for their premium dollars and would opt for the low-carb alternative of life insurance instead of annuities to meet their long-term care needs.

Disability Insurance

Another option some companies offer permits people between the ages of 60 and 70 who have disability insurance to exchange their disability policy for a long-term care insurance policy. A particular advantage is that the policyholder is not required to meet any insurability standards at the time of the exchange.

Surf and Turf

People who have difficulty making up their minds at a restaurant can always choose the surf and turf. When it comes to long-term care planning, mixing long-term care insurance policies, life insurance policies, and annuities in varying degrees to meet your long-term care needs also can be a rather savory choice.

For example, a person might consider buying a long-term care insurance policy with a short benefit period that correspondingly has a lower premium. The need for more extensive long-term care coverage could be met by combining that long-term care insurance policy with a life insurance policy that has a long-term care rider. Another option would be to reverse the emphasis by having a life insurance policy with a long-term care rider cover the initial long-term care needs and supplement that policy with a long term care insurance policy.

As always, the mantra, "Do the math" applies. Have your insurance agent compare the premiums by varying the products and coverage with the ultimate goal of meeting your possible future needs for long-term care in a manner that is most cost-effective for you.

Make the Kids Pay

Maybe our founding fathers had it right. Make the kids pay for your long-term care costs either by picking up the cost of care themselves or by paying for the premiums for your long-term care insurance. After all, what you would otherwise be spending is their inheritance.

Endnote

1. LTC History, www.elderweb.com.

11

Social Security

Just as Mark Twain said the rumors of his death were greatly exaggerated, so it appears that the rumors of the demise of Social Security are also somewhat exaggerated. True, the system needs some drastic fine-tuning, but future retirees can rest assured that they will receive benefits when the time comes, and present retirees can sleep well knowing that they will continue to receive benefits. The voting power of baby boomers and older Americans will help ensure that Congress does the necessary reforms to keep the system going.

History

The Social Security Act was passed into law in 1935, and the first regular monthly payments began in 1940. The first monthly retirement check went to Ida May Fuller, a former legal secretary from Ludlow, Vermont, who received her first check in the amount of $22.54 in January of 1940 and her last check in 1975 when she died at the age of 100 years. Ida May Fuller made out pretty well under the Social Security system. The total contributions to the program on her behalf were $24.75. By the time she died, she had received $22,888.92 in benefits.

Originally, Social Security was intended to be a retirement program, but survivor's benefits were added in 1939 and disability benefits were added in 1956. Medicare became a part of the Social Security program in 1965, with the first Medicare card going to former President Harry S. Truman, a champion of what became the Medicare program.

Cost of living allowances (COLAs) were made a permanent part of the law in 1972, with the first adjustments under this law paid in 1975. Before that time, although inflation ate into benefits, Congress increased benefits irregularly. In 2000, Congress passed "The Senior Citizens' Freedom to Work Act of 2000" by unanimous votes in both the House of Representatives and the Senate. (I guess our elected representatives noticed that senior citizens are pretty good at performing their civic duty of voting.) Under the provisions of this law, senior citizens who were of full retirement age but continued to work would receive full Social Security retirement benefits.[1]

One of the persistent myths about Social Security is that the retirement age of 65 was chosen because that was the age of the German chancellor, Otto von Bismarck, at the time of Germany becoming the first country to establish a national old-age pension program in 1889. Not to sink the Bismarck, but the truth is that the initial age for retirement under the original German law was 70, and at the time the law went into effect, Chancellor Bismarck was already 74 years old.

Eligibility and Benefit Calculations

Just about all of us are in the Social Security system (some government employees are not covered by Social Security), yet a surprisingly large number of people do not know the rules pertaining to eligibility for Social Security retirement benefits. The amount you receive at retirement is based on your earnings averaged over most of your working career. To be fully covered for Social Security, you must have paid into the system for 40 quarters of coverage (QCs, as they are referred to in the Social Security regulations). Some people mistakenly believe that quarters of coverage refer to quarters of the work year, and in fact, at one time, this was correct. Before 1978, employers reported wages to the Social Security Administration every three months. At that time, a worker got a QC, or credit, if he or she earned at least $50 during that three-month period. In 1978, employers started reporting earnings only once a year.

Credits are now based on the total amount of your earnings during the year regardless of when you worked during the year. For 2012, you receive one QC for every $1,130 you earn, but the maximum amount of credits you can get in a year is limited to four. To get the maximum four credits for the year, you need only earn $4,520 in 2012. These figures are subject to change. For the most current amounts, go the Social Security website, which is listed in "Favorite Websites."

The basis for determining benefits is the Primary Insurance Amount (PIA). The higher your earnings, the higher your benefits, although early retirees will receive a smaller monthly payment and those who delay their retirement will receive an enhanced monthly payment. The amount of your retirement benefits is computed by the Social Security Administration according to a complicated formula that initially adjusts your earnings to account for changes in average wages since the year in which your earnings were received. Next, it figures your average monthly adjusted earnings during your highest earning 35 years. Then, the administration applies a formula to these earnings to determine your Primary Insurance Amount. The maximum Social Security benefit for retirement at full retirement age in 2012 is $2,513 per month.

Loophole

Although we most often refer to the benefits received through Social Security as "retirement" benefits, they are actually "old age" benefits for which you are eligible, based on your age, even if you are still working. However, if you apply for benefits while you are between the ages of 62 and 65 (the present age for receiving full benefits), the amount of your benefits will be reduced, depending on the amount you earn at work.

Look for Your Annual Statement

Okay, it does not have the ring of the catchy commercial jingle "Look for the Union Label," which, despite our best intentions, many of us found ourselves singing in our minds back in 1975. But, the annual statement that we get from the Social Security Administration is a key document that contains specific information on our earnings throughout our working lives. When you get your annual statement, review it carefully. Make sure that the information is correct, in general. In particular, make sure that you are properly credited for your highest earning 35 years of wages, because those years determine the amount of your benefit.

You should also carefully review the statement for not just your earnings history, but also your personal information, such as your name and birth date. If a mistake has been made, you can correct it in a timely fashion; it will become an emergency if you wait to correct mistakes until you are about to apply for Social Security benefits. In addition, if you have become a victim of identity theft, where someone is collecting benefits using your Social Security number, the annual statement will alert you to that fact.

Full Retirement Age

Full retirement benefits under Social Security were traditionally paid at age 65. However, in 1983, the law was changed to gradually increase the age for full retirement to 67. As shown in Table 11.1, for people born in 1938, the age for full retirement benefits is 65 years and 2 months. The full retirement age for people born since 1960 will be 67, while for baby boomers born between 1943 and 1954, the age for receiving full retirement benefits will be 66 years.

Table 11.1 Age for Full Retirement Benefits

Year of Birth	Retirement Age for Receiving Full Social Security Benefits
Before 1938	65
1938	65 and 2 months
1939	65 and 4 months
1940	65 and 6 months
1941	65 and 8 months
1942	65 and 10 months

Year of Birth	Retirement Age for Receiving Full Social Security Benefits
1943–1954	66
1955	66 and 2 months
1956	66 and 4 months
1957	66 and 6 months
1958	66 and 8 months
1959	66 and 10 months
1960	67

Early or Late Retirement

It almost sounds like an old quiz show. Do you want the money now or do you want to come back next week and try for the car? Is it better to take less money starting sooner or more money starting later?

If, for whatever reasons, be they financial reasons, health reasons, or any other reasons, you have to retire from work at age 62, you will probably want to start collecting your Social Security retirement benefits at 62, unless you have saved a lot of money. Be aware, however, that if you were born after October 1938 and you take early retirement in 2012, your benefits will be reduced by one dollar for every two dollars over $14,640 you might earn from future employment annually. If you do not need the money for early retirement, you probably will be better off waiting until your full retirement age to claim your Social Security benefits. If you do not need the money at that time, you still may be better off taking the checks and investing the money yourself rather than deferring retirement to age seventy.

The best way to figure out when the best time would be for you to start taking Social Security retirement benefits is by going to the Social Security Administration's interactive website (www.socialsecurity.gov). There, you can use simple calculators to compare different retirement options.

Early Retirement

Although you may not receive full retirement benefits until age 65 and 2 months, if you were born in 1938 and are retiring in 2012, you can retire as early as age 62 and still receive some benefits. The amount that you receive at that age, however, would be reduced by 20.83 percent. Table 11.2 shows how much your benefits will be reduced if you retire at age 62 instead of waiting until full retirement age.

Table 11.2 Reduction in Social Security Benefits if Retiring at 62 Instead of 65 Years of Age

Year of Birth	Percent of Benefits Reduction
1938	20.83 percent
1939	21.67 percent
1940	22.50 percent
1941	23.33 percent
1942	24.17 percent
1943–1954	25.00 percent
1955	25.83 percent
1956	26.67 percent
1957	27.50 percent
1958	28.33 percent
1959	29.17 percent
1960	30.00 percent

Show Me the Money

Many Americans under full retirement age have taken up "Show me the money," Cuba Gooding Jr.'s tagline in the 1996 movie *Jerry Maguire*. They choose to start receiving Social Security benefits as early as age 62 rather than wait until their full retirement age. The age for receiving early retirement benefits was set at 62 for men in 1961. It had previously been lowered in 1956 for women to age 62.

The problem with receiving early Social security retirement benefits is that you receive less money. Or do you? If you elect to start receiving Social Security benefits before you reach the age of full retirement, your monthly benefit check is reduced a fraction of a percent for each month before your full retirement age. On average, if you retire at 62, your monthly check will be about 20 percent less than if you had waited until full retirement age. However, according to the Social Security Administration, based on what some actuary in a cubicle is telling them, taking early retirement benefits will not actually decrease the amount you receive over your lifetime. The reduced monthly check is balanced out by the fact that you begin receiving the money years earlier.

Consider the Social Security Administration as a helpful friend when it comes to helping you determine when to start collecting retirement benefits. The Social Security Administration has interactive benefit calculators on its website (www.ssa.gov) that can provide tremendous assistance in making retirement decisions. These calculators enable you to compare the amounts that you would receive by retiring at different ages with other variables, such as your projections of future earnings.

In making the decision as to whether or not to take reduced early retirement benefits, married men should consider that for many of them, they will predecease their wives and the survivor's benefits that their widows would receive would be reduced from the amount that they would have received had they waited till full retirement age to start receiving benefits.

A Bird in the Hand

Some people believe that it is best to get you money from Social Security as soon as possible (at age 62) so that you can have more control over investing that money rather than leaving it up to Uncle Sam to invest. In addition, taking your Social Security benefits earlier could enable you to leave more of your money to compound in tax-deferred investments, such as IRAs for a longer period of time. On the other hand, with safe investments earning historically low amounts at this time, you may well consider it more prudent, if you can wait, to postpone taking benefits.

Over-Under

In sports betting, you can make a bet called the "over-under," in which you choose to be on whether the total number of points amassed by both teams, such as in a football game, will either exceed or be less than the casino's "over-under" figure. In Social Security, your determination of whether to take your benefits early or later is a similar bet with the Social Security Administration.

In this case, the over-under figure set by the Social Security Administration is its calculation of your life expectancy. Increased benefit amounts for delaying retirement are intended to equalize the total amount that a person would receive if he or she postponed claiming Social Security benefits with someone who retired early and received a reduced amount if both lived to their Social Security Administration's actuarially computed life expectancies. However, the Social Security actuaries do not know you. They do not know your health or the likelihood that you will live shorter or longer than what they believe your life expectancy will be. Strictly looking at the morbid question of how long you expect to live, if you think you will live less than what Social Security projects as your life expectancy, you are better off taking the money early. If you think you will live longer than projected, you should delay retirement.

Take the Money and Run

So, when does it make sense to take the money and run?

The initial no-brainer answer to that question is that if you need the money and do not have other sufficient sources of income, you should take the money early. If you come from a long line of short-lines—that is, your family history is not one of longevity—you may want to take the money early. Similarly, if your health is already poor, go for the early money.

Conversely, if you are healthy and come from a family blessed with longevity, you might want to put off starting your Social Security retirement benefits until you can receive the larger benefit amount available to you if you put off receiving benefits until you are of full retirement age or beyond.

A Work in Progress

If you are still working, you might want to wait to claim Social Security retirement benefits, because the amount you receive from Social Security may be reduced because you are still working. If you elect to early take Social Security retirement benefits before you have reached your full Social Security retirement age, the benefits you receive will be reduced by one dollar for every two dollars earned above $14,640.

Until 2000, people who waited until their full retirement age, but continued working, were penalized by having their benefits reduced by one dollar for every three dollars they earned over $17,000. However, in 2000, with the unanimous passage by Congress of "The Senior Citizens' Freedom to Work Act," which some have cynically called the "Do You Want Fries With That? Act," people of full retirement age collecting benefits are able to work without any reduction in the amount of their Social Security retirement benefits.

Getting a Larger Check Later

Putting off applying for Social Security retirement benefits and getting a bigger monthly check could be enticing if you have considerable longevity in your family or if you married someone who you believe will, most likely, outlive you and collect Social Security retirement survivor benefits.

A surviving spouse of full retirement age can receive his or her deceased spouse's full Social Security retirement benefits. The surviving spouse can receive reduced survivor benefits as early as age 60. A surviving spouse between the ages of 60 and his or her age of full retirement will get between 75 and 94 percent of the deceased spouse's benefits.

As in the classic *Seinfeld* episode in which George was humiliated when he was caught putting the same chip back into a dip after taking a bit out of the chip, "double dipping" is not allowed. If a surviving spouse is entitled to his or her own Social Security retirement benefits in an amount greater than what he or she would receive as a surviving spouse, the spouse is paid the larger of the two eligible benefits.

Spousal Benefits

There are many benefits to being married. One that is easier to quantify is the right of a spouse to receive a spousal benefit equal to half of the other spouse's full Social Security retirement amount. If your spouse is eligible to receive Social Security retirement benefits based on his or her own work history, he or she will receive whichever benefit payment is greater.

Income Taxes

Then, there is the question of income taxes. If you file as an individual and your gross income plus nontaxable income (such as from tax-free bonds) and half of your Social Security benefits are between $25,000 and $34,000, you may have to pay income taxes on half of your Social Security benefits. If your income as just described is greater than $34,000, as much as 85 percent of your Social Security benefits is subject to income tax. When you start taking your Social Security benefits, whether it is early, at full retirement age, or later (up to age 70), you have to consider the money you might lose to income taxes when you figure what you can earn by investing your money. If you file as married filing jointly, and your gross income plus nontaxable income and half of your Social Security benefits are between $32,000 and $44,000, you may have to pay income taxes on half of your Social Security benefits. If your joint incomes, as just described, are greater than $44,000, up to 85 percent of your benefits may be taxable.

Delayed Retirement

Some people choose to delay retirement until even after the age for full retirement benefits, because the longer they put off retiring, the greater the Social Security benefit payments will be. The increase in monthly benefits by deferring retirement, however, stops once a person reaches age 70. Table 11.3 shows the increase in your benefits for each year that you delay retirement up to age 70.

Table 11.3 Increase in Social Security Benefits for Each Year Retirement Is Delayed Until Age 70

Year of Birth	Yearly Rate of Increase
1933–1934	5.5 percent
1935–1936	6.0 percent
1937–1938	6.5 percent
1939–1940	7.0 percent
1941–1942	7.5 percent
1943 or later	8.0 percent

Another Reason to Delay Taking Benefits

For many of us, procrastination is its own reward, and as Mark Twain once advised, "Never put off till tomorrow what you can put off until the day after tomorrow." However, putting off applying for Social Security benefits and continuing to work could be of some benefit to you if the added working years will make a considerable difference in your 35 highest wage-earning years and raise the amount of your benefit. Again, you can calculate this by going to www.ssa.gov.

By the way, with logic only a government bureaucrat could possibly comprehend, if your birthday is on the first day of any month, the determination of your benefits is made as if you were born in the previous month.

COLAs

There were no *Cost of Living Allowances* (COLAs) to combat inflation's effects on monthly Social Security payments until 1950. Social Security recipients were pretty thirsty before they got their first COLA, which increased the payouts by 77 percent. After that, COLAs, as passed by Congress, came along irregularly in 1952, 1954, 1959, 1965, 1968, 1970, and 1971, until, in 1972, COLAs were finally made automatic. The annual increases are based on the consumer price index. The law did not become effective until 1975, so Congress had to enact three more temporary COLAs until it became automatic.

Social Security Retirement Strategies

A surviving spouse who is mathematically inclined might determine that he or she is better off taking an early surviving spouse benefits until he or she reached full retirement age and then switching to his or her own Social Security retirement benefit. The law allows this. Whether this makes sense for a particular person depends on the age of the surviving spouse and his or her earnings, compared to the Social Security benefit derived from the deceased spouse. Fortunately, for those of us who are not mathematically inclined, the Social Security Administration website, www.ssa.gov, has interactive online calculators that can help you find the answer.

Sometimes, the math works out so that a married person can choose to take early benefits at age 62 based on his or her own work history, and then when the other spouse reaches full retirement age, switch to take spousal benefits. In many instances, this results in an increase of total benefits. As always, do the math.

Using a file and suspend strategy, a husband, for example, could file for benefits and then his wife could file for spousal benefits. The husband would then suspend his own benefits, but his wife could still continue to receive her spousal benefits while the husband's benefits would grow until he chooses to start taking payments.

Another strategy involves early restricting of a person's benefits to spousal benefits. For example, if the wife stops working and is collecting Social Security benefits based on her work history, but the husband is still working and not collecting benefits, he could collect spousal benefits based on his wife's benefit payments if he is of full retirement age and then let his own benefits rise as he builds up his own work record until age 70, when he can apply for increased benefits. This strategy works best when both the husband and wife have worked and earned higher Social Security amounts.

Ernest Ackerman of Cleveland, Ohio, received the first check from the Social Security Administration for a lump-sum payment in the princely amount of 17 cents in 1937. Until monthly payments commenced in 1940, the only form of payment between 1937, the time of the first payments of any kind, and 1940 was lump-sum payouts. The purpose of the single lump-sum payment was to provide some amount of payment for people who would be contributing to the program but were not expected to be in the program long enough to receive monthly payments. Don't feel too bad for Ernest Ackerman; for although his lump-sum check was for a mere 17 cents, he only contributed a nickel to the program, which actually is a pretty good return.

Survivor's Benefits

Benefit payments can be made to the surviving spouses or even former spouses of deceased covered workers subject to many conditions. Retirement payments may be made to a widowed spouse of a deceased covered worker at age 60, and ex-spouses of a deceased worker may receive benefits as early as age 62. To qualify as a spouse to receive benefits, the surviving spouse must have been married to the covered worker for at least nine months and must not have remarried before reaching 60 years of age. The nine-month marriage requirement does not apply if the deceased spouse died as a result of an accident, died while on active duty in the military, or if the couple had been married to each other previously for nine months or more and later divorced. To qualify as an accidental death under this law, death must occur as a result of violent, external factors that produce bodily injuries that cause death independently of other causes; this would seem to eliminate the possibility of a gold digger marrying an old man and then scaring him to death. Pushing his wheelchair into traffic apparently would be okay, as long as the death was deemed an accident.

The amount of Social Security benefit to which a surviving spouse is entitled is the full amount of the deceased spouse's benefit amount if the surviving spouse is of full retirement age. A surviving spouse between the age of 60 and the age of full retirement receives between 71 and 94 percent of the deceased spouse's benefits. However, double-dipping is not permitted by law, so if you were entitled to your own Social Security benefits in an amount greater than that which you would receive as a surviving spouse, you would be paid the larger of the two benefits for which you are eligible.

A divorced spouse (or spouses, there is no limit on the number of former spouses who may qualify) must have been married to the deceased covered worker for at least ten years and be unmarried to collect survivor's benefits. If you are a divorced spouse at least 60 years old, you can remarry following the death of your insured-worker former spouse and continue to receive survivor's benefits. Once again, double-dipping is prohibited, and you are entitled to receive the greater of either your own Social Security benefits or one-half of the benefits of the deceased spouse. A divorced spouse who elects to receive benefits before he or she reaches full retirement age will receive a reduced amount of his or her former spouse's benefit (at age 62, this is 35 percent; at age 63, it's 37.5 percent; at age 64, it's 42 percent and at age 65, it's 46 percent).

Trivia

Many people wonder what the sequence of numbers of your Social Security number means. All kinds of bizarre theories abound. The truth is that the first three digits are the only part of the number that have any meaning. They represent the geographical area in which you were living when you got a Social Security card. As to the rest of the digits, they are random.

Notch Babies

As a result of a mistake in 1972 legislation, a double adjustment windfall for inflation was enacted. If the mistake had not been corrected, it was projected that in the future Social Security retirees conceivably could have ended up actually getting paid more in monthly Social Security retirement benefits than they had earned in their entire working career. When Congress corrected the mistake in 1977, it phased in the correction over a five-year period. This resulted in people born between 1917 and 1921, the notch babies, receiving larger benefits than people born after 1921 but less than people born before 1917, who received the benefit of the technical error in the 1972 law. Many well-meaning people who did not understand the situation were under the false impression that the notch babies had been singled out for poorer treatment by the Social Security Administration and that they would be receiving lower benefits than people born before 1917 or after 1921. In fact, not only do all people born after 1916 have their benefits determined according to the same formula, but because of the way the correction was phased in, some notch babies actually received somewhat more than did people born since 1922.

Social Security Disability Income

Social Security Disability Income (SSDI) is a disability benefit paid to disabled workers until the disabled worker reaches the age of 65, at which time the worker's benefits are shifted to retirement benefits. Disabilities can be either physical or psychological but must be expected to keep the insured worker out of work for at least a year. The definition of disability for SSDI purposes is a physical or mental impairment that results in inability to do a previous job or "any other substantial gainful activity that exists in the national economy."

Drug addiction and alcoholism are no longer recognized as disabilities for SSI payments. However, if the disabled person has a disability that was not caused by either drug addiction or alcoholism and that particular disability would still exist even without the use of drugs or alcohol, the disabled person would still be eligible for benefits.

A spouse who is at least 62 years old is eligible to receive benefits based on a disabled spouse's disability benefits.

SSDI is not a needs-based program, so if you meet the QC and disability requirements, you will be eligible for SSDI benefits regardless of your assets or your income. Most often, the QC requirements consist of 20 credits earned in the last ten years. After two years of receiving SSDI benefits, you are eligible for Medicare coverage regardless of your age.

Because of insufficient records, history does not tell us who actually received the first Social Security number. However, the first Social Security number account record comes from Baltimore, Maryland, where John David Sweeney of New Rochelle, New York, was assigned the first Social Security number account. John David Sweeney died in 1974 at the age of 61, never having received a penny from Social Security; however, his widow received widow's benefits for eight years until her death in 1982.

Although John David Sweeney had the first Social Security number account, he did not receive the lowest issued number. That honor goes to Grace Dorothy Owen of Concord, New Hampshire, who was assigned the easy-to-remember number 001-01-000, which, I suppose, is about as close as you can come to an unlisted number. The story of how Grace Dorothy Owen got this number is pretty interesting. The geographic area grouping of the first three digits was to originate in the New England states. You would think that they would start in Maine and work their way down. Instead, the lowest area numbers were assigned to New Hampshire so that the lowest number would be able to be given as a political honor to Social Security Board chairman and former New Hampshire governor, John G. Witant. Chairman Witant, however, refused the offer, whereupon it was then offered to John Campbell, the Federal Bureau of Old Age Benefits' Regional Representative, who also declined to accept the honor. At this point, it was determined to just give the lowest number to whoever first applied in New Hampshire; that turned out to be Grace Dorothy Owen.

Loophole

If you have at least six United States quarters of coverage in the American Social Security program but have worked in certain other countries, the quarters of coverage in those countries are counted in the United States toward eligibility for Social Security benefits here. Those countries are Austria, Belgium, Canada, Germany, Finland, France, Greece, Ireland, Italy, Luxembourg, Netherlands, Norway, Portugal, Spain, Sweden, Switzerland, and the United Kingdom.

Getting a Copy of Your Record

It is important, particularly in the year before you retire, to obtain a copy of your Social Security earnings' record to make sure that you are being credited for your entire work history. If you find that you are not credited for work that you performed, it is your obligation to provide to the Social Security Administration evidence of your past employment so that they can correct the record. Copies of pay stubs, W-2s, income tax returns or even letters from your past employers will be accepted by the Social Security Administration as proof of your employment.

The Social Security Administration will annually send you its computations of prospective benefits to which you are entitled. However, you may also get these documents through the Internet at www.ssa.gov. If you find a mistake, you have up to three years, three months, and fifteen days from the end of the calendar year in which the mistake occurred to request a correction through the local Social Security Administration district office. After that time-period has expired, you can still have a mistake corrected if the mistake was caused by fraud, clerical error or reporting or record errors, which is just about every way that a mistake on your record can occur, so the statute of limitation does not usually present a problem.

Overpayments

Mistakes happen. It is not uncommon for the Social Security Administration to make a mistake in determining the amount of your benefit check. Sometimes, the mistakes are caused by the Social Security recipients who neglect to report important changes in their circumstances that would affect the amount of their check. The most common way for the Social Security Administration to recoup the money overpaid is by deducting money from future monthly payments until the entire amount is repaid.

Loophole

If you can show that an overpayment was not caused by you and that having to repay the money would pose a hardship, the law permits the Social Security Administration to waive the repayment requirement.

Medicare and Your Application for Social Security Benefits

Remember that, when you are dealing with the Social Security Administration, you are dealing with a bureaucracy, so it is wise to file for Social Security retirement benefits a few months before you anticipate receiving those benefits. Even if you intend to defer taking retirement benefits until well after you have reached your full retirement age in order to increase the amount you will eventually receive, it is important to register with the Social Security Administration to make sure you are covered by Medicare.

Endnote

1. History Page—Social Security online, the official website of the Social Security Administration, www.ssa.gov.

12

Medicare

Medicare is the name of the federal government's health insurance program for people who, having paid into the Social Security system, are at least 65 years old or who are disabled.

People often confuse "Medicare" with "Medicaid," although the programs are quite different. Unfortunately, Congress in its infinite wisdom named these programs in a way that would increase confusion. Or maybe they were confused as well. In any event, although Medicare is an entitlement program to which everyone who has contributed to Social Security and is either over 65 or is permanently disabled has a right, Medicaid is a welfare program that is available only to those who meet strict financial qualifications.

One of the biggest sources of confusion between the two programs comes in regard to nursing-home care. Medicare only pays fully for the first 20 days of nursing-home care and then partially pays for the next 80 days with the nursing-home resident responsible for a copayment (in 2012) of $144.50 per day. For the current amounts that Medicare will pay, go to the Medicare website, as described in "Favorite Websites." For those people who qualify, Medicaid pays the cost of long-term nursing home care as long as it is required, with the only copayment being a patient-pay amount that is calculated in accordance with income and need considerations.

The Medicare Alphabet

Medicare comes in four flavors: Medicare A, Medicare B, Medicare C, and—you guessed it—Medicare D. Part A helps pay for hospital care, the limited amount for nursing-home care that I explained in the previous paragraph, hospice care, and some limited home healthcare. Part B primarily covers physician's bills, outpatient services, tests, and medical equipment. Part C deals with newer ways for providing medical services, such as Managed Care Plans and Health Maintenance Organizations (HMOs), and Part D is the Prescription Drug Program.

Part A does not require the Medicare recipient to pay any premiums. Part B is funded partly though monthly premium payments of Medicare recipients; the federal government pays the rest of the cost. Both Medicare A and B require Medicare recipients to make copayments and cover the cost of deductibles for many services provided by Medicare A and B.

A copayment is the amount that you must pay out of your own pocket for a service covered by your insurance. A deductible is the amount that you must pay annually before your insurance will begin to cover any of your needs.

Medicare C was formerly known as Medicare+Choice and is now known as Medicare Advantage. Part C provides increased benefits for a fee through private health-insurance programs, such as HMOs, Preferred Provider Organizations (PPOs), and Private Fee for Service Plans (PFFSs).

History

Some people looking for logic might question why Medicare A and B coverages are separate. The answer is a simple one to which logic does not apply: politics. When Medicare was being debated in Congress before its enactment in 1965, a significant number of legislators were joined by the health-insurance industry and the American Medical Association, both of which were against the idea of a universal healthcare (sound familiar?). As a compromise, physician's services were taken out of the proposed legislation, leaving what was now primarily "hospital insurance" as Medicare A. Later, in another compromise, physician and outpatient services were brought back into Medicare as Medicare B; as a further compromise, Medicare B was made optional and funded partly through monthly premiums to be paid by the enrollees and partly by the federal government.

Medicare A

When you enter a hospital for treatment, Medicare A will fully pay for the first 60 days of what it colorfully refers to (without, I may add, giving credit to Screaming Jay Hawkins, the singer of the old rock classic *I Put a Spell on You*) as a "spell of illness," after the payment by the patient of a deductible; for the year in which this book was written (2012), that amount is $1,156. Again, for the most current figures, go to the Medicare website (as given in "Favorite Websites"). For "spells" that last longer than 60 days, Medicare requires a payment from the patient for days 61 through 90. The amount of this coinsurance payment in 2012 is $289 per day. Those lucky people whose hospital stay extends beyond 90 days can tap into a lifetime reserve of 60 additional days at a daily coinsurance cost of $578 per day for 2012.

Home healthcare for qualifying individuals is also covered under Medicare A. To qualify for home healthcare coverage, you must generally be unable to leave your home to receive medical care without "considerable and taxing effort," the home healthcare for which you are seeking Medicare coverage must be ordered by your physician, and the medical services which you are seeking must be classified as "skilled" (which includes, but is not limited to, part-time nursing services, physical therapy, and speech therapy). There are no copayment requirements for these services, so they come at no additional charge except for a 20 percent copayment requirement for just the medical supplies, the cost of which may be covered by your Medigap policy if you have one.

Medicare recipients with no more than six months to live are eligible under Medicare A for hospice care to be provided at no charge either in the patient's home or at a hospice facility. The services include, but are not limited to, physician's services, nursing care, home health aide, and homemaker services. Because the home hospice-care benefit does not provide full-time coverage, at-home hospice care coverage is only available if there is a caretaker in the home as well. The Medicare A hospice benefit also provides for "respite care" of up to five consecutive days of inpatient care, to allow the patient's primary caregiver a bit of a break during a difficult time. The copayment for respite care is 5 percent of the cost of the respite care. The cost of prescription drugs is an additional $5 for each drug.

Medicare A Premium Penalties

If you fail to enroll in Medicare A when you are first eligible, you have to pay a penalty of 10 percent of your Part A premium when you do enroll in Medicare A, unless you or your spouse did not enroll in Medicare A when first eligible because you were covered by a group health-insurance plan at work. Unlike the penalty for late enrollment in Medicare B, however, the penalty for late enrollment in Medicare A is limited to twice the number of years that you delayed enrolling, so if you did not enroll for two years after initially becoming eligible for Medicare A, you will have a 10 percent premium penalty for four years.

Medicare B

Medicare B's most important coverage involves doctor's bills. Medicare B also includes, but is not limited to, coverage for outpatient hospital services (including emergency-room visits), ambulance services, diagnostic tests, laboratory services, and durable medical equipment, such as wheelchairs and blood (after a three-pint deductible is met).

Medicare has been called a "healthcare system," but it should more appropriately be called an "illness care system," because it does little to provide for care to maintain health or diagnose and treat illnesses early. Rather, it deals with problems after they have become more serious and their treatment is more expensive. Fortunately, since 1998, Medicare B has provided payments for colorectal screenings, pap smears, and pelvic screenings as well as pneumococcal and flu shots.

Unfortunately, Medicare B presently does not cover the cost of most routine dental care, dentures, cosmetic surgery, hearing aids, and exams for fitting hearing aids.

The amount that people who have Medicare B coverage must pay for services is subject to an annual $140 deductible. After this deductible amount has been met, Medicare will pay 80 percent of the Medicare-approved amount for covered services; the patient is responsible for the payment of the remaining 20 percent of the Medicare approved amount. Medicare sets what it considers to be "reasonable charges" for specific, covered medical services. It is a good bet that the amount that Medicare determines as an approved amount is less than what the physician would usually charge for the service. If the treating physician "accepts assignment" of Medicare claims, the physician is agreeing to accept as payment in full the "reasonable charge" as determined by Medicare for the covered service. In that case, the physician would be paid 80 percent of the bill by Medicare and 20 percent from the patient. If, however, the physician does not "accept assignment" of Medicare claims, the physician may charge the patient an additional 15 percent of the Medicare approved amount. This additional fee, referred to as the "limiting charge," will be tacked onto the 20 percent of the reasonable charge that the patient must pay for.

Loophole

Some states require all doctors to accept the Medicare-approved amount as payment in full. If you do not live in one of those states, it is important to ask your physician before you are treated whether he or she accepts assignment of Medicare claims because, if your physician does accept assignment of Medicare claims, your bill will be less.

Medicare Part B Preventive Services

It has been said that we do not have a healthcare system, but rather a sick care system. The difference is that the focus of our system has too often been treating serious illnesses rather than taking steps to prevent or identify illnesses at early stages when they are more readily treatable. Beyond the obvious health benefits, preventive services and early detection of diseases also is less costly, which is something with which we are all concerned.

A number of good preventive health services are available through Medicare B. These services can identify problems early, when they are most correctible.

Medicare B provides an initial "Welcome to Medicare" preventive visit during the first year of coverage. During this visit, a personal long-term healthcare plan can be developed with an eye toward improving your health and preventing disease. In addition, Medicare B offers a yearly "wellness" visit after the first year to update the plan.

Among the preventive services provided by Medicare B are the following:

Bone mass measurement

Breast cancer screening (mammograms)

Cardiovascular screenings

Cervical and vaginal cancer screening

Colorectal cancer screening, including the all-important colonoscopy

Diabetes screening

Diabetes self-management training

Flu shots

Glaucoma tests

Hearing and balance exams

Pneumococcal shots

Prostate cancer screenings

Medicare Part B Premiums

Since the inception of Medicare Part B, the federal government has subsidized the cost of Medicare Part B coverage. In 2006, the covered individual paid 25 percent of the cost of Medicare Part B coverage and the federal government paid 75 percent. However, beginning in 2007, the amount that a person paid for his or her Medicare B premium became indexed according to his or her income. In 2012, individuals with annual incomes of no more than $85,000, and married couples filing joint returns with annual incomes of no more than $170,000, paid $99.90 per month as their Medicare B premium. This premium payment goes up in four income-based increments, with individuals who have annual income of more than $214,000 and married couples filing jointly with incomes above $428,000 paying the highest premium ($319.70 per month) as their premium for Medicare Part B, which is still a bargain. These amounts are adjusted annually in accordance with the Consumer Price Index.

Medicare Part B: Pay Me Now or Pay Me Later

If you are still working when you reach the age of 65, you could be covered by a health-insurance plan at your place of employment and will not need to sign up for Medicare Part B. However, generally, if you are not covered by a group health-insurance policy at work, and you fail to enroll in Medicare B during the initial window of opportunity—the 7-month period that begins 3 months before you reach age 65—the premium for Medicare Part B when you do enroll later increases by 10 percent for each month that you could have enrolled but chose not to. You will continue to pay this penalty for the rest of your life.

Medicare C

Medicare+Choice, which is also commonly called Medicare C, was created through the Balanced Budget Act of 1997 to authorize new types of plans for providing medical services. Among the major Managed Care Plans are HMOs, HMOs with a POS (Point of Service) option, PFFSs (Private Fee for Service Plans), and PPOs (Preferred Provider Organizations). These organizations contract with Medicare to provide care to Medicare beneficiaries in return for a certain amount of money paid by Medicare monthly. How much choice you have as to doctors and hospitals depends on the type of Managed Care Plan you pick. HMOs and PFFSs are more restrictive, requiring you to use the plan's physicians and hospitals. PPOs and HMOs with POS options are less restrictive, allowing you to go to physicians and hospitals outside the plan network for an additional cost.

HMOs, which are the most familiar of the Medicare Advantage plans, include all Medicare Part A and Part B healthcare benefits. In most HMOs, however, you generally can use only doctors and hospitals that are a part of your HMO. In most HMOs, your primary care physician (PCP) is the gatekeeper to further treatment. You must see him or her before you can receive more specialized services under the plan, and you need a referral from your PCP before you can see a specialist. The biggest advantage to the patient is that the cost of participating in an HMO is generally less than with traditional Medicare.

With a PPO, you can see any doctor who is in your plan without a referral. However, if you go outside of your plan to a doctor or hospital, you pay extra.

PFFS plans resemble traditional Medicare where you are generally permitted to use physicians, hospitals and other healthcare providers of your choice so long as they agree to treat you; however, the plan determines the amount that it pays the healthcare providers and how much you must contribute to the cost of your care.

Extra Benefit

Some Medicare Advantage plans actually pay a part of your Medicare Part B premium, which can be a real money saver. Note, however, that whether this benefit will continue is determined annually by the plans that offer it, so you are not guaranteed this benefit each next year.

Bureaucratic B.S.

If you are already a member of an HMO when you become eligible for Medicare and want to continue with the same HMO through its Medicare program, you may not necessarily be able to keep the same PCP you previously used in that same HMO. The same physician may not be designated as a PCP in the HMO's Medicare program. Straining credulity even further, if the PCP you used before enrolling in Medicare is considered to be a "specialist" by Medicare, you will not be able to retain him or her as your PCP.[1] Who makes these ridiculous rules?

Managed Care

Managed care sounds like it should be the best thing since sliced bread, but as George Carlin used to ask, "What's so great about sliced bread?" The idea of managed care is simple. The health plan provider is paid a fixed monthly fee that covers all the patient's medical needs. That is a bargain for the managed care providers if the patient is healthy, but is costly to them if the patient is sick and needs extensive and expensive medical services. With a Medicare managed care plan, the provider receives the fixed monthly fee from Medicare and the patient receives medical care without deductible payments and fewer copayments than usually required under the more traditional Medicare plans (if you can refer to anything that has only been around since 1965 as traditional). Because, with a managed care plan, you do not have as many of these extra out-of-pocket expenses for medical care, the need for a costly Medigap policy vanishes as well. So, what is the catch?

In return for less costly medical care, you give up your right to pick the physician or physicians you wish to treat you. Managed care providers generally have limited lists of the particular physicians and hospitals that are within their network and from which you must choose.

Once you have chosen your PCP, any time that you need the services of a specialist, from a dermatologist to an orthopedist, not only are you limited in your choice of the physician to whom you may go, but you cannot even make an appointment with that physician directly. Just about everything must first be authorized by your PCP, who, frankly, is aware that the profits of his or her employer depend on limited referrals to more expensive specialists. The most contentious area for keeping costs down is the provision that your PCP must get approval from administrators higher up before authorizing many medical treatments. It is not uncommon for the administrators to refuse the treatment, saying that the treatment is either "experimental" or "not medically and reasonably necessary." There are appeals processes, but they can be cumbersome and time consuming at a time when a medical decision must be made quickly. In a major case, a medical plan was sued for medical malpractice for failing to authorize particular cancer treatments for a patient, who, by the time authorization was granted for a less aggressive treatment, was too ill for even the less costly authorized treatment and died.

Once again, if you want to compare the various Medicare managed care plans available to you, the best place to go for much helpful information is the Medicare website (www.medicare.gov).

Medicare Part D

Medicare Part D is the prescription drug coverage that is the most recent edition to the Medicaid alphabet with enrollees first eligible in 2006. You can choose from national plans as well as regional and statewide plans.

Picking an ice cream flavor when your choices are between vanilla and chocolate is relatively easy choice. When the flavor choices start reaching 60 or more, picking a flavor becomes more difficult. The more difficult it is to make the decision, the more likely it is that people will just freeze and not make one at all. Failing to make a decision becomes a decision itself. There is no harm in not being able to pick an ice cream flavor when you dazzled by too many choices. Unfortunately, failing to make a choice when it comes to a Medicare prescription drug program can have serious consequences. In 2013, there are 1,045 different available drug plans. Some plans are limited by state or region. There is an average of 31 plans from which to choose in each region. Nationally, there are 512 Enhanced Alternative (EA) plans that provide not just basic prescription drug coverage, but also supplemental benefits, such as a reduction in cost-sharing in the donut-hole coverage gap, or reduced or reduced coinsurance payments. Regionally, there are an average of 15 EA plans from which to choose. Nationally, there are 533 basic plans with a regional average of 16 of these plans per region.

The cost of plans can vary dramatically. In 2013, there are 466 plans that provide for a zero deductible payment with an average of 14 of those plans from which to choose in each region. The lowest monthly premium for a plan is $15 while the highest premium is $165.40. The average plan premium is $53.26 per month.

A deductible is the amount that you must pay out of your own funds before the insurance kicks in and starts paying. Coinsurance payments are your cost of a covered prescription. Deductibles and coinsurance payments vary from plan to plan. Each plan also has its own particular list of covered drugs, called its formulary. You must pay out of pocket for any of your prescription drug needs that do not appear on your drug plan's formulary.

The Fly in the Ointment

A fly in the ointment is a pretty disgusting image and phrase describing something that interferes with a desired outcome. However the derivation of the phrase goes back to the Bible, specifically the Book of Ecclesiastes, which reads, "Dead flies cause the ointment of the apothecary to send forth a stinking savour."

Having a prescription drug program through Medicare would seem to be a tremendous benefit to older Americans, but the complexity of the program, not to mention its other shortcomings, significantly taints that benefit for many people. Choosing a Medicare prescription drug plan is fraught with problems. Not all plans cover all drugs; so some of your drugs might be covered by one plan, while another plan might cover the rest. Even though you are tied to a single plan for a year, the plan can change the drugs it covers with as little as 60 days notice to you.

Comparing plans can be difficult. The premiums vary significantly from plan to plan. Some plans have deductibles; others do not. Some require copayments; others do not. Even the drugs covered vary from plan to plan. It should be a simple matter to merely compare the total costs to you between the various plans that carry the prescription drugs that you use. If the total cost to you in a plan with a higher premium but lower or no deductibles projects to be less than the total cost of a plan with a lower premium but higher deductibles, the answer should be apparent. I say "should" because so many other variables make it tough to compare. Fortunately, however, an interactive tool on the official Medicare website (www.medicare.gov) can help you choose a plan that is best for you.

Where Do You Get Your Plan?

Medicare prescription drug plans are available either by adding a plan to your traditional Medicare coverage or as a part of the coverage provided by your Medicare Advantage Plan, such as an HMO or PPO. To qualify for a plan, you must live in the appropriate service area for that plan. Not all plans are national in scope.

Tip

If you divide your time between different parts of the country, you may want to enroll in a plan that is national in scope or consider a plan where you can order your prescriptions by mail.

When Can You Join or Switch a Plan

You are eligible for a Medicare prescription drug program when you become eligible for traditional Medicare and can choose a plan anytime during the seven-month period that begins three months before the month you turn 65 and ends three months after the month you turn 65. Once you are enrolled in a plan, you may switch plans during the period between October 15 and December 7. Your switch becomes effective on January 1 of the next year. However, if you move out of your plan's service, you are eligible to switch plans at that time.

What Does It Cost?

Generally, most plans charge a monthly fee that differs from plan to plan. However, many Medicare Advantage Plans, such as HMOs and PPOs, may include prescription drug coverage in your regular monthly premium in the Medicare Advantage Plan at no extra cost. However, just as higher income people pay more for their Medicare B premiums, the same rules apply to Medicare D prescription drug plans. Married people filing their income tax returns jointly with more than $170,000 of modified adjusted gross income (MAGI), which is the total of your adjusted gross income and any tax-exempt interest income, will pay an additional premium, while single individuals and married people filing separately pay an additional premium if their MAGI is more than $85,000. In 2012, the additional premium ranged between $11.60 more per month up to $66.40 for individuals with $214,000 of MAGI and $66.40 more per month for married couples with $428,000 of MAGI.

The Math

You will pay for whatever your deductible is, if you have one, before your Medicare prescription drug plan starts paying. Once you cover your deductible payment, which can be no higher than $325 in 2013, you will also pay a copayment in accordance with your plan's provisions until the amount of payments for your prescription drugs in 2013 reach $2,970. At the point where you and your insurer together have paid $2,970, you are now in the coverage gap, which is often called the donut hole. Once you are in the coverage gap, you pay 47.5 percent of the plan's cost for your brand-name prescription drugs and 79 percent of the cost of generic drugs. Finally, once you have spent a total of $4,750, you now qualify for catastrophic coverage, and you pay only a small coinsurance payment for each covered drug until the end of the year when you start the process over again. For years after 2013, go to the www.medicare.gov website to see the latest figures.

Who Is Keeping Score?

According to Grantland Rice's famous quote, "For when the One Great Scorer comes to write against you name. He marks—not that you won or lost—but how you played the game." That might be true, but while you are alive on this Earth, winning and losing is important, which is why we keep score.

Keeping track of your prescription drug purchases is also important because the amount of your insurance coverage depends upon the total cost of your prescription drug purchases over the year. If you buy your drugs through your plan, the company will maintain a running record of the costs of your drug purchases. However, if you buy your drugs somewhere else, you must make sure that you send the receipts for your purchases to your prescription drug plan provider so your "score" is accurate.

Sticky Little Detail

Only prescription drugs that your plan covers count toward the $4,750 out-of-pocket prescription drug payments that you must make before the catastrophic coverage kicks in. To make things even worse, the cost of any prescription that you bought in Canada or any other foreign country do not count toward your costs necessary to reach your catastrophic benefit coverage. This puts you in the unenviable position of paying less for your prescription drugs by buying Canadian drugs, but never being able to reach your out-of-pocket maximum under the law that would trigger the catastrophic coverage of your drug costs. Thank your congressmen and senators for that one.

Don't Cry for Me Argentina: Tiered Drugs

Every plan determines its own formulary, which is the prescription drugs that will be covered by the plan. Often, the drugs are divided into different tiers with the drugs in the higher tier being more costly for the treatment of the same disease as the drugs in the lower tier. Your plan may require you to first try the less expensive drug in the lower tier, although if your physician indicates that you need the higher-tiered drug, you can use that and apply for an exception in order to get a lower copayment.

Exceptions Process

Each drug plan has its own exceptions process under which you can ask the drug plan to cover a nonformulary drug or to reduce the cost sharing for a formulary drug. In other words, you can ask the drug plan to make a ruling that its formulary requirements apply to all plan enrollees except for you. An unfavorable determination can be appealed. The prescribing physician plays an important role in the exception process because an exception will be granted only if the plan agrees with your doctor's certification that no other drug on the plan's formulary would be as effective for you as the drug in question or that the drugs contained in the plan's formulary would cause adverse consequences to you.

Penalty

As with Medicare A, there is a penalty for not enrolling in a timely fashion and maintaining your coverage in a Medicare prescription-drug program once you are eligible. If you fail to either enroll in your initial seven-month enrollment period, or if you go 63 consecutive days without a Medicare plan, you are subject to a late enrollment penalty when you do enroll or re-enroll. The penalty is determined by taking 1 percent of the national base beneficiary premium (which in 2012 was $31.08), and multiplying this number by the number of months during which you were eligible for a Medicare prescription drug plan, but failed to enroll. This penalty stays with you as long as you are in a Medicare prescription drug plan and, because the national base beneficiary premium may well go up in future years, the amount of your penalty may also go up. The penalty amount is added each month to your monthly premium.

If you are covered for prescription drugs as a retiree under the health plan of a former employer, you can stay with that plan without having to pay the premium penalty, even if your employer withdraws that benefit from your retiree health plan, as long as you promptly enroll in a Medicare prescription drug program with 63 days of losing your prescription drug benefit through your group coverage at work.

Tricare

Military retirees who are covered by the TRICARE for life program have an easy choice when it comes to prescription drug programs. They are not required to obtain a Medicare prescription drug program and will suffer no penalty if they do not enroll. And they should not enroll because the prescription drug benefits they receive through the TRICARE for life program that were negotiated by the federal government with the drug companies are better than any of those in the Medicare prescription drug plans.

Things to Consider When Choosing a Drug Plan

When deciding on a particular program, consider the following:

- Amount of the premium.
- Amount of the deductible. Does the total cost of the prescription drugs you take at least equal the deductible amount plus a year's worth of premium payments?
- Amount of the copayment.
- Does the plan cover the costs of prescription drugs in the donut hole?
- Does the plan's formulary include the particular drugs you need? Also, pay close attention to the strength and dosages of the drugs and the number of days covered in each prescription.
- Are the pharmacies you presently use in the plan's network of pharmacies?
- Is mail order allowed or required? What are the prices for mail order? How many days' worth of your prescription can you get by mail at a single time?
- Does the plan require step therapy, by which you must try other drugs before you are allowed to take the one prescribed by your physician?
- Does the plan use tiered cost sharing, requiring different copayments for generics and brand-name drugs?

- Are there quantity limitations on the number of prescriptions in a month or the number of pills in a prescription?
- Who sponsors the plan? Are they reliable? Are they experienced?
- What are the plan's rules for temporarily providing you with prescription drugs that are not covered by the plan during a transition period? How long is the transition period?
- Do you have creditable coverage through employment or the VA so that you do not need to consider a Medicare prescription drug plan?

Don't Give Up the SHIP

Medicaid recipients who don't have a computer are at a distinct disadvantage when choosing among the available programs. But, don't give up the ship. Throughout the country, there are more than a thousand State Health Insurance and Assistance Program offices (known by the acronym SHIP) that can help people compare plans. The SHIP program sometimes goes by different names in different states. In Massachusetts, the SHIP program is called SHINE, which stands for Serving Health Information Needs for Elder. If you need to access one of the SHIPs, so it does not pass you in the night, go to www.medicareoutreach.org.

Medicare Home Healthcare

With the majority of Medicare recipients living at home, home healthcare is a critical, if often misunderstood, aspect of Medicare. It has been estimated by the Kaiser Family Foundation that 44 percent of Medicare recipients have at least three chronic conditions.

Home healthcare services are available through Medicare A and B without the necessity of any copayments by the Medicare recipient. Home health services are available to people who require care following discharge from a hospital or who have chronic condition that require continuing, but intermittent care if their physician certifies that the "reasonable and necessary" services are required. To qualify for home healthcare, a patient care plan based on a doctor's orders is required.

A primary condition of Medicare coverage is that the patient be homebound, which does not mean that they be bedridden, although the illness or injury must limit their ability to leave their home. A Medicare beneficiary who is able to leave his or her home through the use of a wheelchair, a walker, or special transportation will still be considered to be homebound and thereby qualify for Medicare home healthcare services, so long as the absences from the home do not occur often and are for relatively short duration, as where leaving the home to receive healthcare services.

Home Healthcare Services Provided

Medicare provides a variety of home healthcare services, including the following:

- Physical therapy
- Speech therapy
- Home health aide services
- Medical supplies
- Skilled nursing care on an intermittent or part-time basis that are reasonable and necessary for the treatment of disease or injury

For Medicare purposes, *intermittent* is defined as

...skilled nursing care that is either provided or needed on fewer than 7 days each week, or less than 8 hours each day for periods of 21 days or less (with extensions in exceptional circumstances when the need for additional care is finite and predictable).

Medicare home healthcare services do not cover the following:

- Prescription drugs (although this will be covered through a Medicare Plan D program). However, the services of a nurse to administer such medications may be covered as reasonable and necessary.

- Transportation.
- Housekeeping services.
- Prosthetic devices.
- Administration of routine oral medications.
- Basic skin care.
- Assistance in dressing, eating, and personal hygiene. However, the services of a certified home health aide providing bathing, dressing, grooming, hair care, nail care, and oral hygiene required to facilitate treatment or prevent deterioration of the Medicare recipient's health may be covered.

Post-Hospital Home Healthcare

When a Medicare recipient returns home after at least a three-day hospitalization, he or she may be eligible for up to 100 visits during what Medicare colorfully calls a "spell of illness" through Medicare Part A. The home healthcare services are required to commence within 14 days of being discharged from the hospital; however, if the home-care services do not commence within that time period, they still may be financed through Medicare Part B.

Hospice Care

If your doctor indicates that you have a terminal illness and are expected to live no more than six months, you can qualify for hospice care. There is no cost to you for hospice care; however, there is a copayment of up to $5 per prescription for drugs to reduce pain and manage symptoms. Hospice care may be provided in your home or in a facility where you reside, such as a nursing home. Among the services to be provided through hospice care are the following:

- Medical services
- Nursing services

- Counseling services for not just the patient, but members of his or her family
- Home health aides
- Homemaker services
- Durable medical equipment

Another important part of hospice care paid for by Medicare is respite care, which is when you are cared for at home by a family member, and the caregiving family member needs a break. In this instance, Medicare covers the cost of your stay in a residential facility for up to five days at a time to give your caregiver some needed time for rest and restoration. There is a 5 percent Medicare approved amount that you pay for inpatient respite care.

Premiums

Medicare A is financed through Social Security taxes paid by workers and their employers. If you have worked for at least 10 years in Medicare-covered employment, you do not need to pay a monthly premium for Medicare A coverage. People who worked in Medicare-covered employment for between 30 and 39 quarters of Social Security coverage may receive Medicare A coverage by paying a premium of $248 per month in 2012. Workers with 29 or fewer quarters of Social Security coverage in Medicare-covered employment can receive Medicare A coverage by paying a premium of $451 per month in 2012. Medicare B monthly premiums range between $99.90 per month and 319.70 per month, depending on your income. This amount is adjusted annually, so for the most up-to-date figures, go to www.medicare.gov.

Medicare C premiums vary greatly depending on the particular plan.

Medicare D premiums vary considerably from plan to plan. However, as with the premiums for Medicare D, there is an adjustment to the premium, which—for all but low-income people—can range from $11.60 per month to $66.40 per month. For the latest information and more details, go to www.medicare.gov.

Enrollment

If you are already receiving Social Security benefits, you do not have to do anything to enroll in Medicare A and B. You will be automatically signed up as of the month you turn 65. At that time, you can opt out of Medicare B coverage. There are possible serious consequences to doing so, however, because for every 12 months that you would have been eligible for Medicare B but did not choose it, the cost of your premium goes up by 10 percent. So, if you waited three years to enroll in Medicare B, your premium would be 30 percent higher than the amount you would have initially paid.

Loophole

The increase of premium for people who delay enrolling in Medicare B does not apply if you have group health-plan coverage through employment.

If you do choose not to enroll in Medicare B when you first become eligible, the earliest you can sign up for it is during the next General Enrollment Period, which runs from January 1 through March 31 of each year.

Loophole

If you did not enroll in Medicare B because you were working and covered by group health insurance at the time you enrolled in Medicare A, you can sign up for Medicare B coverage during a Special Enrollment Period at any time you are covered by your group health insurance plan at work. You also can enroll in Medicare B for up to eight months from the time your employment or group health insurance coverage at work ends.

If you are nearing 65 and not yet receiving Social Security benefits or Medicare, you can apply for both together. To prevent your Medicare B initial coverage date from being delayed, you should apply at least three months before you turn 65.

If you are almost 65 and not yet receiving Social Security benefits or Medicare, you may also apply just for Medicare if you want to delay receiving your Social Security benefits. Again, it is important that you apply three months before you turn 65 to ensure that your coverage starting date will not be delayed.

Medicare D

Medicare D is the prescription drug coverage available to all Medicare enrollees.

Picking vanilla or chocolate is a fairly simple choice.

Medigap Insurance

The cost of the various deductibles, coinsurance, and copayments can quickly add up to a tidy sum or a messy amount, but regardless of how you characterize it, it represents a lot of money. Meeting the need for additional insurance coverage to pay for those potentially large costs are insurance policies commonly called "Medigap" insurance policies.

Largely due to legislation passed in 1992, Medigap policies were standardized into ten types of policies, which are presently designated by the letters of the alphabet A, B, C, D, F, G, K, L, and M, which look like they were designated by someone who flunked his or her field sobriety alphabet test. The A policies are the most rudimentary, and the N policies are the ones with all the bells and whistles. As you would imagine, the premiums for the policies also increase as you go up the alphabet. The plans offer varying combinations of benefits that permit consumers to pick the policy that is most appropriate for them. For example, some plans will provide emergency care in a foreign country, other plans cover the cost of certain preventive medical care, Plan N pays the entire Part B coinsurance payment, except for a minor copayment for some office visits and a minor copayment for emergency-room visits that don't result in your being admitted to the hospital.

It is also important to note that Plans D and G sold today provide different benefits than those D and G plans purchased before June 1, 2010. Plans E, H, I, and J are no longer sold, but if you already have one, you are permitted to keep it.

As you can see, picking the policy with just the right combination of coverages for you might appear to be an overwhelming task. However, the Medicare website www.medicare.gov has a section that provides tremendous interactive assistance in choosing a Medigap policy. That section can reduce the task of picking a Medigap policy from overwhelming to merely "whelming," which if it is not a word, certainly should be.

Loophole

Regardless of your health history, you cannot be denied a Medigap policy by the insurance company offering the policy if you apply for the policy within six months of the first day of the month in which you turn 65 or the date you enroll in Medicare B, whichever is later. So, if you are prompt in applying for a Medigap policy, you do not have to meet any medical underwriting standards. The insurance company can neither refuse to issue you a policy nor make you pay a higher premium due to your present health problems if you apply in a timely fashion.

It is important to note that not all present Medigap plan packages are offered in every state.

Traditional Medicare or Medicare Advantage?

An important decision is whether to stay with traditional Medicare coverage or change to one of the new Medicare Advantage plans. Prior to the passage of the Affordable Care Act (sometimes referred to as Obama Care), it was clear that the government wanted to encourage people to switch. How do we know that? It's easy. The federal government was giving billions of dollars to insurance companies to set up these new plans and lure Americans to them in the hope of reducing the cost and increasing the efficiency of the healthcare system.

Although Medicare was opened to private plans 40 years ago with the hope that private insurers would be able to provide benefits in a more cost-effective manner, enrollment in what we now call Medicare Advantage programs did not start to surge until 2006, when the Medicare prescription drug program became effective. Presently, about 27 percent of Medicare enrollees are covered by a Medicare Advantage plan.

In order to be authorized to participate in the Medicare Advantage program, insurers must submit bids to the federal government. The average bid for PPOs are higher than cost of traditional Medicare while the bids of HMOS generally have come in less. Not surprisingly, most people who participate in Medicare Advantage do so through an HMO. However, the future of Medicare Advantage is far from easy to predict because under the Affordable Healthcare Act the subsidies that previously had been paid to insurers as an incentive to get involved in Medicare Advantage have been slashed.

Traditional Medicare has a cost advantage because the federal government has been able to negotiate lower rates from physicians and hospitals than insurance companies have been able to do to date. In addition, many people are attracted to the choice provisions that are at the core of traditional Medicare.

On the other hand, private insurers may well be up to the task and could well be competitive with traditional Medicare even with their subsidies gone. Despite their restrictions of choice, HMOs have been attractive particularly to relatively healthy seniors who are attracted to the lower cost and the fact that their plans generally cover their prescription drugs as well so that they do not have to get an additional plan just for their prescriptions.

Appeals

The initial notice that a Medicare recipient receives informing him or her that payment is being denied by the insurance company is by way of a form misnamed an "Explanation of Medicare Benefits." This form is misnamed because it does not provide much of an explanation. It is often extremely difficult to comprehend and may not even provide a clear explanation as to the specific reason for the denial.

For a while, it seemed everyone was parroting Regis Philbin's oft-repeated line from the original version of *Who Wants to Be a Millionaire?*: "Is that your final answer?" When it comes to denials of Medicare coverage, it may make sense to repeat that sentence again. Decisions as to coverage of particular medical treatments may be denied as not being "medically and reasonably necessary." Appeals of coverage decisions of the insurance companies managing Medicare or the decisions of physicians who make up "peer review organizations" to determine care decisions in hospitals are something that can be done quite successfully. Although few people actually appeal denials of care, the Office of the Inspector General (OIGG) figures for the years between 2008 and 2010 showed that between 50 and 75 percent of appeals of claim denials were resolved in the appealing patients' favor.

One reason that so many appeals by Medicare recipients are successful is that a common basis for the initial denial is a miscoding that occurs when the insurance forms are filled in either by the insurance company or the medical care provider. Every medical procedure has a coded designation used by the insurance companies called a CPT (Current Procedure Terminology) initially developed by the American Medical Association. A number of different factors go into the determination of the proper code. A simple typographical error can result in a medical procedure that would be covered by Medicare being identified as a procedure that would not be covered.

Loophole

Even if you lose an appeal, you may be able to avoid having to pay for the care received for which you sought Medicare coverage if you can show that you did not know or could not have been expected to know that Medicare coverage would be denied. In that case, you may be given a "waiver of liability" absolving you of any financial responsibility.

Endnote

1. Medicare chapter by Diane F. Paulson in *Estate Planning for the Aging or Incapacitated Client in Massachusetts*, published by MCLE, 2002.

13 ————————————————

Medicaid

Medicaid is the only public benefits program that pays for the cost of long-term care in a nursing home. It was never intended by Congress when it was first passed to be the primary provider of the cost of nursing-home care for so much of the elder population, but the combination of more and more people living to older ages and the costs of nursing-home care increasing so much has contributed to Medicaid's prominence for many older Americans.

Over the last 20 years, there have been many changes in the Medicaid program, done more, it would appear, in an effort to reduce costs than to increase the effectiveness of the care provided. In particular, Congress passed the 1996 Kennedy-Kassenbaum law. This law originally contained a provision that made it a crime for lawyers to advise clients about perfectly legal efforts that could be taken to deal with assets in order to make their clients eligible for Medicaid benefits. This provision of the law was challenged and found to be unconstitutional, but it still reflects the thinking of many in Congress, which is to avoid the massive, creative reform that is needed to meet the cost for long-term care in nursing homes in America and instead focus on how a flawed Medicaid program can keep its costs down.

It has been said that change is the only constant. Nowhere is that proverb truer than in the case of Medicaid. The rules regulating Medicaid continue to change approximately every seven to ten years. In 1986, 1993, and 2006, major changes were made in the Medicaid laws, making Medicaid planning by individuals a difficult task.

In 2005, the House of Representatives voted 212-206 to approve the Deficit Reduction Act (DRA) that made drastic changes to Medicaid. Two days later, the Senate approved the bill by a vote of 51 to

50; Vice President Dick Cheney cast the tie-breaking vote. At that time, however, senators who opposed the bill managed to make minor changes to the bill that sent it back to the House for another vote before it could become law; that gave opponents of the bill time to lobby against its passage. On the second go-round through the House of Representatives, the vote was even closer, 216-214, but the result was the same. The vote was primarily along party lines, with Republicans supporting the bill and Democrats opposing the bill. However, 13 Republicans voted against the DRA in its second vote in the House. On February 8, 2006, President Bush signed the Deficit Reduction Act of 2005 into law.

Much of the impetus for the Medicaid provisions of the DRA was the widely held belief that tightening of the Medicaid rules and regulations was required because of large numbers of "Medicaid millionaires," people with large amounts of assets who took advantage of the then present rules to give away their assets to family members and then apply for Medicaid to pay for their long-term care needs. This belief was not based in fact, and Congress did not wait for the facts before passing the DRA into law; however, some opponents of the DRA inserted into the law a requirement that the Government Accountability Office (GAO)—an arm of the government that does unbiased, non-partisan studies for Congress—do a study as to whether this belief about Medicaid millionaires was indeed grounded in fact. In 2007, the GAO issued its report, and it found that the perception as to Medicaid millionaires was totally false. In fact, it found "that nursing-home residents covered by Medicaid had fewer nonhousing resources and lower annual incomes, and were less likely to have reported transferring cash than non-Medicaid-covered nursing home residents." So, what Congress achieved with the DRA was to solve a problem that didn't exist and to make it more difficult and more costly for people who legitimately needed Medicaid to apply for it.

Until the day that Congress finally deals with this issue in a manner that recognizes the serious and compelling needs of the aging American population for affordable long-term care, Medicaid is the only effective option for many people who require long-term care in a nursing home and wish to avoid totally depleting the assets for which they have worked a lifetime.

Medicaid 101

Medicaid is a joint state and federal program that provides payment of the costs of long-term nursing-home care. Among the states, there are considerable differences in how Medicaid operates. A few states, such as Alaska, California, New Mexico, Oregon, Washington, and, most notably, New York, have commendably taken the lead in providing significant benefits for home healthcare. In the great majority of the states, if you might be able to stay in your home with home healthcare provided at a cost that would generally be less than the cost of institutionalization, you could still find yourself having to go to a nursing home because sufficient funds are unavailable through Medicaid to pay for the cost of receiving healthcare in your own home.

Asset Eligibility

Medicaid is a needs-based program, which means that to qualify for benefit payments, you must meet certain financial standards. The federal government sets eligibility guidelines, which then, in many instances, can be modified by the individual states as they operate Medicaid within their own borders. The information provided here is based on the federal guidelines. Individual variations of these rules occur from state to state.

Under Medicaid, a nursing-home resident is permitted to have no more than $2,000 worth of "countable assets." In determining eligibility for Medicaid benefits for long-term care, the assets of both husband and wife are considered if either or both of them require nursing-home care through Medicaid. The terms "countable" and "noncountable" assets are defined within the laws and regulations that govern the Medicaid program. In some states, IRA accounts are considered countable assets, whereas in others, they are noncountable. Noncountable assets include personal possessions, such as clothing, furniture, a television set, and jewelry. Ever on the lookout for loopholes, in a famous Massachusetts case, a nursing-home resident bought a large diamond ring in an unsuccessful effort to convert countable assets (money) to a noncountable asset (jewelry). It was ruled, and rightly so, that this was an improper abuse of the rules.

A car is also a noncountable asset, regardless of its value, if it is used for transportation for the nursing-home resident or a member of his or her family.

The home is generally considered a noncountable asset for determining Medicaid eligibility. The DRA put a limitation on the amount of the equity you may have in a home and still qualify for Medicaid. The states may choose from between $525,000 and $786,000 in determining the maximum amount of home equity a Medicaid applicant may have and still qualify for Medicaid. Some states also require you, the nursing-home resident, to be able to prove that you have a reasonable likelihood of eventually returning to your own home. In the Bible, it says that "The Lord giveth and the Lord taketh away." The Medicaid version of this is that "Medicaid alloweth and Medicaid taketh away." This policy is because, although in most instances, your home will not be a disqualifying asset for Medicaid eligibility purposes, the state will put a lien on the home and, following your death and that of your spouse, who may have lived in the home, the state will generally look to the home for the repayment of every penny paid by Medicaid for your long-term nursing-home care. In many instances, this policy can result in the home being lost to the next generation. I discuss this in more detail later in this chapter.

Also noncountable are prepaid funeral arrangements or small amounts of life insurance designated for use for funeral or burial costs. Because these are things for which money eventually must be spent in any event, many people seeking to reduce the size of their countable assets to qualify for Medicaid benefits will, at the time they apply for Medicaid, set up such prepaid funeral arrangements.

Income-producing property, such as a family farm or interest in a family-owned business, that is used for the self-support of the Medicaid applicant is also noncountable.

Assets that are considered to be, in the terminology of Medicaid, "inaccessible" are also not counted in determining Medicaid eligibility. An example of an inaccessible asset is a piece of inherited real estate that you, the Medicaid applicant, co-own with many joint owners and for which there is no ready market for you to sell your interest.

The spouse of a nursing-home resident applying for Medicaid benefits is allowed to keep a limited amount of the countable assets to support himself or herself. For the year 2012, the year in which this book was written, the maximum amount of countable assets that the community spouse may keep is $113,640. The minimum amount of countable assets that the community spouse may keep in 2012 was $22,728. These figures will change from year to year. To see what the most current figures are, go to the appropriate websites as indicated in "Favorite Websites." Many states allow the community spouse to keep all the countable assets up to a maximum amount of $113,640, while other less generous states permit the community spouse to keep a maximum of one-half of the couple's total assets (up to a maximum of $113,640). These figures are adjusted annually to reflect inflation for people filing applications in future years.

The amount of countable assets that the community spouse is permitted to keep is based on a resource assessment of the assets as they existed on the day that the institutionalized spouse went into the nursing home. This assessment is known as the "snapshot."

The total of both solely owned and jointly owned assets of a couple is considered at the time of determination of Medicaid eligibility, even where only one of them is in a nursing home. Once Medicaid eligibility has been determined, the couple is, for most purposes, considered by Medicaid to be financially separate, such that the community spouse is no longer responsible for the payment of the nursing-home costs of the institutionalized spouse, regardless of how much the assets of the community spouse may increase. In fact, you could win the lottery a few months after your spouse was accepted for Medicaid without affecting your spouse's continuing eligibility for Medicaid benefits.

Life Insurance

Life insurance presents special considerations for families facing a Medicaid nursing-home stay. Cash value life insurance is a countable asset. For policies insuring the life of a nursing-home resident, it often makes sense to cash in the policy and give that money to the community spouse or spend it down. For life insurance on the life of the community spouse, it is important to remember to change the beneficiary of the policy so that if the community spouse dies before the spouse in the nursing home, the policy proceeds are not paid to the spouse in the nursing home. Failing to change the beneficiary to other family members, for example, gives the spouse in the nursing home the life insurance proceeds from the policy and makes him or her ineligible for further Medicaid coverage until the full amount of the life insurance proceeds were spent on the care of the spouse in the nursing home.

Often, it is not advantageous to cash in the policy, so another option is to borrow the cash value of the policy from the life insurance company so that the cash value of the policy for Medicaid purposes is so small or even reduced to nothing. This strategy enables the family to save the difference between the cash value of the policy and the death benefit.

Another possible use of a small life insurance policy is to have it designated for use to cover payments for funeral costs.

Retirement Planning

As with life insurance, making sure that the beneficiary designations are in order is of prime importance. This saves funds from being lost if the spouse in the nursing home inherits the retirement account of the community spouse in the nursing home, and it provides for future tax deferral under the minimum distribution rules described in Chapter 7, "Individual Retirement Accounts and 401(k)s."

Transfer Penalty

Under Medicaid law, there is a period of ineligibility for a person who gives away assets to reduce holdings to a Medicaid-eligible level. Before the enactment of the Deficit Reduction Act, when a person applied for Medicaid, the state determined whether that person made gifts or other transfers of assets within the previous 36 months and then set the appropriate disqualification. For certain kinds of trusts, the look-back period was 60 months, as a further disincentive to using these trusts that in the past had been used successfully to shelter substantial assets.

The specific period of Medicaid disqualification prior to the enactment of the Deficit Reduction Act was determined by going back to the date of the gift and dividing the amount of the gift by the particular state's average monthly private-pay rate, as determined by the Medicaid authority in that particular state. For example, in Massachusetts, where the private pay rate was $8,370 per month in 2012, if a person gave away $83,700, he or she would have had a 10-month disqualification period that would start at the time of the gift before he or she would be eligible for Medicaid benefits.

But, this changed dramatically following the enactment of the deficit Reduction Act. Now, the look-back period has been made a consistent five years instead of the rule of three years for some transfers and five years for others. But, more significantly is the change in the start of the penalty period resulting from any transfers. Now, the penalty period does not even start to run until the Medicaid applicant is in the nursing home and has run out of money and is eligible for Medicaid.

Extending the look-back period to five years and changing the date of the start of the disqualification period for gifts carries a potentially devastating effect for older people who made customary gifts to children or grandchildren for tuition, birthdays, or weddings as long as five years ago when they were healthy, but who now find themselves having to go to a nursing home at a time when the law may characterize those gifts as being impermissible transfers. Even gifts made less than five years earlier to charities or religious institutions could be considered impermissible transfers for a person now entering a nursing home who needs Medicaid coverage. The Deficit Reduction Act in effect seems to require older Americans to be sure that they have funds to cover the cost of five years in a nursing home before making any kind of gifts. With the average cost of a nursing home for a semi-private room at $73,000 per year (and more in many states), this is a tremendous burden for most people.

Exceptions to Transfer Penalties

Not all gifts of assets are subject to the transfer penalty. The primary exception is for gifts to the spouse of the nursing home resident, although other than gifts of the marital home, such gifts would still be counted in determining Medicaid eligibility because both solely owned and jointly owned assets are considered in determining Medicaid eligibility. However, it still makes a great deal of sense to transfer the home, which may be in both names, to the name of the community spouse. Not only can that transfer be made without a penalty, but it also will prevent the home from having a lien placed upon it by the state for repayment at the death of both spouses.

The home may also be given away without penalty to a brother or sister who is a co-owner of the home with the nursing home resident, and who has lived in the home for the year before the nursing home resident entered the nursing home. Another exception from the transfer penalty is when the home is given to a "caretaker child" who has lived in the home, taking care of the parent for at least two years before the parent goes to a nursing home.

People who think they are being amazingly clever sometimes attempt to get around the transfer disqualification by trying to "sell" their home to their children for a dollar. This, they argue with a straight face, is a sale and not a gift. This kind of thinking reminds me of the old saying, "Never try to teach a pig to sing. It is a waste of your time, and it really annoys the pig." Frankly, to attempt to disguise such a gift as a sale is futile and probably insulting to the state Medicaid workers. Credit them with more intelligence. Anyone who would attempt to characterize such a gift as a sale would find that a disqualification period would be calculated by determining the fair market value of the property, deducting the amount of the money paid ($1 in this example) and calculating the disqualification period based upon the difference.

Home Improvement

Home Improvement is not just the name of Tim Allen's popular sitcom that, between 1991 and 1999, never ranked out of the top 10 television shows. It also represents another opportunity for spending down money in a way that can have a direct benefit to the community spouse and ultimately the rest of the family of the institutionalized senior seeking Medicaid coverage for nursing home costs. Many older people have lived in their homes for a long time. Often, those homes are in dire need of repairs, updates, or improvements. Home improvements are a good way to spend down money to make the senior eligible for Medicaid while improving the value of a noncountable asset—the home.

Consideration of Income

To qualify for Medicaid payments, your income minus certain allowable deductions must be paid to the nursing home to contribute to the cost of your care. The state, however, allows nursing home residents to keep a specific amount of their monthly income as a "personal needs allowance." This amount varies from state to state. In addition, deductions from the amount that would otherwise go to the nursing home are allowed for payment of medical insurance premiums, uncovered medical costs and an amount, if necessary, to supplement the income of the community spouse if there is one. Some states, known as "income cap states," limit the amount of income that a person can have and still be eligible for Medicaid. In 2012, for example, that monthly amount is $2,094. However, people with income in excess of this amount may still qualify for Medicaid through the use of trusts that ensure the state will get any excess income.

Protection from Spousal Impoverishment

Although the assets of both a husband and wife are considered in determining eligibility for Medicaid benefits to pay for long-term care in a nursing home, only one spouse might reside in the nursing home while the other remains at home in the community. Medicaid shows some concern for the economic well-being of the community spouse. In response to this concern, the law provides for a Minimum Monthly Maintenance Needs Allowance, which is adjusted annually in accordance with federal poverty figures. As of January 1, 2012, the Minimum Monthly Maintenance Needs Allowance (MMMNA) was $1,838.75 (except in Alaska, where the MMMNA was $2,297.50, and Hawaii, where the MMMNA was $2,116.25). If the community spouse's own income is less than this, Medicaid will permit the community spouse to either take a sufficient amount of the income from the nursing-home resident spouse to reach this level or permit the community spouse, in order to generate further income, to keep a greater amount of assets than otherwise would have to be spent down to reach allowable levels for Medicaid eligibility.

The law provides for the Minimum Monthly Maintenance Needs Allowance to be increased to a Maximum Monthly Maintenance Needs Allowance, which in 2012 was set at $2,841 if the community spouse can show that housing costs require the additional money.

In exceptional cases of extreme hardship, the community spouse is entitled to an administrative hearing at which he or she can request an even larger monthly needs allowance. All Medicaid administrative hearings are called "Fair Hearings," which makes one wonder why when these regulations were written, it was thought necessary to qualify the word "hearing" by the word "fair." The civil courts are not called the "Fair Civil Courts" and the criminal courts are not called the "Fair Criminal Courts." Is not fairness something we assume?

In determining whether the income shortfall of the community spouse will be made up by a larger part of the income of the nursing home resident or by permitting the community spouse to keep a larger amount of assets, some states follow what is called the "income-first rule." This rule requires, as the name implies, that the community spouse first turn to the income of the nursing-home-resident spouse before seeking an additional asset allowance. The constitutionality of this rule was upheld in a 2002 decision of the United States Supreme Court involving the state of Wisconsin's income-first rule. The argument for "assets first" is that the amount of the income that will go to the nursing home is increased because less is deducted from the income of the nursing home resident, which would also reduce the amount that the state would be required to pay monthly. A concern is that with "income first," if the nursing-home-resident spouse were to predecease the community spouse, the surviving spouse might receive reduced Social Security benefit payments and might lose all or a significant part of any pension being received by the nursing-home-resident spouse. Despite this concern, many states continue to follow the income-first rule.

How Much Do You Pay?

A nursing-home resident who has been approved for Medicaid coverage still must contribute most of his own income toward the cost of his or her care in the nursing home. Any pension, Social Security retirement payments, or other income must be paid to the nursing home after deducting a small amount as a monthly personal needs allowance (typically around $72 per month in most states), the cost of uncovered medical costs (including medical insurance premiums) and for married nursing-home residents, an allowance for at-home spouses if they need the money.

Increasing the Allowance for At-Home Spouses

If a community spouse does not have enough money to meet his or her support needs, the law provides in certain circumstances for increased financial assistance to the community spouse in two ways. First, the community spouse could receive some of the income of the institutionalized spouse, such as Social Security or pension benefits, that would otherwise be a part of the institutionalized spouse's patient pay amount (PPA) that would go to the nursing home. Second, as an alternative, the community spouse could keep a greater amount of countable assets to generate the additional income necessary to meet his or her living expenses.

Consider this example the Government Accountability Office (GAO) gave in its 2005 report titled, "Medicaid—Transfers of Assets by Elderly Individuals to Obtain Long Term Care Coverage." A community spouse may be permitted to keep a savings account that earns 2 percent interest annually, resulting in an additional $500 of income that can be used for the community spouse's living expenses. Under the present law, a Medicaid recipient's income must be used first to meet the community spouse's increased needs before a community spouse is permitted to keep more assets than otherwise would be allowed by law.

However, it is important to note that Medicaid requires that the institutionalized spouse's income be used first before the community spouse is allowed to keep a greater amount of countable assets. Although this might not seem, at first blush, to be significant, it can be a critical distinction. Although the income-first rule may allow income of the institutionalized spouse to go to the community spouse, that income may be based on a pension or other income source that terminates at the death of the institutionalized spouse leaving the community spouse, if he or she survives the institutionalized spouse in dire financial straits without enough money to get by. If a greater amount of income earning assets had initially been allowed to be kept by the community spouse to maintain his or her living expenses, he or she would not be in a worse financial position at the death of the institutionalized spouse.

Medicaid Planning

Because of the high cost of nursing-home care, more and more people are doing special estate and financial planning to become eligible for Medicaid coverage of long-term care in a nursing home. This is an area where ignorance of the law is punished severely. People who are aware of the many legitimate planning opportunities that the law provides can protect all or significant portions of their assets, whereas people who are unaware of these "loopholes" will lose assets that they legally could have kept. Medicaid, like the IRS, will generally not tell you what to do to protect your assets. The earlier you plan, the more options are available to you for protecting your assets. However, it is never too late to do effective planning. Even after someone is already in a nursing home, there are, as you will see as you read on, things you can do to protect your assets.

There is nothing illegal, immoral, unethical, or fattening about Medicaid planning, but the decision of whether to take advantage of the laws that permit such planning is one that each family must make for itself.

Many in Congress and the state legislatures are concerned about the effect of Medicaid planning on the costs incurred by both the federal government and state governments, and this is a legitimate concern. Their emphasis too often seems to be on doing what is necessary to reduce the number of people who are receiving Medicaid assistance for their long-term care needs. However, others have focused their interest less on reducing the number of people who must impoverish themselves to qualify for Medicaid and more on the larger question of how to deal in a societal way with the growing long-term care needs of an aging population.

Medicaid's rules are constantly changing. Sometimes, even when the rule has not officially changed, Medicaid changes its interpretation of the law. It is important to remember that Medicaid, again like the IRS, goes by its special version of the "Golden Rule," which is that it has the gold, so it makes the rules. It is also important to remember that because Medicaid is a joint federal-state program, the individual states may and do have laws and rules that differ greatly. Some techniques used in Medicaid planning will work well in one state, but not another. Anyone considering doing Medicaid planning needs to consult a lawyer experienced in this ever-changing area of the law. You can find a lawyer knowledgeable in this area of the law through the National Academy of Elder Law Attorneys at www.naela.org. What follows are alternatives that may be worth considering in Medicaid planning.

Looking for Loopholes

Early movie comedian and atheist W. C. Fields was in the hospital dying when a friend came to visit and noticed that Fields was reading the Bible. When the friend inquired why, Fields replied that he was "looking for loopholes." Fields died on Christmas Day 1946, a holiday this pre-Grinch Grinch was said to despise. But, looking for loopholes is a long and honored tradition for lawyers. Medicaid planning is an area of the law which lawyer have managed to find absolutely legal methods that allow their clients to avoid some of the more Draconian Medicaid rules and protect a small legacy for the families of their clients.

Just Say No

As I said earlier, the assets of both the husband and wife are generally considered in determining Medicaid eligibility, even if only one of them is going into a nursing home. But, what happens if your spouse does not cooperate with Medicaid when you apply for residency in a nursing home? If you have been living apart for many years without divorcing or if you don't know the whereabouts of your spouse, Medicaid qualification will not pose a problem, because under federal law, if a couple has separated for more than a month before a spouse goes into a nursing home, the absent spouse's income and assets are not considered in determining Medicaid eligibility for the person going into the nursing home.

In some states, particularly New York, as a way of protecting their own assets, community spouses often refuse to cooperate. They just say no. If you are in the situation of a non-cooperating spouse, the state steps into your shoes to request spousal support from the spouse living in the community. It varies even from county to county as to whether Medicaid will seek to obtain spousal support from a non-cooperating spouse. Even in states where this tactic is not specifically used, as a practical matter, the assets of a non-cooperating spouse can be determined to be inaccessible assets or considering those assets would cause an undue hardship, so the same end can be achieved.

Estate Planning for the Community Spouse

One of the first things you, the community spouse, should do is to review your own estate planning documents for necessary changes. It is common for a married person to name his or her spouse as the attorney-in-fact under a Durable Power of Attorney, healthcare agent under a Health Care Proxy, and personal representative under a will. If you have done that, you should have all these documents rewritten, removing your spouse from those designations.

In addition, you should have your will rewritten to achieve one of two purposes: to remove your spouse as a beneficiary or to shelter the assets going to your spouse. You do the latter through a special trust that will permit the funds to be used to supplement your spouse's needs without affecting his or her continued Medicaid eligibility. If you do not take one of these steps and die before your spouse dies, assets would pass to your spouse and make him or her ineligible for Medicaid because of excessive assets.

By the same token, you should also review the beneficiary designations on all life insurance policies, annuities, and retirement plans. Make sure that, should you die before your spouse dies, these assets do not pass directly to him or her. If they do, not only could the assets be dissipated, but more importantly, your spouse's continuing eligibility for Medicaid could be adversely affected.

Estate and Financial Planning for the Spouse in the Nursing Home

If your spouse in the nursing home is not mentally able to participate in his or her own estate and financial planning, you can participate for him or her as long as a specifically worded Durable Power of Attorney is in place. In the absence of a Durable Power of Attorney, you would have to go to court to be appointed as guardian for the nursing-home resident spouse in order to do the desired planning. To divest the nursing home resident of assets that would otherwise disqualify him or her from Medicaid eligibility, either the nursing-home resident spouse must be mentally capable of participating in the estate and financial planning or an appropriately written Durable Power of Attorney must already be in place. Obviously, it is much less costly and far less time consuming to be able to do the required planning through the use of a Durable Power of Attorney rather than having to be appointed by the court as a guardian.

Tactics for Reducing Assets Without a Medicaid Penalty

You can achieve Medicaid eligibility in a number of ways that reduce the amount of your countable assets without incurring a transfer penalty.

If you need personal property, such as a television or radio, buy it now. If you do not have a car and you are single, buy a car for no more than $4,500. If you are married and do not have a car, buy one for any reasonable price (no Rolls Royces or Bentleys, please). These items of personal property are noncountable, and there is no transfer penalty for using your assets to buy these.

If you are married and you do not own a home, you may want to consider buying a home and having the home owned in the name of the community spouse. There will be no transfer penalty, and whatever the cost of the home is, it will be sheltered both from consideration of the state in determining Medicaid eligibility and from the state trying to recover for Medicaid payments made on your behalf following the death of yourself and your spouse. You may want to consider buying a life estate interest in the home of one of your children where the community spouse will go to live. For more information about life estates, see Chapter 8, "Planning for the Home." Buying a life estate interest in the home of one of your children has these advantages: You can use money that would be countable and that you otherwise would be required to spend down to reach a level of assets sufficient for Medicaid eligibility; and you convert those funds without any disqualification period into a noncountable interest in a home. The life estate interest would enable the community spouse to live rent-free in the child's home, would protect the money from the state ever having a claim upon it, and would keep the money *All in the Family* (Oh, Archie).

If you have a home and are married, pay off your mortgage. Medicaid, unfortunately, like much of what our government does, is illogical. When the state considers your eligibility for Medicaid benefits, it does not consider your debts at all. It just considers your assets. So, if you have too many assets, pay off the mortgage and reduce the amount. Once you have been approved for Medicaid, the community spouse, if he or she needs the money, can take out a new mortgage, equity credit line, or even reverse mortgage to get access to the equity in the home.

Speaking of logical, why do so many of us continue to keep high balances on our credit cards that, despite every other interest rate at historically low levels, continue to charge, in many instances, exorbitant rates. If you need to reduce your countable assets, pay off the credit cards. Also, if you have a car loan, pay it off. Prepay your real estate taxes, homeowner's insurance, and car insurance. These are things you will have to pay eventually anyway, and Medicaid will allow you to reduce your countable assets by prepaying these debts for a "reasonable period of time."

Pay your lawyer and your accountant. They have their own bills. You have to pay these people eventually, so make your payment when doing so will reduce excess assets that would interfere with Medicaid eligibility.

Have your car fixed. It probably needs it, and every little bit helps.

Repair your home or make improvements to it. Pave the driveway, put on a new roof, paint the house, put on new siding. The list goes on and on. If the community spouse is living in the home, there is no problem in making any repairs or improvements to the home to reduce assets. If neither the Medicaid applicant nor his or her spouse is living in the home, you still may be able to shelter money by repairing or improving the home if you are renting the home and contributing the net rental profits toward the care of the nursing home resident.

Prepay a funeral for the Medicaid applicant and his or her spouse.

Loophole

Buy Series EE or Series 1 U.S. Savings Bonds, which are described in Chapter 5, "Investments." These bonds cannot be redeemed until six months after their purchase date. Buy them immediately before you go into the nursing home. The date used for evaluating the amount of assets that your spouse will be allowed to keep is not the date of the application, but rather the date you entered the nursing home. It is as of that date that the so-called snapshot of assets is taken to determine how much of your joint assets your spouse may keep regardless of how much later the Medicaid application is filed. Therefore, if you buy the bonds just before going into the nursing home, they will be inaccessible assets at the time the application is filed and therefore noncountable. Once the application is approved and six months have gone by since the bonds were purchased, your spouse is free to cash in the bonds. This tactic may not work in every state. Indiana, for example, specifically changed its laws to close this specific loophole.

Early Planning: Personal Care Contract

For early planning before going into a nursing home, you can make a Personal Care Contract with a family member to provide care for you. As you can well imagine, these contracts are strictly scrutinized by Medicaid, and some states are more likely to recognize them than others. In every state, however, Medicaid is skeptical of such contracts, taking the position that family members generally take care of other family members without being paid for doing so.

However, there is nothing inherently wrong with having such a contract. Let's face it. Taking care of an elderly family member is a time-consuming and difficult job. Although many people do not in any way regret doing that job, it does take away time from being able to do other things or even from other jobs. So, there is nothing wrong in having such an arrangement. Being paid for caretaker services is a legitimate way to be paid for the considerable work done in caring for a relative. It is also a legal way to shelter assets that would have to be spent down before the senior would become eligible for Medicaid.

It is critical that such an agreement be in the form of a written contract and that the contract should be executed fully before the caretaker child performs the services. Tax rules should also be adhered to strictly. Consulting an experienced elder law attorney is essential.

Too Late Planning: Divorce

Get a divorce, the ultimate "just say no." Generally, this is not a particularly good idea unless the couple was married in name only and had just never chosen, for whatever reasons, to get a legal divorce. The judge in a divorce case has the authority to order the division of pension benefits that can protect money for the spouse not going into a nursing home. The judge can also divide property in a manner that will preserve the assets for the spouse not going into the nursing home.

A provision in a premarital agreement might say that one of the partners going into a nursing home would result in all the assets going to the other spouse in a divorce. Such a provision would not be binding upon the judge, although the judge could independently make that determination.

There is always an element of risk involved with a divorce when one of the people is in a nursing home. The judge could choose a division of property that might be worse than what you could achieve by proper estate and financial planning on your own. A divorce court judge can order the transfers of assets to the community spouse such that the assets cannot be considered by Medicaid when determining the eligibility of the person going into the nursing home. It is a sad situation when aging couples are faced with the decision to divorce in order to have enough money for the community spouse to survive, but unfortunately this may occur more often under the present, more restrictive Medicaid laws.

Reverse Half a Loaf Giving

Although this particular Medicaid planning tactic is controversial, it still works in different variations in between half and two-third of the states. The essence of reverse half a loaf planning involves the elder making a gift to family members. This gift, if done within the five-year look-back period, will bring about a penalty period. Once the penalty period is determined, which is based on the amount of the gift, the elder will use the rest of his or her funds to buy a non-countable Medicaid annuity or loan the money through a promissory note to family members. The income from the annuity or the promissory note is, in turn, used to cover the nursing-home costs during the penalty period. Thus, the senior is able to save some of his or her money that otherwise would have to be spent down before he or she is eligible for Medicaid.

Trusts

Trusts formerly played a much more significant role in Medicaid planning. Thirty years ago, you could put your home into a simple Living Revocable Trust (explained in Chapter 4, "Estate Planning") and maintain control of your home while protecting it from the state's Medicaid lien upon your death and the later death of a spouse. People could also set up Irrevocable Trusts that would permit the trustee of their choosing to be able, in the trustee's discretion, to give whatever was in the trust in whatever amounts to the senior citizens who had set up the trust. As more and more people took advantage of what some considered to be loopholes in the law, Congress and the various states took steps to close those loopholes. To be effective for Medicaid purposes, trusts have so many limitations put on them by law that they are a good choice for fewer and fewer people.

In the Deficit Reduction Act (DRA) can be found provisions reflecting the opinion of many in Congress that trusts were being used widely for sheltering assets and preserving Medicaid eligibility. The new provisions make it more difficult to create and effectively use a Medicaid Qualifying Trust.

A good indication of Congress' distaste for trusts used for Medicaid planning is that the look-back period use to be longer for assets placed in a trust. Assets given away formerly carried a 36-month look-back period. Transfers accomplished through the use of a trust had a 60-month look-back period, a further disincentive from using this technique. Now, however, the Deficit Reduction Act has made all manners of transfers subject to a 60-month look-back period.

Under the current law, to be effective for Medicaid purposes, a trust you make must be irrevocable, which means that you cannot revoke, terminate, or change it. In addition, to shelter whatever assets you put into the trust from consideration in determining Medicaid eligibility when you apply, the trust must not allow payments to you from the trust's principal, that is, from any of the assets that you put into the trust. The only benefit that you may receive from the trust is the receipt of any income earned by the trust's assets. So, you can receive interest or dividends earned by the trust, but that is all.

You can, however, provide in the trust for the payment of principal, in such amounts as determined by your trustee, in his or her sole discretion, to your children or other people other than yourself or your spouse. You also should have a provision for the trust to be terminated by the trustee if the trustee determines that there is a change in the laws that would negate the purpose of the trust, which is to shelter and protect your assets from being counted in determining Medicaid eligibility. These provisions are important, because it would not be unusual for Congress or the states to change the rules again as to how trusts are considered. And if your trust was an irrevocable trust that could not be remedied to comply with new rules, you would be facing a serious situation.

Protecting the Home

In addition to the exempt transfers of giving your home to a community spouse, an equity-holding brother or sister, or a caretaker child, all as previously discussed, you also may want to protect your home by giving the home to your children with or without reserving a life estate. If you are planning early enough, the five-year look-back period should not pose a problem. At its essence, a life estate is an arrangement by which the elderly homeowner keeps the right to use and control his or her home throughout his or her lifetime. At death, the property passes automatically and outside of probate to the named individuals, who are called remaindermen. Some states fully recognize life estates while others do not. The advantage of retaining a life estate when you give away your home in those states that permit such a technique is that the value of what you are giving away when you retain a life estate is less than if you gave away a complete interest in the home. Therefore, there may be a disqualification of less than five years as a result of the gift. The reason is that when you retain a life estate interest, you are giving away an interest in the home to the people for whom the full benefit of the gift does not take effect until you die.

This putting off of possession of the property allows you to value what you are giving away in accordance with IRS charts based on your age at the time you make the gift. For example, if a person who is 75 years old gave away a life estate interest in his home, according to the IRS table, the value of the gift is only 43 percent of the value of the house. The savings would be increased even further if, as can be done in many states, the starting point for the home's valuation is not its fair market value, but rather the assessed value, which is often considerably lower.

In addition, if the home was given to children without the reservation of a life estate, the children's basis in the home for income tax purposes would be the cost of the home when the parent bought the home, with some minor adjustments. The children would incur a substantial income tax if they later sell the home.

For example, suppose you bought the home many years ago for $25,000. When you now give it to your children, it is worth $200,000. The tax basis for the children would be $25,000. If your children later sell the home for, say, $250,000, they would have to pay capital gains taxes on $225,000 ($250,000 minus $25,000). However, if you gave the children the home subject to your life estate, their tax basis when they receive full title to the property upon your death would be the stepped-up basis, which is the fair market value of the home at the time of your death. So, in our example, the $25,000 home valued at $200,000 when you gave a remainder interest to your children, reserving a life estate for yourself, is worth $250,000 when you die. If the children sell the home, then their basis for income tax purposes is $250,000, and they would not owe anything in income taxes on the sale.

In addition, a life estate can avoid probate and, during the lifetime of the nursing-home resident, provide income that can be used to pay a portion of the nursing home costs which would reduce the amount Medicaid pays to the nursing home.

The only thing that makes this in any way a difficult call for people in states where Medicaid permits the use of life estates is that there is no guarantee that the state will continue to do so. Congressional legislation specifically permits states to change their laws as to whether life estates will escape the claims of the state following the death of the life tenant.

Another creative way to use a life estate for Medicaid planning involves having an elderly parent buy a life estate in the home of one of his or her children. In this instance, the parent would pay for the right to live with the child in the child's home for the rest of his or her life. This technique will permit the elderly parent to shelter from Medicaid consideration the money used to pay the child for the life estate. An important condition of such an arrangement is that to be fully effective for Medicaid asset sheltering purposes, the parent must live in the home of the child for at least a year.

The Medicaid rules for life estates vary significantly from state to state, so make sure that you consult with an experienced elder law attorney to see whether this might be right for you or your parent or grandparent. A good place to find an elder law attorney is the website of the National Academy of Elder Law Attorneys (www.naela.org).

Loophole

A law permits the transfer of title without any disqualification period to a brother or sister who is a co-owner of the home and who has lived in the home for at least a year before the Medicaid applicant goes into a nursing home. The law has no required period for which the brother or sister must have been a co-owner before the home may be given to him or her. Therefore, it may be good planning to add a brother or sister to the title to your home if you are single and are living with that sibling. Or, if your sibling is not living with you, it may make financial sense to have him or her move in with you so that you can meet the requirement of how long he or she must have lived in the home before you go into a nursing home.

Another alternative for planning for the home when you do not have much time to plan is to sell the home to a family member. If you receive cash for the sale, the money you receive may serve to disqualify you from Medicaid eligibility, but if the payment is by way of a private annuity, which I will explain later, the value of the annuity, if properly structured, is noncountable and would allow you to protect the house.

If there is no community spouse, it still might make sense to keep the home and use the money to make the necessary repairs so that the home can be rented during the time that the elder is in a nursing home. This results in a win-win situation, because the profit that is derived from renting the home will be applied to the elder's nursing home costs and will correspondingly reduce the amount that Medicaid has to pay for the elder's nursing home costs. Further, if, through proper planning, ownership of the home is done in a manner that avoids the state's estate-recovery lien upon the death of the Medicaid recipient, the home will most likely be an asset that increases in value over time and is available as a legacy to the next generation.

The law only permits Medicaid applicants to protect a maximum home equity amount of $525,000 in some states; however, other states have increased the amount of the maximum home equity amount protection to as high as $786,000. The DRA leaves it up to the individual states to determine the amount that is protected within these parameters. Fortunately, if there is a community spouse still living in the home, excess equity will not disqualify the homeowner from Medicaid benefits.

Tips for the Home

When a husband and wife own their home together and one goes into a nursing home, the excessive home equity problem can be avoided by simply changing ownership of the home to just the community spouse. This tactic makes sense on many levels. It will not involve a gift tax. It will guarantee that the home's value will not harm the institutionalized spouse's eligibility for Medicaid benefits and, quite importantly, at the death of the institutionalized spouse, that state has no rights of estate recovery against the home. It is important for the community spouse to remember to change his or her will so that in the event that the community spouse predeceases the institutionalized spouse, the home will not pass to the institutionalized spouse and ultimately be subject to estate recovery.

Tactics for Increasing Assets to Achieve a Greater Spousal Resource Allowance

In some states, the amount of countable assets that a community spouse can keep is limited to one-half the assets to the maximum amount, set in 2012 of $113,640. In those states, couples with countable assets of less than $227,280 would be well served if they could find ways to increase their countable assets at the time the Medicaid snapshot is taken so as to keep more of their assets rather than spending them down to achieve eligibility.

It is important to remember that the critical date for determining how much of the countable assets the community spouse will be able to keep is the snapshot—the date when the institutionalized spouse first entered the nursing home, regardless of a later date on which a Medicaid application is filed. The snapshot date is the date that you want your countable assets to be at least $227,280 in order to keep the maximum amount of assets. Postpone paying your regular bills so that your accounts have as much money in them as possible. If you need to pay for something at that time, pay for it by credit card so that at the date of the snapshot, your assets are worth as much as you can make them. Remember, Medicaid is not interested in what you owe—only what you own. If you own a home, take out an equity credit line and take out enough money from the credit line to make your countable assets reach $227,280 at the time of the snapshot. Once the institutionalized spouse has been accepted for Medicaid, you can pay back the money you borrowed on the equity credit line. Of course, in those states that permit the community spouse to keep all the joint assets up to $113,640, it is not necessary to attempt to increase the assets over that amount prior to the time of the snapshot.

Annuities

Annuities are a helpful Medicaid planning tool in many states, although again, just as with trusts, as more people use annuities, we are finding more states placing limitations upon them. The laws governing the Medicaid use of annuities vary significantly from state to state. However, in most states they still present many planning opportunities.

As I said earlier, when someone gives assets away in order to qualify for Medicaid benefits, there is a disqualification period, the duration of which depends on the amount that is given away and the figure used by the particular state for the average cost of nursing home care in that state. However, certain kinds of annuities qualify as noncountable assets, so you can exchange what would otherwise be countable assets for a noncountable annuity, regardless of the amount and regardless of when it is done, without adversely affecting Medicaid eligibility.

Purchasing an annuity is not considered a disqualifying gift, but rather a proper exchange of countable assets for a noncountable asset. To qualify as an annuity, which will be a noncountable asset for Medicaid purposes, the annuity must be irrevocable, unassignable, and actuarially sound, with immediate payments to the community spouse. Irrevocable means that once the annuity has been purchased, it may not be cashed in during the lifetime of the community spouse. Unassignable means that ownership of the annuity may not be transferred to someone else. Actuarially sound means that its regular payments, which for Medicaid purposes cannot be delayed, must be based upon the life expectancy of the community spouse in accordance with IRS life expectancy charts.

Although the rules vary in some regards from state to state, the last-minute purchase of an annuity is an effective way for an elderly couple to protect assets for the community spouse without jeopardizing Medicaid eligibility for the spouse in the nursing home while turning countable assets into a noncountable asset.

Here's how this works: Other assets that are countable for determining Medicaid eligibility, such as stocks, bonds, or bank accounts, are cashed in. The money is used to purchase an annuity for the benefit of the community spouse that meets specific Medicaid requirements. When done properly, excess assets that would be countable and disqualifying for Medicaid purposes are converted into a stream of income for the community spouse that is not counted in determining the eligibility of the institutionalized spouse. Because converting the otherwise excess disqualifying assets into an annuity for the community spouse is properly considered the exchange of countable assets for a noncountable asset of equal value (the annuity), no gift is involved; therefore, there is no transfer penalty. For this reason, the purchase of an annuity for Medicaid purposes is not something that need be done, or should be done, long before applying for Medicaid.

Not all annuities qualify for Medicaid purposes. Specifically, such an annuity must be actuarially sound; that is, its payout must be based upon the age of the community spouse. In addition the annuity must be irrevocable and cannot have a life insurance component.

Much was made in the media of the provision of the Deficit Reduction Act that requires the state to be named as a beneficiary of the annuity, to be reimbursed at the death of the nursing home resident for whatever the state has paid on his or her behalf. However, many in the media overlooked the fact that that if the annuity is purchased for the benefit of the community spouse and not the spouse in the nursing home, the state is eligible only for reimbursement if the community spouse later requires Medicaid to cover his or her own nursing home costs. So, annuities can still work to save money, particularly for the community spouse.

As with all legislation, the Deficit Reduction Act appears to have loopholes. These loopholes might be able to be exploited to save assets for the elderly. However, anyone using the more aggressive techniques runs the risk of having the courts interpret the law in a way that closes the loophole. With that being said, it would appear that the law permits a person to give a portion of their money to their children and buy an annuity with their remaining money sufficient to cover their costs in a nursing home for the period of disqualification brought about by their gift to their children, thereby saving money for their family that would otherwise have to be spent on their care.

Commercial annuities are done by insurance companies, which in exchange for the payment of your premium, provide you with a steady stream of income. For more information about annuities, refer to Chapter 5.

Another way of avoiding the problem of the premature death of the community spouse as well as the very high sales commissions and fees that are involved with a commercial annuity is to have your attorney draft a private annuity. A private annuity is an annuity contract between the community spouse and a member of his or her family. Under the terms of a private annuity, the community spouse and the spouse residing in the nursing home transfer assets they have in excess of the amounts permitted by Medicaid to a family member. In return, they receive an actuarially sound annuity that makes regular payments to the community spouse. With a private annuity, there would be no need for a term-certain because if the community spouse were to die prematurely, the value of the annuity would pass automatically to the family member, who would be the most likely recipient of the community spouse's estate in any event.

Promissory Notes

Another technique that had been used effectively prior to the passage of the DRA and still remains a viable, if less advantageous, strategy is the transferring of property to a family member in return for a promissory note so that the transfer would not be considered a disqualifying gift. The DRA set forth three conditions that must be met in order for such transfers in return for a promissory note to be considered an uncountable asset. First, the term of the loan may not be longer than the life expectancy of the senior. Second, the payments must be made in regular equal amounts during the period of the promissory note; no deferrals of payments or balloon payment provisions are allowed. Third, the debt evidenced by the promissory note may not be cancelled at death. However, by effectively using this strategy, you can change the character of assets into a stream of income, thereby enhancing Medicaid eligibility.

Do Nothing Strategy

The primary choice of procrastinators everywhere is to do nothing. However, for exceptionally old or terminally ill homeowners facing a nursing home, it might be the better option than selling the home. As I indicated earlier, Medicaid pays nursing homes at a rate that is significantly less than the private pay rate throughout the states. The lien that Medicaid has on the home is for the cost of the care for which it has paid on behalf of the nursing home resident. Therefore, if faced with the choice of selling a home to get money to pay directly to the nursing home at the higher private pay rate, or keeping the home and applying for Medicaid and letting a lien be placed on their home for the lesser amount of the state's monthly Medicaid payments, the option of not doing anything and paying the state back through the sale of the home after the death of the home owning Medicaid recipient may be the choice that preserves the most assets for the family. The more likely that the nursing-home resident will not be in the nursing home for many years, the better this option becomes.

As if You Don't Have Enough to Worry About

Sometimes, what you don't know can hurt you. Many people are blissfully unaware that 30 states presently have laws that permit adult children to be held financially responsible for the support of their aging parents. It is not beyond the realm of possibility for the states to look toward the children of nursing-home residents to pay for the cost of their care when new, more restrictive Medicaid laws act to disqualify indigent elderly people from Medicaid coverage. These laws have been rarely, if ever, enforced and are of questionable constitutionality, but the bottom line is that in desperate times, the states might take desperate measures.

Partnership for Long-Term Care

An innovative program that, prior the enactment of the Deficit Reduction Act (DRA), was available only in California, Connecticut, Indiana, and New York, is the Partnership for Long-Term Care. This joint program between the private and public sectors helps pay the costs of long-term care while preserving some of the person's assets as a legacy to children and others. Until the 2006 effective date of the DRA, states other than those just named were not permitted to enact Partnership for Long-Term Care laws without adopting an estate recovery provision that effectively removed the attractiveness of the program. In the hope that Congress would change its mind on this valuable program, 16 states passed laws to set up Partnership for Long-Term Care programs if and when the federal laws were changed.

These efforts were rewarded when expansion of the Partnership for Long-Term Care was made a part of the DRA. A key provision of the DRA requires long-term care insurance policies to contain compound inflation protection for policyholders up to age 75 to qualify for the Partnership for Long-Term Care program. As discussed in Chapter 9, "Alternative Housing," inflation protection is an important option in a long-term care insurance policy.

Although the specific provision in the states that do have Partnership for Long-Term Care programs vary, under the Partnership for Long-Term Care, people involved in their state's plan can increase the amount of the assets that they are allowed to keep and still qualify for Medicaid. Usually, the amount that they are allowed to keep is equal to the amount of coverage provided by a long-term care insurance policy that they purchase privately. The New York program, for example, allows a participating individual to keep all of his or her assets if the person purchases a qualifying long-term care policy. Although an individual in a state that is not involved in the Partnership for Long-Term Care program is allowed to have only $2,000 worth of countable assets (not including the value of a home that has equity of no more than a minimum of $525,000 or a maximum of $786,000, as determined by the individual state) and still qualify for Medicaid, under the Partnership for Long-Term Care program, an individual buying a long-term care policy that provides $100,000 worth of benefits would be able to keep $100,000 of assets and still qualify for Medicaid. This provides a tremendous incentive to purchase long-term care policies. It also reduces the amount of taxpayer money that would be needed for Medicaid to pay for long-term care.

Obviously, this is not a solution for everyone. Some people will not be able to afford a long-term care policy and others might not qualify for long-term care policies because of health problems. However, for significant numbers of middle-class people seeking to find a way to pay for long-term care without going broke while preserving some sort of legacy for the next generation, this is an option worth considering.

Estate Recovery

Although the home of a Medicaid recipient is not a disqualifying asset in the determination of Medicaid eligibility, if the home is owned by the Medicaid recipient, the state will have a lien upon it, giving the state a claim at the death of the Medicaid recipient or, if there was a community spouse, at the death of the community spouse, whichever event occurs last. Through this claim, the state has a right to be reimbursed for everything it has paid for the long-term care in a nursing home of the Medicaid recipient. Because, generally, the only asset of any value in the estate of a Medicaid recipient is the home, the state recovery program effectively allows the state, in many instances, to require that the home be sold to reimburse the state for money advanced through Medicaid for the long-term care of its former owner.

In many states, this claim is limited to only assets that are held in the probate estate of the Medicaid recipient, which means that if the home was held in a life estate or jointly with the community spouse and the community spouse survived the spouse in the nursing home, the state's lien would be extinguished forever. However, federal law permits individual states to make their own laws to extend the property to which the claim will apply to include property held in a life estate or joint ownership. Since 1993, the federal government has required the individual states to recover funds expended for Medicaid recipients from whatever may be in the estates of those recipients in an effort to offset some of the cost of Medicaid Congress did, however, give the states some leeway in establishing their own estate-recovery programs, but they are required to have some program in effect. The individual states are, however, also allowed to limit the assets from which they would seek payback to the assets contained in the probate estate of the deceased Medicaid recipient. The probate estate of a deceased person consists solely of things that were owned by the deceased in his or her name alone. Joint property and property with beneficiaries, such as insurance policies and trusts, are not considered probate assets. The estate-recovery programs of states that limit their recovery efforts to probate property permit Medicaid recipients and their families to avoid estate recovery by using planning techniques, such as life estates. Alternatively, states have the option to enact laws that expand the definition of the estate from which they may exact estate recovery to include such non-probate assets, such as joint tenancies, trusts, and life estates.

According to the 2002 Medicaid Estate Recovery Work Group Report to the Pennsylvania Intra Governmental Council on Long-Term Care, 30 of 48 states surveyed used the less-intrusive probate standard for estate recovery. Florida and Texas, in particular, have laws that are protective of the home from estate recovery.

Exceptions

Federal and state laws do, however, permit the estates of some Medicaid recipients to avoid estate recovery. Surviving children of the long-term care Medicaid recipient who are disabled are not subject to estate recovery. Nor are brothers and sisters of the long-term care Medicaid recipient who are living in the home and were co-owners of the home with the Medicaid recipient and had lived in the home for at least a year before the Medicaid recipient was institutionalized. Also exempt are adult children of the Medicaid recipient who had lived in the home with the Medicaid recipient and who took care of the Medicaid recipient for at least two years before he or she entered a nursing home.

If the surviving spouse still lives in the home and was a joint owner of the home with the spouse who was in a nursing home receiving Medicaid coverage for the costs of long-term care, the states do not attempt to recover the cost of the Medicaid funds for that person's care from the value of the home. However, some states place a lien on the home and merely defer their right to be repaid until the surviving spouse has died.

An easy way to avoid any estate-recovery complications when the long-term care Medicaid recipient is a homeowner is merely to have the Medicaid recipient give his or her interest in the home to the community spouse. In this way, at the time of the nursing home resident's death, the home is entirely in the name of the surviving community spouse. This is a real no-brainer with no downside, because there is no Medicaid disqualification for gifts between husband and wife. The only significant asset of most married couples that is not countable when determining initial Medicaid eligibility is the house; thus, it is the only significant asset that can be successfully sheltered from estate recovery by merely giving it to the community spouse.

States are also required to not pursue estate recovery when to do so would result in an undue hardship. The definition of "undue hardship" is left up to the individual states to determine for themselves. Generally, though, this rule applies to homes of particularly modest value and income-producing property, such as a farm that is necessary for the support of surviving family members.

From the onset, estate recovery has been a controversial policy that appears to many people to be a mean-spirited attempt by the government to steal often-meager inheritances. Many people consider a home, in particular, to be more than just bricks and mortar and wood. It takes on a greater emotional meaning. The ability to pass on this legacy, often in lieu of anything else, is important to many older people and their families. In addition, the perception exists that the estate recovery laws are applied inordinately to the poorer citizens of our county. Finally, much evidence suggests that estate recovery does not bring in sufficient funds to make it worth the human toll.

The Latest Information

Medicaid law is constantly changing, both on the federal level and on the individual state level. For the most up-to-date information on Medicaid, go to the appropriate websites indicated in "Favorite Websites."

14

Veterans' Benefits

Although the last of the American veterans of World War I, Frank Buckles of West Virginia, died in 2011, there are still an estimated three million veterans of World War II who are still alive and, even though it is hard to believe for America's baby boomers, those who served during the Vietnam War era are now generally old enough to be eligible for many veterans programs. Many lawyers are still not conversant in the various veterans' benefit programs for which their elderly clients may be eligible, but more people are becoming aware of these potentially important benefits.

Veterans Adminstration (VA) pensions are generally available to veterans who served during wartime who have limited income and assets and who are at least 65 years old. Wartime veterans of any age who are permanently and totally disabled, reside in a nursing home, or are presently receiving Social Security Disability payments are also eligible for VA pensions. In addition, disabled veterans may also be eligible for additional benefits through the Aid and Attendance and Housebound programs.

Among the most unused and yet most helpful of veterans programs available to many of today's veterans and their families is the Veterans' Aid and Attendance Improved Pension. This program provides financial benefits for not just veterans who need assistance with activities of daily living (ADL), such as eating, bathing, and moving, but also for their surviving spouses. Patients in nursing homes and blind veterans are also covered, as are eligible veterans or their spouses residing in Assisted Living Facilities. A key factor in Aid and Attendance benefits is that they do not require that the assistance be required as a result of a service-related illness.

In addition, veterans who may not require Aid and Attendance benefits for themselves, but have an ill spouse, may qualify for benefit payments if the spouse's medical expenses pretty much takes up their entire joint income. In such cases, the veteran can apply for benefits as a veteran with a sick spouse.

Although the amounts change periodically, presently unmarried veterans are eligible for Aid and Attendance benefits of as much as $20,447 per year and a surviving spouse is eligible for up to $13,128 per year. An eligible married veteran is eligible for as much as $24,239 per year.

VA pensions are calculated by totaling the veteran's income for VA purposes and after making the appropriate deduction including, most prominently, the total of other countable income, deducting that amount from the maximum pension amount as shown in the previous paragraph to arrive at the figure for the specific individual. Aid and Attendance benefits, however, are paid in addition to the benefits paid under a basic VA pension, although the veteran must be eligible for a basic pension in order to qualify for Aid and Attendance benefits.

Veterans Eligible for Veterans Administration (VA) Pension Benefits

Four classes of veterans are eligible for VA benefits:

- Veterans who have a disability that either began or was made worse during their military service.
- Veterans at least 65 years old who served during World War II, the Korean Conflict, the Vietnam Era (which is defined as service between the dates of August 5, 1964 and May 7, 1975), and the Persian Gulf War, which also includes hostilities in Afghanistan beginning on August 2, 1990 and continuing to date.
- Veterans who served during the above-described periods of war who are permanently and totally disabled as a result of a non-service related disability.
- Veterans who have a disability that began or was made worse by VA medical treatment.

To qualify for VA pensions, members of these classes of veterans must also have income below the maximum annual pension rate to receive VA pension benefits. This maximum annual pension rate is set annually by Congress. In 2012, the maximum annual income limit for an unmarried veteran applying for a basic VA pension was $12,256; for housebound benefits, $14,978; and for Aid and Attendance benefits, $20,447. For a married veteran, the maximum amounts of income for a veteran applying for a basic VA pension was $16,051; for housebound benefits, $18,773; and for Aid and Attendance benefits, $20,447. In addition, a surviving spouse applying for basic pension benefits had a limit of $7,868 of annual income; for housebound benefits, $9,616; and for Aid and Attendance benefits, $13,128. Countable income includes, but is not limited to, income from earnings, disability, and retirement income, interest income, and dividend income.

Spouses and Family Members Eligible for VA Benefits

Four classes of relatives of veterans are also eligible for VA benefits based on the military service of their family member:

- A widow of a veteran or child of a veteran who died during his or her military service or later as a result of a service-related disability.
- A widow of a veteran or child of a deceased veteran who served in the military during one of the periods of war described above.
- A widow of a veteran or child of a deceased veteran whose death was caused by a disability that started or was made worse by VA medical treatment.
- Parents of a veteran who died during his or her military service or who died as a result of a service-connected disability.

As you can see, there are many groups of seniors who may indeed be eligible for VA benefits of which they may often not be aware. In fact, many people are not aware that any veteran who served on active duty for at least 90 consecutive days and now is suffering from amyotrophic lateral sclerosis, which is commonly referred to as Lou

Gehrig's disease, has been categorically eligible for VA benefits since 2010 without having to prove a service-related connection. In addition, many Vietnam Era veterans who served in Vietnam, certain areas of Korea, or certain areas of Thailand where they were exposed to herbicides, such as Agent Orange, are categorically eligible for VA benefits if they now suffer from disabilities that have been tied to exposure to herbicides, such as Parkinson's disease, coronary artery disease, diabetes, mellitus, or specific cancers. In addition, widows and widowers along with their children of veterans who died as a result of diseases only now recognized as being service related can also be eligible for VA benefits. Note that, in order to be eligible for spousal benefits, the veteran's surviving spouse must remain unmarried. There are no minimum age requirements for an unmarried widowed spouse to receive spousal benefits.

Basic Requirements for Veterans' Benefits

The beginning point for eligibility for veterans' benefits is that the benefits are based on service on active duty in the Army, Navy, Air Force, Marines, or Coast Guard. The service must have been for a minimum of 90 days with at least one of those days being during wartime. In addition, to qualify for VA benefits, the veteran upon whose service the benefits are based must have received a discharge not classified as dishonorable. Thus, either an honorable or general discharge will be sufficient to meet the condition of an eligible discharge.

Spouses

Veterans' benefits are not restricted to the veteran himself or herself, but also may extend to his or her spouse. Because the federal government does not recognize same-sex marriage, in order to qualify for spousal benefits, the spouse of a veteran must be of the opposite sex. Only about 15 states recognize common-law marriages, and some of those states have limitations on their recognition; however, if a couple who never obtained a marriage license or had a marriage ceremony live together as husband and wife, and the marriage is recognized by the state in which they reside as a common-law marriage, the VA will recognize the marriage for VA benefit purposes.

Pension Benefits for War Veterans and Their Families

Veterans of those wars previously mentioned who are 65 years of age or older and disabled may qualify for pension benefits regardless of whether their disability is service related. Wartime veterans of any age who are both permanently and totally disabled may be eligible for a pension. (Again, it is important to remember that the veteran's disability does not have to be service related.) The payment is needs-based, such that there are qualifying limitations of both the veteran's assets and income. Although the qualifying formula is not simple (what government formula ever is?), generally, to qualify for benefits, the veteran's assets cannot be of a value of more than $80,000, although it is important to note that, in computing this amount, the VA does not count the value of a home owned by the veteran. In addition, when computing income eligibility, if a veteran's out-of-pocket medical expenses are sufficient, he or she might qualify for VA benefits where he or she would otherwise be disqualified due to excessive income.

Benefit Amounts

It is important to remember that the amount of a VA pension is reduced on a dollar-for-dollar basis by other "countable income," although the pension amount is increased if the veteran or his or her survivor is housebound, in a nursing home, blind, or requires the aid and attendance of someone else. The most important deduction in determining the veteran's countable income is his or her out-of-pocket medical expenses which, for VA purposes, are referred to as Unreimbursed Medical Expenses (UME). In addition, the cost of premium payments for private health insurance or Medicare is also deductible in determining countable income. Out of pocket medical expenses also include the cost of unlicensed at-home attendants.

Total Disability

For VA purposes, total disability means that the veteran is unable to be gainfully employed. The VA defines permanent disabilities as those disabilities that are expected to continue for the duration of the veteran's lifetime. With logic only a government bureaucrat could understand, but which works to the benefit of many older veterans, a person who is less than 100 percent disabled may still qualify as totally disabled if at least one disability is rated at least 60 percent or has a combined disability rating of at least 70 percent, with one disability rated at least 40 percent.

Housebound Benefits

Veterans or their surviving spouses who are substantially housebound may be eligible for housebound benefits, which are in addition to the pension benefits for which they may be eligible. To be eligible for housebound benefits, the veteran must be eligible for a basic VA pension. A housebound spouse does not receive any housebound benefits until such time as his or her spouse dies; at which time, he or she becomes eligible for housebound benefits. The maximum annual household benefits are $14,457 for an unmarried veteran; $18,120 for a married veteran; and $9,696 for a surviving spouse of a deceased veteran.

Eligibility for VA Prescription Drug Coverage

Veterans who are receiving housebound benefits are also eligible to have their prescription drug needs met through the VA at a significantly reduced cost when compared to other prescription drug plans. However, the veteran's spouse or widowed spouse is not eligible for this benefit.

Aid and Attendance

Many in the public are unaware of Aid and Attendance benefits, which are paid to veterans and their surviving spouses who are blind, residing in a nursing home, or are in need of regular aid and attendance of another person in regard to activities of daily living (ADL). These payments are often made to veterans or their surviving spouses residing in an Assisted Living Facility. A surviving spouse may be eligible for benefits upon the death of his or her veteran spouse. The annual payment for a single veteran is $19,736; a married dependent is $23,396; and $12,681 for a surviving spouse. Like housebound benefits, these benefits are payable only to veterans or their surviving spouses eligible for a regular VA pension benefit and are payable in addition to those payments.

Service-Connected Compensation Payments

Veterans who incurred disabilities or had disabilities worsened during the course of their military service are also eligible for benefits called "compensation" by the VA. It is important to note that disabilities that relate to military service do not have to occur while the veteran was on active duty, but can even manifest themselves many years later. These payments are not needs-based and are tax-free, although military retirees may have their compensation benefits offset by any military retirement pay they receive.

In many instances, Vietnam veterans are presumed to have many disabilities related to their service, particularly as they relate to the effects of herbicides, such as Agent Orange. As I indicated earlier, any veteran who served at least 90 days in the military who develops Lou Gehrig's disease will have the condition covered as a service-connected disability.

Effect of VA Benefits on Other Benefits

Veterans and their spouses who do receive VA benefits should be cognizant of the fact that such benefits will affect their eligibility for need-based programs such as Supplemental Security Income (SSI), food stamps, and housing assistance. However, VA pensions do not affect a veteran's eligibility for Social Security benefits. Conversely, receipt of Social Security benefits will not affect eligibility for VA compensation.

Nursing-Home Services

The VA maintains nursing-home facilities for eligible veterans and contracts with private nursing homes in some circumstances to provide for the nursing-home needs of eligible veterans. Veterans who require nursing-home care as a result of a service-related condition or veterans with service-related disabilities of 70 percent or more are eligible for such services. In some instances, a copayment of the veteran is required.

Note

For current VA information, including the latest figures, rules, and regulations, go to the Veterans Administration website: www.vba.va.gov.

15

Being Patient

Patience is said to be a virtue. But, if you find yourself a patient in a hospital, good medical insurance may be of more help to you than merely being virtuous. At one time, corporations were more generous in continuing medical insurance coverage for retired employees, particularly those early retirees who did not yet qualify for Medicare, but today, as many companies look for ways to cut costs, reducing health insurance coverage for retired workers is becoming one of the ways companies achieve that end. And other companies that may have had the best of intentions have gone bankrupt, causing retirees to lose health insurance benefits as well. Another problem occurs when companies change their health insurance benefits for retirees after they have retired. It seems unfair, but it is perfectly legal. Some of the changes intended to reduce costs include tying health benefits to the length of time the retiree worked for the company or just flat out reducing coverage payments by the company.

As for retirees already receiving Medicare, it will not startle anyone to learn that Medicare does not even come close to covering the medical insurance needs of people, which is why Medigap policies to fill the gaps in coverage are so prevalent. In the past, companies were more likely to provide this insurance, but not as much anymore.

So, what can you do? Unfortunately, little. In the fine print of most retirement packages is the right of the employer to reduce or eliminate healthcare coverage. You can try to make a binding right to certain levels of health insurance a part of your retirement package. However, unless you are in a particularly good bargaining position, this is not a viable option. About the best you can do is be aware of the situation and be constantly on the lookout for other healthcare options. You may need them someday.

Privacy and Medical Records

In these days of greater concern over the privacy of our personal information, it is fairly common for people to regularly monitor their credit reports. But, how many of us ever bother to check our medical record to make sure that the information contained within it is accurate? The information contained in your medical record can affect whether you get long-term care insurance or other kinds of insurance.

In 2003, regulations were enacted as a part of the federal Health Insurance Portability and Accountability Act (HIPAA), which clarifies our rights to our medical records. HIPAA was intended to strike a balance between our privacy rights with the needs of the health-care industry for access to patients' records. Many states already had medical privacy laws in place. These laws were not supplanted by HIPPA, and in fact, if they provide more personal privacy protection, the state law will supersede. You probably have already received a HIPPA-required notice of your rights from your physicians and health insurer. If you are like many of us, you did not even bother to read the fine-print-intensive notice, just like the financial information sharing privacy notices we receive annually, pursuant to the federal Gramm-Leach-Bliley Act, telling us of our right to opt out of some of the privacy-invading, financial-information-sharing programs of the various banks, credit-card companies, and insurance companies with which we do regular business.

Some financial institutions with a straight face actually trumpet the fact that so many people do not opt out of information sharing because, they say, we consumers are in favor of giving our personal financial information to other companies. The truth is that it requires someone to actually first read these complicated, confusing notices and then follow the directions for opting out of financial information sharing. For many of us, that is just too hard and too much work. It is easier to do nothing. That is what the banks and other financial institutions counted on when they lobbied Congress to make these rules an opt-out program rather than an opt-in.

But, back to our medical record privacy rights: The HIPAA notice you have received tells you the policy of your particular medical care provider or insurance company in regard to patient privacy. Generally, it indicates that they share information for administrative purposes in regard to your treatment and payment of medical bills.

Access to Medical Records—By You and Others

A most important part of the HIPAA regulations is your right to have access to your medical record and to have a copy made of your record for yourself. This is particularly important when you are applying for any kind of insurance, particularly long-term care insurance, for which your medical record is a critical factor in determining whether you will be granted insurance. Just as with your credit report, you have the right to ask your physician to correct any mistaken or misleading information that may be contained in your record.

You also have the right under HIPAA to refuse to have your medical record shared with anyone when the purpose for the information sharing is not related to your treatment, billing, or administrative purposes, such as where your physician wants to use your information for research purposes. In furtherance of your other rights, you have the right to learn who has received your medical information in order to confirm that any information sharing was appropriate.

16 ———————————————————

Scams

Willie Sutton, a bank robber, was once asked why he robbed banks, to which he replied, "Because that's where the money is." Older Americans own more than half of the financial assets in the country, which may explain why, according to the U.S. Subcommittee on Health and Long Term Care, that although the elderly only account for 12 percent of the population, they account for 30 percent of scam victims. Today, the innocent (and sometimes not so innocent) prey of con men may find themselves victimized primarily through scams on the Internet and by fraudulent telemarketers. Older Americans make up a disproportionately large number of the people who are swindled each year. According to a study of the National Institute of Justice, close to 12 percent of people 60 years or older have been financially exploited. MetLife, Inc. did a report in 2011 that found that scam and financial abuse of the elderly totaled close to 3 billion dollars. Some people have hypothesized that it is because senior citizens both are more trusting and less apt to complain after being cheated out of money (often due to embarrassment) that they are the victims of choice for so many criminals. Seniors also may often be more polite than younger Americans and not hang up on the telemarketer marketing a scam. But, knowledge is power, and learning about the common scams out there can go a long way toward helping people avoid becoming a victim.

Interestingly, a recent study by the University of Iowa has actually indicated that there might be a physiological reason that the elderly are so often the victims of scams. The studies point to the ventromedial prefrontal cortex (vmPFC), which is an area of the brain that controls belief and doubt. According to the study,

In our theory, the more effortful process of disbelief to items initially believed is mediated by the vmPFC, which in old age, tends to disproportionately lose structural integrity and associated functionality.

The deterioration of the vmPFC begins as early as age 60 although, of course, the degree of deterioration can differ significantly among individuals. The study went on to conclude that

...vulnerability to misleading information, outright deception, and fraud in older adults in the specific result of a deficit in the doubt process that is mediated by the vmPFC.

This explains how intelligent older people may often be perceived accurately as being more gullible and susceptible to the entreaties of scam artists and identity thieves.

Identity Theft

Identity theft is now the number-one consumer fraud complaint, according to the Federal Trade Commission. Identity theft occurs when personal information, such as your Social Security number or a credit-card account number, is stolen by someone who can then steal your identity and run up huge charges in your name. If you find that you are a victim of identity theft, you should promptly contact the fraud department of each of the three major credit-reporting bureaus (Equifax: 1-800-685-1111 or.www.equifax.com; Experian: 1-888-397-3742 or www.experian.com; and Trans Union: 1-800-916-8800 or www.tuc.com) informing them of the theft. You should also ask that a fraud alert be placed on your file and that no new credit be granted without your specific approval. Identity theft can ruin your credit, so it is important to notify all three credit-reporting bureaus, because they operate independently of each other.

As soon as you find that either an existing account has been accessed or a new account has been opened in your name, you should contact the security department of the company and promptly close the account. Put passwords on any new accounts you open to replace the former accounts, and make sure you do not use your Social Security number as the password, because the identity thief may already know your number. It is also important to file a report of the crime with your local police, because any bank or company with which you may deal may require proof of your complaint. The necessary notification of everyone with whom you may do business can be a frustrating, time-consuming task; however, the FTC has recently created a model identity theft affidavit form that you can use to simplify the process of reporting information to many companies. This form was developed by the FTC together with banks, credit companies, and consumer advocates. You can get a copy of the form either by going to the FTC's website at www.consumer.gov/idtheft/affidavit.htm or by calling 1-877-ID-THEFT (toll-free).

Affinity Fraud

We all tend to trust people who are just like us. That is a truism. With a knowledge of psychology that would make Sigmund Freud envious, scam artists, the only criminals we refer to as artists, use that trust to their advantage. Scammers know that once they have a potential victim's heart and trust, his or her wallet will soon follow.

In recent years, there has been an epidemic of fraud that targeted particular nationalities, ethnic groups, racial groups, fraternal organizations, and religious groups. Religion-related scams are particularly common. Bernie Madoff was guilty of tremendous affinity fraud within the American Jewish community. A scam artist may join a particular church, synagogue, or mosque and gain the trust and confidence of the congregation by making a significant contribution to the religious organization. But, this is just seed money. Scammers often target members of a religious, ethnic, fraternal, or other group to which they appear to belong and offer "special" investment opportunities that ultimately turn out to be worthless.

Trust me, you can't trust anyone. Before investing, people should do their homework and check out both the investment and the person touting it. The endorsement of someone you know and trust is no substitute for real research into any investment. It is also important to never invest in any investment that you do not totally understand. This was a mistake made by investors with Bernie Madoff. They trusted him despite the fact that they did not understand how he claimed to be operating his investments.

The Grandparent Scam

Despite more and more people being aware of this scam, it never seems to go away. Law enforcement believes that many of the scammers inflicting this scam upon unwary grandparents are located overseas. Generally, the scam starts when a grandparent receives a telephone call from someone purporting to be their grandchild, who has encountered problems, such as an automobile accident or an arrest while traveling in another country. The "grandchild" then pleads with the grandparent to send money to assist the grandchild in need. The money is requested to be wired, which is an early sign of a scam because it is hard to trace and all but impossible to get back. Often, the scammer will provide details that the grandparent thinks proves that the person to whom they are speaking is their grandchild; however, this proof may have been merely taken from social media sites or other easily accessible sources. A significant number of grandparent-scam telephone calls have followed a death in the family where family names may have appeared in an obituary.

Anyone receiving such a call should immediately contact the child or parent of the child to verify the child's location.

Social Security Scams

Confusion about government benefit programs is fertile ground for scammers. Social Security has been the basis for many con artists, who use this confusion to take advantage of unwary seniors.

Social Security Refund Scam

In this scam, scammers promise their victims that they can get back from the government the victim's lifetime worth of Social Security tax payments. For the proverbial "small fee" and a percentage of the refund that never comes, the con artist promises to file the proper claims forms with the IRS. The truth is that there is no such program. Social Security tax payments are not refundable under any circumstances. The victims pay their fees and wait for a refund that never comes

Direct Deposit Verification Scam

This scam involves a call or an email you receive from someone purporting to be from the Social Security Administration who says that he needs to verify your direct deposit banking information. It is easy to fall for this type of scam and provide your Social Security number and bank account number, but if you do, you will end up becoming a victim of identity theft and having your bank account stolen.

No one should ever provide information over the phone to people whom they have not called and are not absolutely sure are legitimate. In this case, the Social Security Administration never contacts people by email requesting information. Neither would it ask for personal information by phone. If someone were to receive an email or call requesting information and have even the slightest thought that the contact may be legitimate, they can always contact Social Security by phone at a number that they know is accurate to confirm that their previous contact by a scammer was indeed a scam.

Windfall Scam

Another Social Security scam occurs when the victim is told that his or her benefits are being reduced because the victim has inherited a home or money from a deceased relative. The victim is told that he or she must pay back the benefits he or she received. The truth is that Social Security is not a needs-based program where you must qualify by having a limited amount of assets so the basic premise is false. Yet, unwitting victims pay the amounts demanded by scammers who say they are collecting on behalf of the federal government.

Social Security Identity Theft Scam

In this scam, people receive an email that appears to have come from the Social Security Administration warning the recipient that they are the victim of identity theft and that someone is using their Social Security number. They are then directed to a phony website that looks like the official Social Security Administration website, where they are directed to confirm their identity not only with their name and Social Security number, but also with bank information, credit-card information, and sometimes even PIN information. This should be a tipoff that this is a scam, because under no circumstances would the Social Security Administration ever ask for your credit-card information or your PIN.

Social Security COLA Scam

COLA is an acronym for Cost of Living Adjustments, which are annual additions to Social Security benefit payments that get paid automatically to recipients. Each year, scammers take advantage of news stories about COLAs to scam people through identity theft. Typically, the victim receives an email indicating that there will be a cost-of-living adjustment beginning in January of the next year. However, the victim is also told that, to receive their COLA, the victim must update personal information with the Social Security Administration. To make things worse, the victim is told that if he or she does not update his or her information by a specific date, that his or her benefits will be suspended. However, the victim is also told that he or she can merely click a link to the Social Security Administration website where the victim can update his or her information online and continue to receive benefits and any increases to which the victim is entitled. Once again, the website is phony, and you are turning your information over to an identity thief. The key is to remember that COLAs are automatic. You do not have to do anything to receive a COLA. Also, the Social Security Administration will not contact you by phone or email. Finally, if again you have any concerns that what you are being told is correct, merely call the local Social Security Administration office where you can confirm that it is a scam.

Medicare Scams

Many Medicare recipients have received telephone calls from someone purporting to be from Medicare notifying them that new Medicare cards are being issued and that, to maintain their Medicare coverage, they need to confirm personal information, such as their Social Security number or checking account number. This is a scam. Medicare is not issuing new cards (although they should because present Medicare cards prominently display the holder's Social Security number, thereby making them more vulnerable to identity theft), and Medicare never contacts people by phone. In addition, the real Medicare already has your personal information with the exception of your bank account information, for which they have absolutely no need. As with any telephone call to you that requests personal information, no one should ever give such information over the phone because you can never be sure who is calling.

Medicare Open-Enrollment Scam

The annual Medicare open enrollment period occurs each year between mid-October and early December. The open-enrollment period is the only opportunity Medicare recipients have each year during which to change their Medicare D prescription drug plan. Medicare D prescription drug plans often change their coverage within the year, yet the only time you can change your plan is during the open-enrollment period to make sure that you are enrolled in the best plan for you. Plans may change their formulary, which is the list of covered drugs. They also may change other terms of the plan including the amount of any deductible so it is important to review your plan each year and compare it against other plans to make sure that you have the best plan for you. Scammers take advantage of the open enrollment period to contact you by email or phone purporting to be from a Medicare prescription drug provider. The scammers then request personal information, such as your Medicare number (which is the same as your Social Security number). If you provide this number to the scammer, he or she will use that number to turn you into a victim of identity theft.

Always zealously guard the privacy of your Social Security number and Medicaid number. Do not give out this information by phone or on the Internet to someone who contacts you. You should also be aware that Medicare rules prohibit real prescription drug providers from contacting you by unsolicited emails or telephone calls so if you receive such a communication, you can be sure that it is a scam. For all the information you need to compare and choose a plan that is right for you, go to www.medicare.gov.

Charity Scams

Seniors are often generous when it comes to contributing to charities. Immediately after a natural disaster, such as a hurricane or tornado, scammers pop up through phony websites, emails, or phone calls posing as representing a charity. All too often an empathetic senior will fall prey to the scammer and send money to the phony charity. It is also important to remember that even if you are on the federal Do-Not-Call list to restrict calls from telemarketers, you still are allowed to be contacted by charities. It is also good to remember that when you are contacted by a telemarketer on behalf of a charity, not only do you have no way of knowing if the caller legitimately represents a real charity, but even if they do, you may want to consider that in that situation the caller is generally working on commission so that any amount you contribute through the telemarketer to the charity of your choice is reduced by his or her commission. The better course to follow is, as always, never give out your credit-card number on the phone to someone whom you have not called and are sure is legitimate. Before giving to any charity in response to an email, phone call, or any other solicitation, you should check out the charity to make sure that it is legitimate. Go to www.charitynavigator.org, which not only tells you whether the charity is legitimate, but also how much of your contribution goes toward salaries and expenses of the charities management and how much actually goes toward its charitable activities.

Investment Frauds

There are no free lunches or breakfasts. Many scam artists offer free lunches or seminars to lure seniors and others to a high pressure sales environment where the investment is misrepresented, the benefits exaggerated, the risks downplayed, and the suitability for the investor rarely discussed. A study by the Securities and Exchange Commission (SEC) found that only about 5 percent of the time were the seminars conducted in compliance with regulatory agency standards.

Never invest at a free seminar, and don't even consider investing with the sponsor of the seminar until you have investigated the sponsor and the type of investment. Never invest in any investment that you do not fully understand. It also is a good idea to get an independent third-party evaluation of a particular investment of which you become aware at a free seminar before considering investing.

Variable Annuities

Variable annuities are curiously a legal investment that every year turns up on lists of the top-ten scams affecting senior citizens. Variable annuities carry high commission rates, so there is an incentive on salesmen to try to sell them, but they also come with many fees buried in the fine print, including high surrender fees that may make them an inappropriate investment for a senior citizen.

Charitable Gift Annuities

Many charities, most notably the Salvation Army, offer charitable gift annuities whereby someone makes a donation to the charity, receiving, in return, an annuity that provides payments to the charitable donor for the rest of their life. At the end of the life of the charitable donor, the remaining value of the annuity passes to the charity. These are a good way of doing well while doing good. When these are done by legitimate charities, such as the Salvation Army, the donor is able to achieve some income tax savings by donating appreciated assets, such as stocks, that can be sold by the charity without any income tax liability and, at the same time, receive a lifetime stream of income; all while benefiting a charity after the donor's death.

However, in the hands of a scammer who is not representing a legitimate charity, the money may go right into the scammer's bank account. Often, these are run as Ponzi schemes with the early investors being paid out of funds from later investors. The key to determining whether a particular charitable gift annuity is real or not is to only deal with charities that are legitimate and to deal with the charities directly and not through an intermediary salesperson. You can check out the legitimacy of a charity at www.charitynavigator.org.

Churning

Churning is the name for the illegal practice of brokers who make excessive stock trades that are not appropriate for their clients in order to generate sales commissions rather than make trades that are in the best interest of their clients. Some seniors become more susceptible to this type of scam, because they do not even open their monthly brokerage statements while others may not understand the statements. The key here is to always check your monthly statements and make sure that you understand each trade and the reason for it.

Stranger-Owned Life Insurance (SOLI)

This scam is actually legal in some states, but in general, it reminds me of the old saying, "If it looks like a duck and walks like a duck and quacks like a duck, it's a duck." In this case, it certainly looks like scam. It may even quack.

This scam starts when a senior is approached by someone telling them that they can want to provide them with a sizable free life-insurance policy. The person approaching the senior will loan the money to the senior interest-free to pay for the life-insurance policy. If the senior dies during the two years, the death benefit will be paid to the family of the insured senior minus the loaned money used to purchase the policy. If the senior lives beyond the two-year period, the senior has the choice to either pay back the loan and keep the policy or turn the policy over to the person who loaned them the money and even receive a payment for turning over the life insurance policy. It sounds good. It sounds innocuous...until you start taking the transaction apart.

First of all, why is this third party doing this? They are doing this to get you to buy a life-insurance policy that you will turn over to them and which they will then sell to either investors who will hold the policy and pay the premiums until your death, or they will gather a large number of policies and actually have them consolidated into bonds that can be sold to investors. They do this rather than purchase a policy on you directly because the law for hundreds of years has prohibited people from buying life insurance on the life of strangers, which makes sense, because when it was allowed in England hundreds of years ago, people bought life insurance on strangers and then killed them in some instances.

But, where is the harm?

The determination of the premiums for life-insurance policies is a complicated task done by actuaries of the life-insurance companies after consideration of many factors, including consideration of the large number of people who will purchase life-insurance policies during their lifetimes and then stop paying the premiums and let the policies lapse such that the insurance company never has to pay out the death benefit. If large numbers of people entered into

SOLI arrangements, the cost of life insurance premiums for individuals would rise precipitously. In addition, if you do this and sell your policy and then later develop a need for life insurance, you may not be able to buy another policy because insurers will often decline to issue new policies if there is already substantial insurance in place. Also, complicated tax laws (surprise, surprise) could result in your owing income taxes on the interest-free portion of the loan for the two years that you owned the policy as well as the money that you were paid as a bonus for turning the policy over later to the stranger. Finally, conscious of this use of life insurance for a purpose for which it was never intended, life-insurance policies are now often asking on applications whether or not a person is purchasing the policy in order to sell it later. Lying on the application could bring both civil and criminal liability.

Sham Tax Forms

Con men are ever so clever in tricking unsuspecting people to reveal personal information that can lead to identity theft. A common scam involves sending you phony forms that appear to be from either banks or the IRS that request such personal information as marital status, place of birth, bank account numbers, employment history, and parents' names: Information that can readily be translated into identity theft. The form appears to be official and is often similar to genuine forms. One such form, which purports to be from a taxpayer's bank, says that it is a Reporting and Withholding Exemption Form and asks for PIN numbers and the maiden name of the taxpayer's mother. No IRS form requires such information, so be wary if you receive such a form.

Another fake form that is being circulated is a Form W-9095 entitled Application for Certificate Status Ownership for Withholding Tax. It looks similar to the legitimate IRS Form W-9 Request for Taxpayer Identification Number and Certification with which taxpayers, particularly those who have obtained mortgages with tax escrow accounts, are familiar. Again, however, the phony form asks for more personal identifying information than does the legitimate form.

Phony Prizes

Phony prize scams are abundant. According to the National Consumers League's National Fraud Information Center (www.nclnet.org), they represent one of the three most common telemarketing frauds perpetrated against older Americans. Sometimes, the scam involves your being required to buy something to get your prize. Usually, what you buy is extremely overpriced. Other times, you are told that to claim your fabulous prize, you must first pay the income tax on the prize to the company. Wrong! Prizes are indeed generally subject to income taxes. However, you would pay taxes directly to the IRS through an estimated tax payment or the taxes would be deducted from the prize itself. In either case, you should receive a Form 1099 from the company giving you the prize. The form would state the value of the prize and the amount to be reported on your income tax return. Under no circumstances should you be required to make a tax payment to the company providing the prize.

Slavery Reparations

A particularly insidious tax scam that has been pervasive over recent years is the one in which promoters claim that for a fee they will aid African Americans in obtaining a substantial tax credit or refund as a reparation for slavery. This is totally false, although it has a tenuous historical basis. Following the end of the Civil War, Congress passed a bill authorizing the payment to all former slaves of forty acres and a mule as compensation for their enslavement. However, President Andrew Johnson vetoed the bill, and it was never made into law.

People making a claim for slavery reparations on their federal income tax returns run the risk of being assessed a $500 penalty for filing a fraudulent tax return. In the past, the IRS has said that it would not assess this penalty unless a person had submitted the slavery reparation claim more than once after being informed that the claim was invalid. However, the IRS is now saying that it may assess the penalty against anyone who fails to withdraw a slavery reparations claim.

Despite what we are told has been the IRS's best efforts to educate the public about this scam and the con men preying on unsuspecting African Americans, as recently as 2001, the IRS received more than 77,000 tax returns claiming a slavery reparation refund or credit—an increase of more than 64,000 tax returns over the previous year. To make things worse, an embarrassed IRS finds itself publicly (and correctly) proclaiming that there is no slavery reparation credit while admitting that it mistakenly paid out as many as 200 of these claims for a total of $30 million. Unfortunately for those people who received any of the mistakenly granted tax credits, the IRS is taking steps to recover any improperly issued refund checks along with interest and even penalties.

IRS Impersonators

Speaking of the IRS, another common scam is the con man at your door saying that he is from the IRS coming to collect your taxes. If someone comes to your home saying he or she is from the IRS, you should be wary. In today's world, hardly anyone, from your doctor to even the IRS, makes house calls. If an actual IRS field auditor did go to your home, that person would generally call first and would have a picture ID. Do not open your door to anyone you believe to be an IRS imposter.

Credit-Card Protection

One of the more common Internet and telemarketing scams involves the sale of unnecessary credit-card protection services. Often, under this scam, victims are told that their credit-card numbers can be found on the Internet and that they are therefore vulnerable to unauthorized charges. They are then told, in a blatant misrepresentation, that their credit cards provide no protection against such theft or that because of Internet fraud, their liability for unauthorized charges is no longer limited to $50. The con men then sell a program for hundreds of dollars that promises to protect the consumer from unauthorized charges.

The truth is that not only is your credit-card liability for unauthorized charges generally limited to $50, in most instances, you are not held responsible for even $50 of charges. Most often, your liability is zero. In response to these scams, the Federal Trade Commission started a special program called Operation Protection Deception, by which it investigates and prosecutes perpetrators of such frauds.

Chain Letters

Aretha Franklin (one of my favorite singers and the first woman inducted into the Rock and Roll Hall of Fame) had a hit song, "Chain of Fools." Remember the song to remember that chain letters, whether they are the old-fashioned snail mail variety or the newer Internet chain letters, are a bad bet.

Chain letters are a scam that has been around for ages with a little updating here and there to make it look different or even legal (which it is not), but the bottom line is always the same: You send a small amount of money to four or five people whose names appear on the list you receive and replace one of the names on the list with your own name before you send the list back out to more people.

Not long ago, the Federal Trade Commission (FTC) sent out its own mass mailing to 2,000 people involved in an Internet chain letter that promises participants a minimum of $46,000 within 90 days. The FTC notice informed these people, who should have known better, that this scheme, like other chain letters involving money, was illegal. If you start a chain email or letter or even send one, you are violating the law. The chain letter that was the focus of the FTC's action was pretty much a standard chain letter, except that participants allegedly received something of value for their payments, namely, instructions on how to start their own chain letters over the Internet and recruit tens of thousands of participants. That particular chain letter even claimed that the program was perfectly legal and urged participants who questioned its legality to contact the FTC's Associate Director for Marketing Practices to confirm its legitimacy. This was entirely a bluff. The Associate Director for Marketing Practices at the FTC has specifically said that that particular chain letter and others like it were illegal.

The FTC has taken legal action against a number of email chain letter offenders. Chain letters for pay, whether they are over the Internet or through the mail, are illegal and carry the potential for substantial fines or even imprisonment.

Pyramid Schemes

Pyramid schemes are so named because, if you diagrammed the scheme, it would resemble a pyramid with ever-increasing members descending from its initiator. But, they also could have received this name because this particular scam has been around so long that it might well have been present at the time the pyramids in Egypt were being built.

Pyramid schemes keep surfacing with slight variations in terminology and subtle changes in substance to make them look legal. But, they are not. A recent incarnation of the pyramid scheme involved a "gifting club" where people made cash "gifts," which really were not gifts, to high-ranking members of the club with the promise that as they recruited new members to the club, they would rise through the ranks to a position where they would be receiving "gifts" from new members in large amounts. The problem with this is the same problem with any pyramid scheme. Eventually, you run out of people and those left on the bottom of the pyramid lose everything. It is a scam, pure and simple.

Cramming

Cramming is a term with which you may not be familiar outside of the peculiar pasttime of the 1950s in which young people tried to see how many of them could fit into a telephone booth. Or maybe you remember the last-minute studying for an exam in school. However, cramming as a fraudulent activity is one that is so sneaky that many people are not even aware that they have been scammed. Cramming is the name for unauthorized charges appearing on your telephone bill. The charges may be a one-time charge or they may be repeated monthly. With telephone bills so complicated to read and understand, many people entirely miss these charges on their bill and just pay them.

A common place from which crammed charges originate is a contest entry form that may appear to be innocuous on its face. However, in the fine print of the contest-entry form, which is both small and often confusingly written, is a notice that by completing the form, you agree to a telephone calling card or some other service that will be added to your telephone bill. Sometimes, you get the service. Sometimes, you just get the bill. In both cases, it was nothing you wanted or intended to order.

Cramming also is commonly found in sweepstakes promotions that you may receive in the mail directing you to call an 800 number to claim your prize. Again, the devil is in the detailed fine print of the promotional material, which may say that if you call the 800 number, you automatically become enrolled in whatever program they are providing. Once again, you may or may not ever receive the service for which you have enrolled, just the charges added to your phone bill.

Tip

Review your telephone bill carefully each month. Look for charges described as "Miscellaneous Charges and Credits" or fees described as "Min Use Fee," "Activation Fee," "Member Fee," "Voice Mail Fee," or any other similar fee. If anything appears on your bill that you did not authorize, follow the instructions on the bill for disputing the bill and removing the charge.

Credit Repair Services

We have all seen the ads for credit repair services, some of them legitimate and others quite illegitimate. According to the law, adverse credit information remains on your credit report for seven years except for bankruptcies, which stay on your credit report for ten years. Despite what you may be told by some credit repair services, information that is correct and verifiable cannot be removed from your credit report. If you find incorrect information on your credit report, you may request the credit reporting bureau to investigate the item and remove it if it is either shown to be incorrect or even if it merely cannot be verified.

The Federal Trade Commission has been cracking down on illegitimate credit repair companies. In 2001, it took action against almost 200 phony credit repair promoters. In Federal Court in Texas, Clifton W. Cross was not only ordered to pay $171,000 in restitution to defrauded customers, but was also sentenced to 49 months in federal prison. Clifton Cross, through his company Build-it-Fast, used a website to entice customers to hire him to show them how they could erase their old bad credit by getting a new clean credit report. At the crux of this scheme was an old technique called file segregation. Cross sold instructions to customers that told them how they could obtain an employer identification number from the IRS to use instead of a Social Security number. This number has the same number of digits as a Social Security number and was used in the past by people to hide bad credit and establish a new, clean credit report. Obtaining an employer identification number for this purpose is a federal crime. In addition, advising consumers as to how they can hide their true credit histories is also a violation of the federal Credit Repair Organizations Act.

Another tactic advised by the phony credit repair services is to dispute all adverse information on your credit report because under federal law when this is done, the credit-reporting agency must, within 30 days, investigate your claim. If the credit reporting agency is unable to verify the debt, it must delete the item or items from your credit report. The hope is to clog the system with so many false claims that they are unable to be processed within the statutorily mandated 30-day period. This tactic is also illegal.

The bottom line is that curing a bad credit report that contains accurate but adverse information is just a matter of time.

Travel Fraud

I'll bet that you, like me, have "won" a fantastic free or ridiculously low-cost vacation. Whether you learned of your "good fortune" by way of a telemarketer, email, fax, or a postcard, the old adage continues to be true. If it looks too good to be true, it usually is. Even the "free" trip is rarely free. The deals are generally fraught with hidden charges, conditions, and additional fees you must pay to receive the trip you think you were promised. The trip you actually get can look different from what you anticipated. It is never a good idea to give your credit-card number or bank account information to anyone over the phone if you are not absolutely sure who that person is. Unscrupulous travel con men may say they need that information for verification purposes only. They are lying.

If you are still interested in the vacation package, do not fall prey to high-pressure sales tactics by which they insist that you must act immediately. Take your time. Check out the company with the consumer protection division of your state's Attorney General's office as well as the Federal Trade Commission, but even that may not be enough, because these companies often merely change their names and it is not to protect the innocent.

Reloading

You better watch out, you better not cry, you better not pout, and I'm telling you why. No, Santa Claus isn't coming to town, but fraudulent telemarketers are. And they have a list and they have been checking it twice, not to find out who is naughty or nice, but to find out who has been previously scammed. A nasty trick played by fraudulent telemarketers is to call people who have been previously cheated and cheat them again. Often, the way this works is after you have been scammed by a con man through telemarketing, you may receive another call, this one purporting to be from a government agency or private consumer organization offering to help you recover the money you had been scammed out of previously.

If this happens to you, you should be wary because what fraudulent telemarketers do is create sucker lists of people who have lost money to phony telemarketing schemes. These lists include names, addresses, telephone numbers, and other personal information gathered by the scammers who in turn sell these lists to other con men (or con people, if we are to be politically correct). These lists are valuable property because unfortunately, if you fell for the con in the first place, you are probably vulnerable to being taken advantage of again.

Fortunately, there are some telltale signs to help you identify the good guys from the bad guys. First and foremost, if the caller offering assistance asks for a fee, he is a fraud. Government agencies and legitimate consumer organizations do not charge for their services.

This technique of tricking victims twice is called "reloading," and it is not restricted to phony consumer assistance schemes. Another reloading scam involves using prize incentives to induce you to buy more stuff. Once you have made a purchase, you will get a call implying if you buy even more stuff, your chances of winning a valuable prize will increase. Don't fall for it—particularly twice.

Some Good Advice

It is a good idea never to give your credit-card number over the phone to anyone with whom you did not initiate the contact. If, however, you find that you have been defrauded by a telemarketer and you paid with a credit card for goods or services you never received, you should contact your credit-card company, explain what happened, and ask that the charges be removed from your bill. Do not pay the disputed amount because doing so will limit your rights.

If you did not follow my advice the first time and gave one of these con men your credit-card number over the phone and then you did not follow my advice the second time and paid the disputed charge, there is still something you can do. Under federal law, if you did not receive purchased goods or services, you can dispute the charges as a billing error. In that instance, the credit-card company is required to investigate your claim and take off the charge where appropriate.

Be a careful consumer and remember that, when the phone rings, there are a lot of phonies on the phone, many of whom apparently are guided by the quote often attributed to P.T. Barnum, "There's a sucker born every minute."

Identity Theft from the Dead

Not even the dead are immune from identity theft, and this particular type of identity theft is now on the rise. One way this occurs is when identity thieves merely check out the latest obituaries and then go to a free data bank called the Death Master File maintained by the Social Security Administration. Using the Death Master File, the identity thief is readily able to obtain the deceased person's Social Security number, which then can be used along with other information gained from the obituary to establish credit, make purchases, or take out loans in the name of the deceased person. This, obviously, can create tremendous problems for the family of the deceased.

To avoid this problem, is it important to limit the amount of personal information contained in any obituary in order not to provide information that can be exploited by an identity thief. Also, the executor or personal representative of the estate should contact the major credit-reporting bureaus and notify them that the person is deceased and not to issue any further credit. All creditors of the deceased, such as credit-card companies, should be notified of the death and the accounts closed as soon as possible.

A Few Tips

You can avoid many telemarketers by signing up for the federal Do-Not-Call List by calling 888-382-1222. It is important to remember, however, that scam artists ignore the Do-Not-Call list, so you still have to be vigilant.

Shred important documents that you do not need in order to help avoid identity theft.

Do not give out your Social Security number to anyone or any agency that does not absolutely need it, and never give it out over the phone to anyone who calls you. For that matter, don't give out your credit-card number or any other personal information over the phone or through the computer to anyone who contacted you, because you can't be sure if he is legitimate.

Do not carry your Social Security card or your Medicare card in your wallet or purse unless you need it on a particular day because if your wallet or purse is stolen or lost with either of those cards in it, you run a serious risk of identity theft.

Never click links in emails, even if they are emails from friends, unless you know that the email is truly from someone you trust. Remember your trusted friends can have their email accounts hacked. Clicking links in hacked emails or phony websites may download key-stroke-logging malware that can steal all of the information from your computer.

Never invest at a free seminar.

Never invest in anything that you do not understand fully and never invest with anyone until you have investigated both them and the investment itself.

When making charitable contributions, don't do them through a telemarketer. Only make such contributions directly to the charity and only after checking out the charity at www.charitynavigator.org.

17

End-of-Life Issues

"Death and taxes and childbirth!
There's never any convenient time for any of them!"

—Margaret Mitchell

Although there certainly does not appear to be a convenient time for death, a terminal illness may be an appropriate time for a person to make important decisions regarding various end-of-life issues.

Health Care Proxy

It is important to make sure that your Health Care Proxy or Advance Care Directive is in order and that it reflects your wishes as to medical care you wish and do not wish to receive. However, too much specificity in a Health Care Proxy can unfortunately serve to complicate your situation in the event of unforeseen circumstances that do not neatly fit into your wishes as expressed in your Health Care Proxy. Perhaps the better way to go is to wisely choose the person who will make healthcare decisions on your behalf if you become incapacitated. Also, make sure that you provide duplicate originals of your Health Care Proxy to that person as well as to your primary care physician (PCP).

Note from Steve: The statutes refer to this document as a Health Care Proxy.

Hospice Care

The first American hospice program was set up in Connecticut in 1974. Now, there are more than 3,100 hospice programs throughout the country.

Hospice care involves care for terminally ill people outside a hospital setting, with the goal of providing comfort and dignity in a person's final days. Generally, hospice care is done when a person is expected to live no more than six months. Medicare will cover the cost of hospice care. You can get more information about hospice by going to the website of the Hospice Foundation of America at www.hospicefoundation.org.

Organ Donation

If you have a Wurlitzer, you certainly can donate that to someone, but by donating your heart, kidneys, pancreas, lungs, liver, intestines, corneas, or bone marrow, you can give someone in need the greatest gift of all: a new chance at life. You also can donate your body to a medical school to help advance medicine.

Perhaps the most important thing to do if you are considering an anatomical gift is to learn about it. The U.S. Department of Health and Human Services has a website with much helpful information about this topic. It can be found at www.organdonor.gov.

If you decide that you wish to make an organ donation, it is important that you not only fill out a declaration of anatomical gift form, but also that you make sure that your family and physician are aware of your decision.

Durable Power of Attorney

Durable Powers of Attorney were discussed earlier in Chapter 3, "Substitute Decision Making." If you have a Springing Durable Power of Attorney, one that does not come into effect until your incapacity, you may want to have that Durable Power of Attorney changed to become immediately effective. You should also review your Durable Power of Attorney as to any limitations you may or may not wish to place on the person you appoint to make financial decisions on your behalf. In particular, you may wish to revisit any provisions within your Durable Power of Attorney that authorize your attorney-in-fact (who does not have to be a lawyer, but merely your agent) to make gifts. You also may wish to take the lead yourself in making gifts while you are alive and able to enjoy seeing people appreciate your generosity.

Beneficiary Designations

It is important to make sure that the beneficiary designations on any life insurance policies, annuities, or retirement plans are in order and specify the people to whom you would want to leave those assets. Often, for the sake of convenience, people will add the name of a friend or relative as a joint owner on a bank account or other asset, not intending to leave those assets to these people at death, but rather just to permit these assets to be managed more easily during life. This can create problems at death, because the presumption is that jointly owned property automatically passes to the surviving joint owner. A better way to deal with this issue would be through the use of either a Durable Power of Attorney or a Living Trust. Either option enables your assets to be managed on your behalf during your lifetime, but will pass the assets to the people you desire at your death.

Monetary Needs

If you do not have readily available assets at this time, you may be able to either tap into your life-insurance policies if they have accelerated death benefits or sell your life-insurance policy to a Viatical Settlement company to receive necessary cash. Both of these alternatives were discussed in Chapter 10, "Long-Term Care."

Wills

It also is important to make sure that your will is in proper order. You should make sure that the people named in the will either as personal representative, executor, or beneficiaries are in accordance with your wishes. You also may wish to make a separate list of all of your tangible personal property and to whom you wish these assets to go. This list may be referred to in your will and incorporated into your will through that reference.

Planning Your Funeral

It's your funeral, you should be able to plan it. But, if you do not make your wishes specifically known, family members can find themselves arguing at this inappropriate time. Do not let what happened to Ted Williams happen to you. As you may remember, Baseball Hall of Famer Ted Williams' family conducted a prolonged court fight as to what to do with the remains of Williams. Make your wishes clear. If you wish, you can prepay your funeral and pick out exactly what you want or you can describe what you want and leave the money in a Funeral Trust to be used at your passing. Perhaps you want to be cremated or perhaps you want to be buried, in which case you should pre-purchase a cemetery plot. You also may wish to consider leaving your body for scientific research that could benefit mankind. In that case, you would certainly want to carefully take the time to research to what facility you would prefer to donate your body.

If you do prepay your funeral, you want to make sure that you understand the terms of the contract and what services and goods are provided pursuant to the terms of the contract. If your state does not regulate prepayments for funerals, you will want to make sure that your prepayment is properly protected in the event of the funeral home going out of business or declaring bankruptcy. Your lawyer can assist you with this.

The Federal Trade Commission enacted what is referred to as the Funeral Rule, which provides for greater disclosure of your options for a funeral.

Funerals can be expensive. It is not uncommon for funerals to cost more than $10,000. If the choice of what to do for a funeral of a family member is left up to the family to deal with immediately and, perhaps on short notice, following the death of a loved one, the family is left with little time or inclination to do the kind of comparison shopping they would do before spending that kind of money on a purchase made during a person's lifetime.

Wills to Live By

A will is an important document by which you can make clear to whom you wish to leave your worldly possessions—your stuff. Everyone should have a will. But, each of us is more than the sum of the "things" that we have managed to accumulate during our time on Earth. What is important and more enduring are the principles and values by which we live. These are our greatest legacy, and yet many of us, caught up in the details of day-to-day life, neglect to take the time to reflect upon these important matters and even fewer of us take the time to put these important thoughts on paper. These are the words which can, long after we are gone, serve both as a guide to future generations and a continuing close, comforting contact with the people we love.

It should come as no surprise that, when in the summer of 2002, nine coal miners, trapped below the surface, faced their own mortality and chose to write messages to their loved ones who, at that time, seemed so far away, these messages were not about "things." They were about more important matters. Miraculously, all these miners were saved and got the chance to tell their loved ones in person how they felt. All of us can do that, too. I call these messages, "Wills to Live By." They are not legal documents. They are more important than that. They provide an opportunity for you to tell the people in your life how you feel about them. You can leave an account of the principles and values that you hold dear. You can express your beliefs and your faith. You can also recount some of the stories of your life for others to remember when you live on in their memory. There is no one way to do a "Will to Live By." Once you start, you will find your own way.

Glossary

A

Activities of Daily Living (ADLs)—Regular daily activities that people generally do on their own, such as bathing, dressing, moving, and feeding oneself. The inability to do a certain number of these ADLs triggers the payment of benefits of a long-term care insurance policy.

adjusted basis—An income-tax term that relates to the initial price of property adjusted for certain additional costs related to the property (for example, a house to which the cost of improvements, such as a new bathroom) are added. Adjusted basis is used in the computation of capital gains taxes.

adjusted gross income—An income-tax term that relates to your total taxable income minus certain adjustments. This is the figure at the bottom of the front page of Form 1040.

administrator—The designation for a male appointed by the Probate Court to administer the estate of a deceased person who died without a will. A female performing that job is referred to as an administratrix.

alternate valuation date—A date six months from the date of death. Used for estate tax purposes to value the assets in the estate. This term is used most often when the value of the estate has gone down during that time.

Alternative Minimum Tax (AMT)—A way that the IRS gets money from people who the government considers to have high incomes, but have managed, through the use of various deductions, to drastically reduce their tax burdens. The law creating the AMT was never indexed for inflation and thus applies to many people to whom it was never intended to apply. It is confusing and costly.

Ancillary Administration—The name of the probate procedure required to clear the title to real estate in the name of a deceased whose real estate is located in a state other than the state in which the deceased made his or her primary home.

Annual Gift Tax Exclusion—The maximum amount a person may give to as many individuals as he or she wishes during a calendar year without incurring a gift tax or even having to file a gift tax return. This amount is indexed for inflation and stood at $13,000 in 2012.

assessed value—The value that your local tax official has placed on your real estate for real estate tax purposes.

assets—Your stuff, from real estate to stocks to bank accounts. If it has a value, it is an asset.

assisted living facility—A form of housing arrangement that provides some assistance with activities of daily living.

B

benefit triggers—The term for particular situations that will cause a long-term care insurance policy to commence paying benefits.

C

Charitable Remainder Trust—A type of trust that provides for payments to a person during his or her lifetime. At death, whatever remains in the trust passes to a designated charity.

Codicil—An amendment to a will.

cognitive impairment—An inability to do deductive reasoning, disorientation as to person, place, and time, a serious loss of short- or long-term memory.

COLA—Cost-of-living adjustments reflecting annual increases in the consumer price index added to the benefits paid to Social Security retirees.

Commercial Annuity—A contract with an insurance company by which, in return for premium payments by you, the insurance company agrees to make payments to you regularly for a specific period or for the rest of your life.

community spouse—The at-home spouse of a nursing home resident receiving Medicaid benefits. He or she receives an allowance of income and assets in the process of determining Medicaid eligibility for the spouse in the nursing home.

continuing care retirement community—A term that encompasses a broad spectrum of alternative housing arrangements with a common thread of providing housing, meals, nursing home, and other health services, as well as social and recreational facilities.

Credit Shelter Trust—Also called a Bypass Trust or an AB Trust. Allows married couples to leverage their federal estate tax credit or exemption ($5,120,000 million in 2012) so that they get double the protection of their assets from federal estate taxes.

Crummey Power—A provision found in a trust, most commonly an Irrevocable Life Insurance Trust, that allows beneficiaries of the trust to take out assets from the trust at their option.

D

Defective Trust—A bad name for a good trust. It permits the person setting up the trust to have trust income taxed on his or her individual income tax return while at death the assets will not be included in the taxable estate.

designated beneficiary—The person indicated on a form that specifies the beneficiary of an IRA following the death of the owner of the IRA.

disclaimer—A technique by which a person who would inherit something through a will, a joint tenancy, a life-insurance policy, an IRA, or legal document specifically renounces the right to receive some or all of what he or she would otherwise inherit.

Dividend Reinvestment Plan—A plan by which dividends from a stock or mutual fund are automatically used to purchase additional shares.

Durable Power of Attorney—A document by which you appoint someone else to act on your behalf in financial matters. A Durable Power of Attorney can be written either to be effective immediately or to take effect should you become incapacitated.

E

elimination period—The period of time during which a person must pay privately before a long-term insurance policy will commence payments.

Employee Retirement Income Security Act of 1974 (ERISA)—A federal law that regulates some pension and health care benefit programs.

Equal Credit Opportunity Act—A law that prohibits banks from age discrimination when granting discriminating credits or loans.

equity—A measure of the value of interest in a home, which is calculated by subtracting from the value of the home the amounts of any mortgages.

Estate Administration—The procedure for settlement of an estate by gathering the assets of the deceased, paying the bills of the deceased, and distributing the assets.

estate tax—A tax on the assets in which a deceased had an interest at the time of his or her death.

executor—The designation of a male person who is named in a will who is then appointed by the Probate Court to administer an estate. If that person is a woman, she is referred to as an executrix. Many states now refer to this person as a personal representative.

exemption—An amount of money that you may deduct from your income in determining your taxable income for yourself and any dependents.

F

Fair Hearing—The designation of the administrative law hearing when you appeal a Medicaid decision.

Family Limited Partnership—An estate and financial planning vehicle that also has significant asset protection capabilities.

FICO—Although it sounds like it should be the name of a dog, FICO is an abbreviation for the Fair Isaac Company, which provides a credit-worthiness scoring system used by the major credit-reporting agencies.

fiduciary—Someone who acts on your behalf in a position of trust, such as an executor, personal representative, or a trustee.

filing status—Uncle Sam believes it is important in determining your income tax rate to know whether you are single, married filing jointly, married filing separately, or a head of household.

G

gift tax—A tax imposed in some situations on the giver of a gift.

Glossary—A collection of specialized terms. I wondered exactly what this word meant, and since I was writing a Glossary, I thought I better know its meaning.

Golden Rule (government version)—If you have the gold, you make the rules.

grantor—The name for a person who sets up a trust. This is synonymous with settlor, donor, or trustor.

guardian—A person appointed by a court to manage an incapacitated person's personal and financial affairs.

H

Health Care Proxy—Also known as an Advance Directive for Healthcare. This is a document by which you are able to appoint someone to make medical care decisions on your behalf in the event of incapacity.

Health Insurance Portability and Accountability Act (HIPAA)—A federal law that provides, among other things, for medical information privacy and tax benefits for long-term care insurance.

Home Equity Conversion Mortgage (HECM)—An FHA (Federal Housing Administration)-insured Reverse Mortgage.

Home Equity Loan—A line of credit, secured by a mortgage on your home, that allows you to borrow money as you need it.

I

Incentive Trust—A type of trust that distributes your assets after your death upon the fulfillment of conditions that you establish through the trust.

Incidents of Ownership—Indications of ownership of a life insurance policy by such things as paying the premiums, changing beneficiaries, and taking out a loan on the policy. Life insurance is subject to estate tax if the deceased had incidents of ownership of the policy.

Income First Rule—The Medicaid rule for raising the income of the community spouse of a Medicaid recipient in a nursing home. A portion of the income of the nursing-home-resident spouse is given to the community spouse to provide additional income instead of having the spouse outside the nursing home retain more of their joint assets.

Intervivos Trust—A living trust. Any trust that is created during your lifetime as contrasted to a testamentary trust that is a part of your will. As an unwritten rule, the more Latin your lawyer uses, the more you pay.

intestacy laws—The laws that determine who inherits property when a person dies without a will.

intestate—Dying without a will.

IRA—*See* **Roth IRA** *and* **Traditional IRA**.

Irrevocable Life Insurance Trust—A type of trust that will permit life insurance proceeds to avoid estate taxes.

J

jejune—This word means childish or juvenile. It does not really relate to legal and financial planning, but it is a nice, obscure word that you can use to impress your friends when you drop it into everyday conversation. Thanks to Attorney Marc Padellaro, I have learned this word and many others.

Joint Tenancy—Also known as Joint Tenancy with Right of Survivorship. A way of multiple owners owning property. Upon the death of one owner, the surviving joint owner or owners automatically receive the deceased joint owner's interest in the property without the property being subject to probate.

L

Life Estate—The right of a person to use and control property during his or her lifetime. Upon that person's death, the property automatically passes to a person or persons designated as remaindermen.

Living Revocable Trust—The most basic form of trust. You can be the creator of the trust, trustee, and beneficiary; you have the right to change or revoke the trust. It is often used as a way to avoid probate.

Living Trust—The name for any trust that is created and effective during your lifetime.

load funds—Mutual funds that carry a sales commission and are generally sold through a broker or financial planner.

look-back period—The five-year period that Medicaid reviews to find any gifts that a Medicaid applicant made to reduce assets to qualify for Medicaid nursing home benefits. A disqualification based upon the amount of the assets given during the look-back period begins when the person is in a nursing home and otherwise eligible for Medicaid.

M

marital deduction—A provision of the estate tax that does not tax anything passing to a surviving spouse. They get you later.

Marital Deduction Trust—A trust that holds assets for the benefit of a surviving spouse and avoids estate taxation until the death of the surviving spouse.

Medicaid—A joint program between the federal government and the states that substantially provides for long- term care in a nursing home. It is the only public benefit program of this type.

Medical Expense Deduction—A provision of the income tax law that allows you to deduct medical expenses if they are more than 7.5 percent of your adjusted gross income.

Medicare—The federal government's health insurance program for people who contributed to the Social Security system and are at least 65 years old or who are disabled.

Medicare A—The part of the Medicare program that helps pay for hospital care expenses.

Medicare B—The part of the Medicare program that helps pay for doctor bills and medical tests.

Medicare C—Also called the Medicare+Choice program. It provides for new types of plans for providing medical services, such as Health Maintenance Organizations (HMOs).

Medicare D—The part of the Medicare program dealing with prescription drugs.

Medicare Supplement Insurance—Sometimes called Medigap insurance. It is private health insurance that supplements Medicare coverage.

Minimum Distribution Rules—IRS rules that determine the amount of money you must take out of an IRA or other retirement account as well as the age at which you must take those distributions.

N

No-Load Fund—A mutual fund that does not add a sales charge.

nonprobate property—Property that passes at death to beneficiaries outside the probate process. This generally is property with a designated beneficiary, such as life insurance.

notch babies—People born between 1917 and 1921, many of whom believe they are discriminated against in regard to their Social Security retirement benefits.

P

Patient-Pay Amount—The amount of money that Medicaid recipients in a nursing home must contribute monthly toward the cost of their own care.

Patient Self-Determination Act—A law, passed in 1991, requiring that anyone admitted to a hospital receive at admission written information regarding advance care directive laws in that state.

POD account—Payable on Death. Designates that when the owner of a brokerage account dies, ownership of the account passes to the person specifically named by the account owner to inherit the account.

points—Prepaid interest on a mortgage loan that you pay when you take out a mortgage loan. Each point equals 1 percent of the loan. In other words, the more money you borrow from the bank, the more you get to pay them for the privilege of doing so.

Pourover Will—A will that moves (pours over) your assets into an already existing trust that will control the disposition of your property.

Private Annuity—An annuity contract that is made between a person and another individual, often a family member, rather than an insurance company. A private annuity is often used in some states to shelter assets from Medicaid.

probate—The process by which the Probate Court oversees the settlement of an estate.

Q

QTIP—Not something you stick in your ear. It is an acronym for a Qualified Terminable Interest Property Trust. This is a form of a marital deduction trust often used to manage assets for a surviving spouse as well as to protect those assets for the later benefit of surviving children.

R

remainderman—Not the name of a hero from a Saturday-morning cartoon, but rather the designation of the person who succeeds to ownership of property when the person who has a life estate dies.

required beginning date—The latest date by which a person who has an IRA must begin taking distributions from the IRA. The date is April first of the calendar year after the year in which the IRA holder reaches 70-and-a-half. Now, isn't that logical?

reverse mortgage—A mortgage loan by which the bank pays a senior citizen money either as a line of credit or on a regular basis. A reverse mortgage is generally paid back at death.

Roth IRA—A type of IRA in which no tax deduction is taken for contributions to it, but no taxes are paid on distributions from it. *Contrast with* **Traditional IRA.**

S

Second-to-die life insurance policy—A life insurance policy on the joint lives, generally of a husband and wife, in which the policy does not pay any benefits until the death of the second person to die. This is a low-cost way to provide money that may be needed for estate taxes.

Section 529 Plan—A tax-advantaged way to save for the costs of higher education.

self-proving affidavit—An affidavit of witnesses to a will that attests that the will was properly executed. The affadavit is made a part of the will This affidavit can make the probate process quicker and less costly.

Single Premium Life Insurance Policy—A life-insurance policy that is paid for by a single premium payment. This type of policy can be used to provide long-term care benefits.

spousal rollover—The transfer of funds from the IRA of a deceased person to an IRA of that person's surviving spouse.

Springing Durable Power of Attorney—A Durable Power of Attorney that takes effect only when the person assigning that power becomes incapacitated.

T

tax credit—An amount of money designated by the IRS as a benefit for particular situations. Every dollar of a tax credit is applied directly to the amount that you would otherwise owe in taxes. It is more valuable than a tax deduction, which is a deduction from your total income that is subject to tax.

tax deduction—An amount that is subtracted from your total income in determining the amount of your income that will be subject to income tax.

Tenancy by the Entirety—A way for a husband and wife to own real estate that is protected from the creditors of either the husband or the wife.

Tenancy in Common—A way in which two or more people can own property such that when one co-owner dies, his or her share passes to his or her estate rather than to the other co-owners.

term life insurance—A life insurance policy that provides pure insurance coverage for a specific number of years. It has no cash value.

testator—A male who makes a will. A female who makes a will is a testatrix.

Traditional IRA—A retirement account, which, if you are eligible for it, will permit you to take an income tax deduction for contributions to it. Your contributions and the interest grow tax deferred; the money is taxed when you take it out, which must start to occur by age 70-and-a-half.

trust—A way of owning property in which the people who get the benefit of the property, "beneficiaries," are designated separately from the people who control the property, "trustees." In some trusts, such as a simple living revocable trust, the same person may be both the trustee and beneficiary.

trust protector—Someone other than the primary trustee who is named in a trust and given special powers, such as the authority to remove a trustee or amend the trust in response to changing laws or other changed circumstances.

U

Uniform Transfer to Minors Act—A law that simplifies the holding of assets for the benefit of minors. It is best used for assets not of substantial value.

universal life insurance—A relatively new kind of life insurance with cash value, but that permits you to change the coverage amount and the premium payments.

V

viatical company—A company that buys the life insurance policy of a person with a short life expectancy. The company gives the insured person cash now and receives the policy proceeds at the death of the insured.

W

waiver of premium—A provision in an insurance policy that eliminates the requirement of continued premium payments while you are receiving benefits under a policy, such as long-term care insurance.

whole life insurance—A basic life insurance policy with a cash value.

will—A document executed in strict accordance with state law to provide for the disposition of a person's property. A will also names the personal representative or executor, the person in charge of the settlement of the estate.

Favorite Websites

The Internet is a great source of timely information. However, sometimes the breadth of the material that can be located online can be somewhat daunting. How do you know if you can trust the information? The websites I include here are all sites that I have personally found to be helpful, reliable, and—most importantly—understandable. The websites are listed in no particular order. They represent an assortment of sources for up-to-date information, which is important because, in the world of elder planning, change is constant.

www.benefitscheckup.org

Created by the National Council on the Aging (NCOA), which is a nonprofit organization, www.benefitscheckup.org is an exceptionally helpful website. It provides a relatively simple way for you to identify local, state, and federal programs for which you may be eligible. Over a thousand programs provide various services to older Americans, but if you are unaware of these programs, they can do you no benefit. The NCOA estimates that more than five million senior citizens are not receiving benefits for which they are eligible just because they do not know about them.

This website provides a way for you, at no charge, to find out which programs apply to you. Some of the programs pertain to financial assistance, healthcare programs, property-tax programs, prescription-drug assistance, housing assistance, home-energy assistance, in-home services, and legal services.

To find out which programs you are eligible for, all you need to do is answer about three dozen online questions. The process takes about 15 minutes, and the information is kept confidential. In addition, no personally identifying information is taken. You do not have to provide your name, address, telephone number, or social security number.

The process is entirely anonymous and, after a few minutes, you have a personal report that lists the various programs from a data bank of more than a thousand programs for which you may be eligible.

www.pbgc.gov

This is the website of the Pension Benefit Guaranty Corporation (PBGC), which was set up by the federal government to help locate people who may be owed defined benefit pension money from companies that either went out of business or ended their defined benefit pension plans.

Since 1996, the PBGC has found close to fifteen thousand people owed more than $61 million in pension benefits, and the PBGC is trying to locate thousands of more people who are eligible for another $80 million in pension benefits from defined benefit pension plans that have terminated. Benefits paid by the PBGC have been for as little as a dollar and as much as $123,498.

People who think that a pension plan might owe them some money should go to this website for information and assistance.

www.medicare.gov

This is the federal government's authorized source for information on Medicare. This website provides answers to questions about eligibility, enrollment, and premiums for the various programs covered by Medicare. In addition, it has helpful information about nursing homes, Medigap policies, prescription-drug assistance programs, and many other healthcare issues of interest to older Americans.

www.medicare.gov/NursingHomeCompare

This website is a part of the overall official Medicare website and provides specific information to help people compare the more than 17,000 Medicare and Medicaid certified nursing homes throughout the country. Included in the information found on this site for all the covered nursing homes is material on the number of beds in the facility, inspection information, and staffing information.

www.hmos4seniors.com

This independent website contains Medicare HMO cost comparisons that let you obtain information from Medicare HMOs and private fee for service (PFFS) plans available throughout the country, along with tips for choosing a Medicare HMO.

www.medicareadvocacy.org

This is the website of the Center for Medicare Advocacy Inc., which is a private nonprofit organization. The website contains much helpful material for Medicare beneficiaries.

www.aarp.org

When you turn 50 years of age, who do you think will be there right away sending you birthday wishes? If you guessed the American Association of Retired Persons, you were right. You don't have to be retired or even a member of the organization to use the website's useful information on a host of topics of concern to senior citizens and even those not so senior.

www.irs.gov

"Helpful" and the "Internal Revenue Service" are not words that are commonly found in the same sentence; however, the website of the IRS is truly a very helpful website filled with information that explains the tax laws (as well as a government bureaucrat can). The website also provides downloadable tax forms.

www.taxsites.com

Once you go to the IRS, if you still have a tax question or even if you just want to get a second opinion, this website is an easy place to go to. From here, you can choose from any large number of specific websites that deal with tax issues.

www.ftc.gov

This is a terrific website full of information of great interest to consumers, old and young alike. The "consumer protection" section of this website of the Federal Trade Commission is useful and has an abundance of free information on many important consumer issues.

This website is particularly helpful if you are the victim of identity theft, and it has specific advice and forms online that can help victimized consumers. The website also has information to help people be more aware of the various fraudulent schemes and scams that are so prevalent today.

www.scamicide.com

This website is another good source of information about fraud, scams, and identity theft. In addition to information on a variety of scams and identity-theft schemes, this website/blog is updated on a daily basis to provide information about the latest scam and identity-theft threats.

www.reversemortgage.org

This website of the National Reverse Mortgage Lenders Association has a great deal of information that clearly explains how reverse mortgages work. In addition, the website has an online mortgage calculator that can help you easily see how much money you could get through a reverse mortgage.

www.ssa.gov

This is the official website of the Social Security Administration with more information than you could shake a stick at (if that is your idea of fun). In addition to clear, helpful information explaining and guiding you through the various Social Security Programs, such as Retirement, Disability, Survivors, and Supplemental Security Income, this website has much additional interesting information, including a fascinating history of Social Security.

www.healthfinder.gov

This is the website of the American Association of Homes and Services for the Aging, which is an organization of 5,600 nonprofit nursing homes, continuing care retirement communities, assisted living, and senior housing facilities. This site contains a good section of tips for consumers and family caregivers to help in the choice of facilities and services.

www.uslivingwillregistry.com

This is the website of the U.S. Living Will Registry, a private organization that electronically compiles and stores advance care directives (Living Wills and Health Care Proxies), which are then made available, as necessary, to hospitals, nursing homes, and other healthcare providers. The service is free to the public. The cost of the service is paid by the healthcare providers and attorneys, financial planners, and other professionals who use the service for their clients.

www.naela.org

This is the website of the National Academy of Elder Law Attorneys (NAELA), which is a nonprofit association of attorneys who work with older citizens on the many issues they face. Through the website, you can locate a NAELA member attorney in your geographical area that is knowledgeable in elder law.

www.equifax.com

This is the website of the Equifax credit reporting bureau. Through its website, you can obtain your credit report and report identity theft. It is important to obtain your credit report from each of the three credit-reporting agencies, because they operate independently. Each report may differ significantly.

www.experian.com

This is the website of the Experian credit-reporting bureau. Through its website, you can obtain your credit report and report identity theft.

www.transunion.com

This is the website of the Trans Union credit reporting bureau. Through its website, you can obtain your credit report and report identity theft.

www.treasurydirect.gov

This official United States government website permits you to set up an account with the U.S. Treasury through which you can buy and redeem Treasury bills, notes, and bonds. The website also provides a great deal of information about various savings bonds and how to purchase them. The website provides easy-to-use calculators that can assist you in determining the value of bonds which you may have.

www.sec.gov

This is the official website of the U.S. Securities and Exchange Commission (SEC). It is a good source of reliable information on companies in which you may be considering investing as well a good source for other investor information. Informational corporate filings, required to be filed with the SEC, can be accessed through the site's EDGAR database.

EDGAR stands for Electronic Data Gathering, Analysis, and Retrieval system. How long do you think it took someone to come up with that acronym?

personalreports.lexisnexis.com

This website has a section where you may obtain a claims history report for real estate you may be considering buying. This information is not only helpful in evaluating the condition of the home; it also is important in evaluating what the cost will be for obtaining homeowner's insurance on the property. Cooperation of the home's present owner is required.

www.bankrate.com

This website provides a range of helpful consumer financial information, including comparisons of credit cards and mortgages presently being offered. It provides a treasure trove of information.

www.help4srs.org

This is the main website for the Healthcare and Elder Law Programs Corporation (HELP). Although the site is primarily concerned with elder issues for California residents, it also has extremely helpful information on a broad range of concerns of older Americans.

www.organdonor.gov

This website, sponsored by the U.S. Department of Health and Human Services, provides important information about organ donations.

www.hospicefoundation.org

This is the website of the Hospice Foundation of America, which is a nonprofit organization. The website is a good source of information on hospice programs that provide care to people in the advanced stages of terminal illnesses.

Forms

Many people live by the motto, "One of these days, I'm going to get organized." Perhaps the biggest source of procrastination in getting organized is not knowing where to start. The "Document Location" form is a good first step toward organizing your affairs. Locating all of the important documents in your life not only helps you arrange your life now, but helps your family tremendously when they face the difficult task of administrating your estate after your death.

The form titled, "Procedures to Follow Upon the Death of _____," serves as a simple and thoughtful guide to your family after your passing. It provides ready access to information that will ease the confusion at that difficult time and make the estate settlement process less difficult.

DOCUMENT LOCATION

ITEM	LOCATION

Will _____

Tangible Property Memorandum _____

Codicil to Will _____

Durable Power of Attorney _____

Health Care Proxy _____

Trust _____

Funeral Instructions _____

_____

_____

_____

Anatomical Gift Declaration _____

_____

_____

_____

Cemetery Deeds _____

Insurance Policies _____

_____

_____

Employee Benefit Plan Statements _____

_____

_____

Financial Statement _____

_____

_____

Deeds _____

DOCUMENT LOCATION

ITEM	LOCATION
Leases _____	
Bank Account Information _____	
Stocks & Bonds _____	
_____	
_____	
Birth Certificate _____	
Marriage Certificate _____	
Prenuptial Agreement _____	
Divorce Decree _____	
Separation Agreement _____	
Military Service Record _____	
Social Security Card _____	
Medical Records _____	
_____	
Will to Live By _____	
Other _____	
_____	
_____	
_____	
_____	
_____	
_____	
_____	
_____	

PROCEDURES TO FOLLOW UPON THE DEATH OF

---

1. Notify family members and friends.
2. Confirm if provisions for anatomical gifts.
3. Arrange for care of pets.
4. Evaluate security of deceased's residence and need for care.
5. Make funeral and burial arrangements.

    Consult memorandums of deceased's wishes.

    Contact funeral director.

    Contact clergyman.

    Notify family and friends of date, time, and place of funeral service.

6. Prepare obituary notice.
7. Maintain records of callers and letters.
8. Contact the following:

    Lawyer

    Guardian

    Executor

    Trustee

9. Obtain multiple copies of death certificate.
10. Make arrangements for mail delivery.
11. Locate safe deposit box, if any.
12. Locate important documents.
13. Notify Social Security Administration.
14. Available fund locations:

    Checking account

    Savings account

    Money market account

State Income Tax Deductibility of Section 529 Plans

Each state has its own Section 529 Plan for saving for higher education expenses. Although it is possible to use the plan of a state in which you do not reside, some states permit you to take as a deduction on that state's income tax the amount of your contribution to its Section 529 Plan. Therefore, consider the value of using your own state's program if it provides tax deductibility. The amount of the deduction differs among the states that do permit you to take a deduction for 529 contributions on your state income tax.

Listed here are the states that do and do not allow a state income tax deduction for contributions to their 529 Plan. Alaska, Florida, Nevada, South Dakota, Texas, Washington, and Wyoming are listed as not providing a deduction, because they do not have a state income tax.

States That Allow Tax Deductions on Their State Income Tax Returns for Contributions to That State's 529 Plan

Alabama	Maine	Oklahoma
Arizona	Maryland	Oregon
Arkansas	Michigan	Pennsylvania
Connecticut	Mississippi	Rhode Island
Colorado	Missouri	South Carolina
Georgia	Montana	Utah
Idaho	Nebraska	Vermont
Illinois	New Mexico	Virginia
Indiana	New York	West Virginia
Iowa	North Carolina	Wisconsin
Kansas	North Dakota	
Louisiana	Ohio	

States That Do Not Allow State Tax Deductions for Contributions to 529 Plans

Alaska	Massachusetts	Tennessee
California	Minnesota	Texas
Delaware	Nevada	Washington
Florida	New Hampshire	Wyoming
Hawaii	New Jersey	
Kentucky	South Dakota	

Index

2/13
646.79
WEISMAN

In an increasingly competitive world, it is quality
of thinking that gives an edge—an idea that opens new
doors, a technique that solves a problem, or an insight
that simply helps make sense of it all.

We work with leading authors in the various arenas
of business and finance to bring cutting-edge thinking
and best-learning practices to a global market.

It is our goal to create world-class print publications
and electronic products that give readers
knowledge and understanding that can then be
applied, whether studying or at work.

To find out more about our business
products, you can visit us at www.ftpress.com.